Franklin

Franklin

The man behind the United States Commando Dogs

MATTHEW DUFFY

ISBN-13: 9780692062708
ISBN-10: 069206270X

Praise for "Franklin"

"An exhilarating look into the fascinating story of a true pioneer behind S.O.F. dogs trained for the U.S. Military. Jeff's story is a remarkable one that needs to be heard for future generations of patriots to emulate."
—Mike Ritland, New York Times Best Selling Author of Trident K-9 warriors, Navy SEAL Dogs and Team Dog

"This book is particularly unique because it fills a void in current military literature about how military Special Operations Forces use military commando dogs, as well as how they are acquired and trained. Matthew has written as if he is invisibly seeing into all of the action by watching the developer of the Special Operations commando dog teams, Jeffrey Franklin, as well as making Jeff into the real person that he is. Matthew Duffy's book is a superlative read and at the same time a textbook on the operations of Special Operations Forces and their integration of man/dog teams. 'Damn Skippy!'"
Paul F. Nagengast Jr., LT. Colonel, Armor Branch, U.S. Army (Retired), Regimental affiliation: U.S. Army Second Cavalry Regiment

"A powerful story that needed to be told. This adventure explains what is capable if you refuse to settle for mediocracy and faithfully dedicate yourself to the dogs and people that you train."
Brendan Callaghan, Special Operation Lead Canine Handler,
Operations Iraqi and Enduring Freedom
(6 combat deployments)

"Matthew Duffy provides the reader with a wonderful insight on the background of Jeffrey Scott Franklin, the man behind the United States Commando Dogs. We are given the opportunity to understand the origins of a dedicated and efficient individual who has the unique ability to train man's best friend into not only a disciplined soldier, but also an effective weapon against terrorism and those that seek to harm the United States. Beginning with the fundamentals and foundations of ethics laid out by his father and his true bond with canines, we see the beginning of his evolution with his first love, Lucy. Hard lessons learned from her have not been forgotten as this former United States Marine and police officer moves forward with the development of cobra

Canine into the arena of military/police working dogs. We are allowed to get an idea of the financial strains, sourcing and acquisition practices for these elite canines through both international markets and domestic breeding programs. Through continual transformation and the 'fix the problem that is right now and in front of us' mentality, we are able to follow Mr. Franklin into Iraq, Ecuador, Afghanistan and feel as though we are there and can visualize a snippet of the training and usage of these finely tuned machines, the United States Commando Dogs."
Dr. Andrew Baker, DVM MRCVS

"Imagine Jeff as a young kid being told one day the United States Military would choose to task him with the honor of creating and developing the first and only Spec Ops K-9 program, thus making U. S. Military history. Being a Military Wife, I sleep better knowing Jeff's dogs and handlers are with my husband."
Kelly Carlson, Actress (Nip/Tuck), Navy Wife, Political Activist

"Mr. Duffy has captured the character, personality and subtle nuances of Jeff with masterful elegance. The detailed and descriptive narrative of Jeff's life made me feel like I was walking alongside him through each experience, from his heart pumping altercations to his moments of grief. Jeff's love for canines is unmistakeable and his humility as one of the world's top trainers is admirable. Serving both stateside and overseas, he has left an indelible mark on the working dog community. He truly embodies the essence of an American patriot."
Nathan Ghoens, Chief Petty Officer, USN

"This book illustrates the selfless and unparalleled dedication to duty of the Special Operations Canine Teams and their trainer, Jeff Franklin. Jeff is an innovator and has led the way in the canine industry. Franklin's commitment to his craft has resulted in war dog teams that have saved countless lives worldwide."
Lt. Roby Rhoads, Arkansas State Police, Canine Coordinator

"Chapter Eight stimulates every reason I became a K-9 Officer, and the remaining chapters represent the reasons I still am. A great book!"
Daniel Cliff, Patrol Captain K-9 Commander
Morristown, TN Police Department

Franklin
The Man behind the United States
Commando Dogs

Jeffrey Scott Franklin

Dedication

To the K-9 Team and the timeless relationship between man and dog!

Two Warriors

Table of Contents

Harder Dogs

Recognition

This project would have been too daunting for me to manage without my mentor, Dr. Kate Horsley and her fountain of composition wisdom. I am indebted. And I hope to keep writing, if for no other reason than to better use the skills that Kate has taught me.

I owe endless gratitude to Dr. John Parker, my silent partner in writing. Without his hours of meticulous editing and his encouragement to tell my stories in print, there would be no book. John's efforts extended well beyond friendship.

My longtime friend and client, Dr. Steven Wright, was my one faithful test-reader. I greatly appreciated the honest feedback and the confidence he contributed to the project. Steve's two gifts inspired me to be creative.

Then came Ron Buschmann. His artistic mastery of photo enhancement and text manipulation put the finishing touches on the narrative. Ron's creative application of the cover-image alone captured the full drama of Jeff's story. I will always be indebted to my friend.

I would also be at fault if I didn't mention Jeff Franklin's enormous contribution to this writing project. He patiently recounted stories over and over again until

I sufficiently absorbed their full content, especially when it came to military protocol and jargon.

I wish for this book to stand as a salute to all of the canine handlers who have served and who are currently active in the military or law enforcement. Too few people who benefit from their employment appreciate the extra effort required of the men and women called to this special duty.

Sincerely,
Matthew Duffy

Declaration

Franklin
The Man
Behind the
United States
Commando Dogs

This story is based on the life and times of Jeffrey Scott Franklin as it was relayed to me. Significant names, locations, and dates have been altered to protect identities and sensitive information. Preserving the integrity of non-disclosure was a top priority.

Although the people, dogs, and events you'll read about were created for this narrative, they were all fashioned from legitimate beings and experiences that define Franklin's life. Illustrating Jeff's tale presented an opportunity to showcase the faithful warrior who bravely and selflessly stands between the enemy and the innocent.

The contents of this book, including any misrepresentations are the sole responsibility of the author.

Matthew Duffy   June 14th, 2014

Introduction

In June of 1991, Jeffrey Scott Franklin received his first tutorial on aggressive working dogs from me. Jeff was not yet twenty years old when we first met, and he had just returned home from active duty as a Marine Tank Operator during the Desert Storm War. Jeff worked closely with me as a professional dog trainer for more than a decade while also serving as a K-9 Officer before he was once again called upon to aid his country.

Whether he knew it or not, Franklin committed to making history in 2004 when he agreed to develop one of the world's first top tier Canine Commando programs for the preeminent branch of the United States Military. Having no template to guide him, Franklin was compelled to develop his own canine selection criteria as well as the necessary training protocols to meet the "high octane" demands of a covert task force.

With the exception of me and Jeff, each character (both human and animal) represented in this narrative is a composite of real personalities that impressed Franklin at some point along the way in his journey. Each chronicled mission or training exercise was a fusion of numerous components extracted from many engagements and woven together for the purpose of telling a complete story about extraordinary canines and the exceptional men who handle them. Given that Franklin has worked with myriad K-9 Teams within the police and military worlds throughout the course of his career, I chose to highlight exceptional aspects of human and canine performance extracted from hundreds of missions in order to distil Jeff's story into a palatable length.

Jeff Franklin was adamant about the practice of non-disclosure when recounting his life's experiences in order to safeguard the integrity of sensitive and secured information. He regrets being unable to give specific recognition to the courageous and hardworking warriors so deserving. Jeff believes that the testimony of valor demonstrated by the men and dogs represented in these pages lives on with the active K- 9 teams currently standing against antagonists both at home and abroad.

Each dated episode in this book occurs in only approximate chronographic order. Countless hours of conversation and recollections went into the written construction of each tale. Ultimately, this narration is related as Jeff wished it to be; a salute to the good men and dogs with whom he had the privilege of working.

In writing about each K-9 team, I hoped to have successfully portrayed the uniquely close bond that can exit between people and animals who work intimately together. If one is exposed even for a few moments to a specially trained human/dog team, the witness would surely testify that the synergy between the canine and his handler is palpable. With rare exception, the attention and respect given to a police or military dog by their handlers approaches that which is given to their human counterparts. In the working/service-dog world, a handler typically cares for and depends upon his animal just as the animal cares for and depends upon his handler.

By the autumn of 2012, twenty-one years from our first meeting, Jeff reached a pinnacle in professional dog training. He was charged by the United States government with the responsibility of overseeing the selection and instruction of all the elite canines assigned to competing special tactics groups stationed on opposite sides of the country. He is the only man ever to have held such a position, and I am honored to narrate this story about my friend, Jeffrey Scott Franklin.

An elite Canine Commando Team.

One

ALONE

H ot on the heels of eight trained police dogs that he had shipped a week earlier, Jeffrey Scott Franklin's 767 landed in the darkness of the Quito airport. It was February of 2009, and he was attempting to fulfill the first contract for his newly formed company, Cobra Canine. For the previous several years he had lived and trained exclusively with a highly secretive combat group within the preeminent branch of the United States Military, while developing the first of its kind, K-9 Commando. This "Special Tactics Force" is arguably the world's most elite combat element, and Jeff created a war- dog program that was uniquely designed for their covert operations.

From the program's inception deep inside a secured military compound, to the battle-proofing in the Middle East, Jeff was enveloped with resources as he instructed the commando-team handlers and trained their canine counterparts. This trip to South America was an undertaking of a different sort, however. Operating as a civilian and a self-contained entity, Jeff was flying solo without the lavish support of the U.S. government. Far from all that was familiar, Jeff was about to enter a culture where he rarely heard his native language and violent eruptions were commonplace. Even before his plane landed, Jeff realized that he had never really operated alone before.

Born and raised in the countryside of Kentucky, Jeff was clean-cut, thirty-seven years old, and a devoted family man. He could have been a poster child for working class America. Up to this point in his life, he had only traveled under the protective umbrella of the United States military, first as a Marine, and later as the canine instructor for the "Special Tactics Group." Even his early dog buying trips to Europe were orchestrated and financed by the United States Military. It occurred to Jeff as he was walking into the Quito airport that he had been well supported and protected thus far in life. In all of his thirty-seven years, Jeff had truly never felt that he was "by himself" in anything he did. However, here in the Capital of Ecuador, with over two million Spanish speaking people, the young man from the country was beginning to feel on his own right out of the gate. It was midnight in the Mariscal Sucre, International airport and the place was buzzing. There were no escorts or translators waiting to greet Jeff; no State Department representative or Officer in Charge there to usher him to the next station. His first International trip as an entrepreneur, under the name Cobra Canine, felt like an entry into chaos and culture shock.

Jeff's specifically selected police dogs were already in-country and waiting for their trainer. With no more than the clothes on his back, his passport and a small amount of money, Jeff had to abandon the idea of securing the bag with all his essential accoutrements. He couldn't afford to wait any longer on luggage that could be in Australia. Almost panicky, Jeff hurried for the custom's security line. Not yet one step out of the baggage area, he hears a roar from the crowd left behind. A truck had dumped a small mountain of luggage in the middle of the floor, and people were diving headlong into the melee to retrieve their or some-one else's possessions. Unwilling to participate in what looked to be a piranha feeding frenzy, Jeff chose to continuously circle the hysterical crowd and prepare to ambush whomever attempted to walk off with his bag. Under his breath, while monitoring the baggage allocation, Jeff made a vow to never be delayed for a mission again because of lost gear. From that day forward the pledge became a matter of principle: if it can't be carried on, it stays behind.

An interminable wait for his flight's luggage to be delivered was unbearable. No one in the entire International complex seemed to be on a schedule or care in anyway about time. Jeff wondered around the airport for what seemed like an hour looking for an English-speaking official with some information. Coming up empty handed, Jeff was con-vinced all his training gear had landed in another country. The frus-tration over the potentially missing luggage was compounded by the anxious thoughts of failing to meet his only contact in South America, Captain Hector Liano. Jeff could not afford to miss this connection because he was headed to the dangerous border region where Ecuador meets Columbia, and Hector would be his "lifeline." This region was a virtual war zone, and not the familiar military operation Jeff was accus-tomed to. The area was engulfed in a raging battle between a ruthless, "far reaching" terrorist organization known as F.A.R.C. (Revolutionary

Armed Forces of Colombia), and a contingent of Ecuador's highly skilled, Special Police Force referred to as the G.I.R. (Intervention and Rescue Group).

Even though his luggage surveillance plan ate up precious time, he was too close to taking possession of his tactical clothing and training equipment to walk away. And as fate would dictate, one of the last bags of the luggage mountain to be wrestled over was his. So, ripping it from a pair of greedy hands, Jeff took off for customs only to find more snags. His bag made it through the check point but he didn't. As he was escorted by security from the customs to the visa check station, the chatter around him was intense. Understanding virtually none of the language being directed at him, Jeff gathered by the finger pointing and hand gestures that American dollars were needed to purchase a visa before he was free to return to customs and start the process all over. By the time he had cleared all of the security requirements, Jeff had spent virtually half the night trying to get out of the Quito airport. With little hope of finding Hector, who no doubt gave up on the American dog trainer long ago, Jeff weaved his way through the busy crowd of Spanish speaking people to find his way outside at last.

Just like the interior of the airport, the city streets of Quito were crawling with people. Ecuador was proving to be nothing like Jeff had imagined. His naïve, mental pictures of South America were of small villages with sparse populations. But Quito was a "city" in every regard. Even the smell which has lingered in Jeff's olfactory memory since his first visit, was of industry and mechanics rather than food and animals. Although Jeff's images of Ecuador were somewhat distorted and his preparations were lacking, his resolve to get on with the mission was strong. In accordance with his nature, Jeff quickly dismissed any thoughts or worries over obstacles that may lay in front of him. He was on a mission in South America, and nothing was going to keep him from finding the dogs that were sent down a week earlier and helping them adjust to their new handlers.

Early in this mission Jeff came to a realization about himself. His minimal preparation, "charge ahead come what may" approach, is a repeated and consistent theme throughout his entire life. To the exclusion of everything else, only the mission matters! Truly perplexed, and almost bothered by this revelation, Jeff realized for the first time what everybody around him accepts as his normal persona. Once, when recounting this adventure to a colleague, he was asked if he'd thought about learning a little Spanish before embarking on the trip, or considered arranging for an English-speaking escort, or packing bug spray and emergency rations. He thought for just a moment and answered, "It never crossed my mind". He said, "I know that makes me appear stupid, but I didn't really care about those considerations. I had a job to do, and I was utterly focused on one thought, find my dogs and the Anti- Kidnapping Special Forces Group, period! Although, I wasn't exactly sure how I was going to get that done, one thing I knew, nothing was going to keep me from doing my job. No doubt, I have made many aspects of my life more difficult than they had to be with this unwavering 'task mindedness.' In order to warrant those obsessive tendencies, I tell myself they must account in some way for the successes throughout my career!"

Fishing for his passport and newly acquired visa, Jeff was fully prepared for more security checks. As the two officers approached they gave no outward signs of friendliness, just business. One of the men engaged Jeff with questions that he didn't comprehend of course, but as the man repeated the series of questions Jeff thought he picked up on a key word, "Liano", Hector's surname. Jeff slowly pronounced "Captain Hector Liano". The officer immediately responded with, "Si"! With Jeff's best attempts at asking for Hector's whereabouts, the only response from either officer was "no Capitan Liano." While offering their clipped responses, one of the officers motioned Jeff to follow him to an old, beat-up Toyota Hilux parked out on the road, and the other grabbed his luggage. Tension and hurry marked the encounter which heightened Jeff's growing sense of paranoia. Maybe he had attended one too many of the State Department's briefings on abductions and violence in that part of the world. With paramilitary groups and terrorists on his mind, Jeff was beginning to feel a little vulnerable. One thing was certain, two men armed with MP5, submachine guns slung across their chests, making no attempt to identify themselves, did nothing to make him feel less uneasy. Hector could have sent these two as transporters. Hector could have been called away, and these two officers remained behind to look for Jeff. Those were real possibilities, but so was the possibility that Captain Liano, Jeff's "lifeline", was now just another national statistic. It was quite possible that Hector had been abducted by a para military group or a terrorist organization that routinely captured and impersonated law enforcement officers. In reality, Jeff had no options any way. He was alone, unarmed and in unfamiliar territory where he didn't speak the language!

Jeff reluctantly approached the pickup truck and saw a middle-aged man, dressed in civilian, business clothes sitting in the back seat. The man appeared to be Ecuadorian with a head full of thick black hair and a heavy mustache. As Jeff was directed to climb in next to the stoic passenger, he commented out loud, "I'm not sure if this situation is getting better or worse!" Since his remark generated no kickback, Jeff extended a greeting to the stranger that also went unnoticed. In fact, the man who was purposely staring straight ahead, offered no words or gestures of any kind to comfort the person they have just taken charge of. The apparently grim situation seemed to be getting darker by the moment, and Jeff was barely able to stave off despondency. After a hard week of dog training in the field, followed by a sleepless night of traveling a third of the way around the world, it's no wonder that Ecuador's strange and unfriendly reception was causing an antagonistic mood to fall over the American dog trainer.

Unable to help himself, Jeff leaned into the unsmiling passenger and says "you can call me Franklin, that's what Captain Liano calls me." With no reaction from the stranger still, Jeff leaned in a little closer, "I'm going to call you Mingo." Finally, the stoic man responds by shifting his hard stare directly into Jeff's eyes, which are only inches away. Purposefully, without retreating a millimeter, Jeff gave Mingo his signature half smile that flashed just a hint of lip curl, and said, "I win!" Jeff's pushy behavior contributed nothing towards friendly relations. It did, however, make him feel more in control of his situation, and that feeling satisfied his competitive side enough to allow him to relax a little.

While sitting in the dark and painfully quiet Toyota as it barreled out of Quito, the ex-police officer side of Jeff decided to cognitively reconnoiter. At the time of this first visit to South America, Jeff had only limited knowledge about the hostility in Ecuador and neighboring Columbia. Through briefings by the U.S. State Dept. (during the contract procurement process), all contract bidders learned that the Ecuador's Special Intervention and Rescue Group (G.I.R.) were in need of eight trained working dogs to locate explosives and assist in human apprehension. The G.I.R. represents a highly skilled contingent of their National Police, which was formed primarily as an anti-kidnapping organization. The trained detection and apprehension canines would be utilized by G.I.R. almost exclusively to combat the terroristic efforts of the Revolutionary Armed Forces of Columbia (F.A.R.C.).

Classified as a Terrorist Organization by the USA, European Union, Canada and Columbia, F.A.R.C. was officially formed in 1964 by Manuel Marulanda Velez, a long-time guerilla leader, and 47 other members of the Columbian Communist Party (P.C.C.). These 48 battle-tested guerillas represented the foundation of what has become the largest and oldest insurgent group in the Americas, boasting an armed strength of more than 8,500 members. The United States launched its initial counterinsurgent effort in the region (Plan Lazo) under the Special Warfare leadership of Commander General William P. Yarborough back in 1962. This action marked the beginning of more than 50 years of adversarial relations between the Revolutionary Army and the United States. Contractors were forewarned that U.S. citizens in that region of the world were prime targets for abduction. If captured, a government employee/contractor would most likely endure torture in exchange for information, while being held prisoner for years in hopes of collecting ransom. The "Fundacion Pais Libre", a non-governmental anti-kidnapping organization, estimated a total of 6,778 people had been kidnapped by F.A.R.C. between 1997 and 2007. Just a few years prior to Jeff's plane landed in Quito, the United Nations published a report on the F.A.R.C. and their egregious breaches of human rights, citing the many cases of murder, hostage taking and torture.

Around the time of Jeff's visit there was also no shortage of reports in the U.S. news about Columbian violence. Our own Attorney General, Alberto Gonzales, was working on the prosecution of 50 F.A.R.C. leaders indicted for smuggling more than $25 billion worth of cocaine into the U.S. during the spring of 2006. With an estimated annual revenue of approximately 300 million dollars (the majority of which came from taxation of the illegal drug trade, ransom and extortion), the Revolutionary Army was a regular feature in the global news. Racing out of Quito in the predawn hours, Jeff had legitimate reasons for feeling apprehensive. His reception party could have easily been terrorists looking for an American hostage, and his destination was left entirely in their hands. In fact, the Intervention and Rescue Group's training compound where he was hopefully headed was logistically located in the Northern region of Ecuador near the border with Columbia, and comprised the same country that the Revolutionary Army called home. Because of this juxtaposition, Jeff would not be sure which side of the battle line he landed on until he stepped out of the Toyota.

The geographic location of the G.I.R. headquarters, which was also the principle conflict zone, was nearly as intimidating as the enemy itself. At the base of the Andean mountains lies an immense, contiguous stretch of equatorial forest. From its inception, the original 48 members of the Revolutionary Army retreated to this region for concealment and protection. By the time Jeff was fulfilling this first contract, the F.A.R.C. fighting force had swelled to thousands, and they were divided into a multitude of heavily armed camps that were strategically dispersed throughout 190,000 square miles of unforgiving jungle. Once one is abducted and hidden away in this oppressively, thick area of vegetation (imagine for scope, an area that runs 435 miles north to south, and 435 miles east to west), history has shown that rescue from the clutches of terrorists is not very likely. To further complicate rescue and apprehension efforts for groups like G.I.R., the Revolutionary Army (as well as some other paramilitary organizations in the area) continuously move camps, resources and prisoners from one inaccessible place to another. Oftentimes these migrations are nothing more than a convenient death-march for the hundreds of malnourished and abused prisoners that are held captive at any given time. Given the immediate situation, these heavy thoughts rolled through Jeff's head like enemy tanks. So He turned his tired mind towards the choice dogs he would hopefully be seeing again, imagining that they were alive and well regardless of who had them.

After long miles of body numbing travel, the driver diverted from the main road onto an obscure country lane, without discussion or comment from anyone in the truck. The diversion in course should have piqued Jeff's interest, but maintaining awareness of the surroundings had become extremely difficult by this point in the trip, and registering a change in the route seemed unimportant. He'd been two full days without sleep, and although in close company with possible enemies, complete strangers at best, he could barely ward off unconsciousness within the dark, truck cab. Pulling up to a grocery store, the two uniformed men exited the truck and signaled for Jeff to do the same. Cooperating with the captors, or escorts whichever they may be, Jeff reached for his bag as he attempted to climb out of the pickup, but Mingo held onto the bag and motioned Jeff to move along while he and the pack of belongings remained behind. Again, with no other options, Jeff reluctantly released his bag and stepped between the armed guards who escorted him into the store.With both hands on their MP5s, the uniformed men walked Jeff around the country store step by step. Although they gestured to grab some food and drink, they never diverted their eyes from scanning the crowd who were oblivious to the armed men. The last thing on Jeff's mind was finding something to eat, but to placate his escorts he picked up some jerky, a couple bags of nuts, and as many bottles of water as he could carry, all items that he could stuff into his pockets since he had no idea where this trip would end. With no concern over paying for the items, the highly paranoid escorts shuttled Jeff toward the front door, apparently anxious over keeping things moving.

Once through the door and turning for the Hilux, Jeff saw Mingo outside the pickup. He was standing in the middle of the sidewalk with his hands crossed at the belt buckle, holding a Sig Sauer, P226, 9mm handgun for all the world to see. Mingo's air of indestructible hardness created a commanding presence that dared all onlookers to a challenge. Jeff stopped in his tracks, struck by this image of a middle-aged Ecuadorian, dressed in khaki slacks and a blue blazer, flaunting a high capacity pistol. With no expression, Mingo stared at the three men as they approached while surveying the environment.

Again, other than giving the gun toting man a wide berth, the general public walked by without so much as a suspicious glance. The local laissez faire philosophy over the public display of submachine guns and 9mm pistols reminded Jeff he was nowhere near Kentucky. Ecuador, like most countries in a state of developmental flux, was accustomed to violence and the drama that goes with it. The culture in this part of the world had already adopted into their norm these scenes that Jeff found so bizarre. Extreme fatigue contributed to this strange experience in front of the store, and made it surreal enough that Jeff thought it might just be a really bad dream. Whether he was dreaming or not, it dawned on him that the three escorts were beginning to show signs of concern in regard to his welfare, more like unfriendly bodyguards than captors. Maybe that was the case; but, without the prospect of communication he could only guess whether or not they were all on the same side. "Wait and see" was his only plan.

Back on the road, the sun was starting to peak over the horizon when the uniformed man in the passenger seat, at last, initiated some chatter with the driver. Although Jeff comprehended none of the conversation, the sound of human voices fluctuating with a little emotion was enough to drag him out of the sleep deprived stupor he'd been in for the last 100 miles. Daylight provided another boost in energy, especially since it allowed him to study the hardened countenance of Mingo's substantially pocked face, weapon capacity inside the truck, and clothing details. After a short lifetime of combat-readiness instruction from the Marines, the Police Academy, and most recently the Special Tactics Force, Jeff found that he couldn't keep himself from meticulously evaluating the situation. His calm awareness, quick assessments, mental reconnoitring, and detail recognition, resembled a top tier operator more than an ordinary dog trainer. Even though feeling very much alone there in Ecuador, Jeff was continuously preparing to take whatever action necessary when and if the dung hit the fan.

After a few miles of Spanish jabber, Jeff heard the name "Bosco" jump out from between two words, and then "Natz". These were more than just familiar words to Jeff; they were two names from his group of dogs that arrived in this country days ago. When Jeff interjected the names "Lobo", "Sniper" and "Charlie", both uniformed men turned around with actual smiles on their faces, "si, los perros robustos!" Their smiles and the names of his familiar canine charges soothed the weary dog trainer. Of course, Mingo preserved his stone-like posture and contributed nothing to the exchange. By now, Jeff was convinced that not only was this guy impossible to read, he must be some kind of professional hit- man or body guard. Regardless of Mingo's line of work or the fact that Jeff had no idea where he was being taken, the morning sun and the smiles from the uniformed men had a positive effect on his attitude.

At long last, Jeff's Southward journey came to its termination at a remote and thoroughly secured installation, very much like the military facilities he was used to. In fact, as the Hilux slowly pulled up to the guard post, Jeff's thoughts drifted back to Virginia, and the first time he was escorted into the secured compound of the Covert Operations Group where he first developed U.S. Military's elite dog program. A double row of eight-foot high fencing topped with concertina wire enclosed the entire outpost. There were innumerable sentries patrolling the grounds and positioned in sniper towers. Each of them was outfitted in full battle gear. From every angle this was a fortress prepared for all manner of siege, and a glaring calling card for the territory of which it was part.

From the back seat of the Toyota, Jeff could make out on one of the Spartan, concrete buildings an insignia along with the words "Groupo de Intervencion y Recate". He recognized those Spanish words from a few State Department communiques: Group of Intervention and Recovery or its acronym, G.I.R. The relief that fell over Jeff after seeing those words was like being wrapped in a warm blanket after days of marching in the cold rain. Somehow, despite his scant preparations, thousands of miles of travel, and no use of the native language, he had ended up at the appropriate destination. He was now, and had been all along, in the company of friends. This was to be his home away from home for the next week.

Hector had indeed taken care of his American friend. Captain Liano not only sent two of his best "shooters" to transport Jeff, he had also hired Mingo to act as a bodyguard. Jeff later found out that his stoic companion was no ordinary protector. Mingo was a seasoned professional whose livelihood as a sentinel in the presidential detail involved protecting high profile persons against the likes of the F.A.R.C. For the length of Jeff's mission in Ecuador, he went nowhere without his bodyguard. Although lacking in social skills, Jeff's entourage was the best in the protection business, in a corner of the world that housed some of the most prolific kidnappers in history.

In Jeff's case, his identity and the purpose of his trip made him a highly prized abduction target in terms of ransom or revenge. Captain Liano was well aware of this. He was also very aware of the likelihood of leaked information about the arrival of anti-terrorist dogs from the United States. Jeff could almost hear the Captain's orders: "Eyes and ears gentlemen, lock and load your weapons, and don't leave Franklin's side. Make only one stop for food, and under no circumstances deter for anything or anyone until my friend reaches the safety of this compound! Everyone crystal?" Jeff knew how Special Forces groups operated, and G.I.R. was internationally considered a top tier organization. With their high caliber soldiers, the face to face directive from their Captain conferred in no uncertain terms that the transportation task would be completed as ordered; everyone involved understood, if there happened to be a glitch, no excuses would be offered, and none would be accepted!

Still no sign of Hector as Jeff was shepherded directly from the truck to his barrack. He thought for sure he would be shuttled straight away to Captain Liano. As has been customary, there were no attempts at explanation from his escorts, just hand and head gestures. Jeff was walked to a stark, concrete and tile building, one of several that comprised the garrison. Undoubtedly built for lodging, this structure was completely devoid of inhabitants. His barrack door opened into a small musty room that was furnished with a broken-down cot, a single wooden chair next to a child–size desk, and a tiny bathroom with running water. The quarters felt more like a prison cell than a dorm room. Jeff did notice a few amenities right away though including new sheets for the bed, toilet paper and soap. Those were no doubt gifts or luxuries arranged by his friend, who had recently traveled to the U. S. and was keenly aware of an American's customary conveniences. Even though Jeff was inside the G.I.R. fortress, Ecuador's most elite fighting group's headquarters, he was still within a legitimate Third World country where these kinds of things are considered luxuries. Although this geographic area was shaped by political instability, poverty and violence, it was still far more civilized than the Middle East theaters Jeff had experienced. He was very grateful for his friend's thoughtfulness.

Lying back on his cot and trying to take advantage of his solitary quarters, Jeff hears a rap on the door. One of the G.I.R. soldiers was sent over to summons Jeff to breakfast. He would have much preferred sleep, but the thought of real food did trigger a little growl in his stomach. So out the door he went leaving sleep and unpacking for later. Walking across the parade grounds toward the chow hall, the men caught the smell of bacon and other fried foods wafting in the air. Jeff's hunger pangs exploded with the smell of hot breakfast food which had always been his favorite meal of the day. Entering the hall, Jeff and the soldier stepped in line and slowly made their way to an anticipated feast. The closer the men got to the serving table, the clearer the servings became. As Jeff's plate was being filled he was overwhelmed with dismay, looking down at two hotdogs over white rice with a cup of mystery soup on the side instead of eggs and pancakes. To add insult to injury, all the food was cold to the touch. Sitting at the table with the other enlisted men, Jeff was still smelling delicious bacon and eggs, yet all he saw was rice and hotdogs. Casting his gaze across the hall he spied a table full of what must be officers helping themselves to all of the dream food. Another little taste of culture shock was experiencing a real divide in a two-class society, even within this very special group of the National Police. No apologies from the "haves", no noticeable looks of envy from the "have nots." In fact, no one acknowledged the disparity except for Jeff. He wasn't sure if the monumental disappointment in the menu for the enlisted men killed his appetite, or if it was the bitter juice that came with his meal; all he knew was after rearranging his cold hotdogs and rice for a bit, he was ready for some sleep.

Stepping outside his barrack, after recharging with a few hours of sleep, Jeff intended to get his baring and maybe some exercise. He found the entire installation motionless. Not a soul to be found anywhere as he moved about. Somewhat like a ghost town in an old "Western", or a facility left in the aftermath of an apocalypse, Jeff felt like the last being on earth walking across the compound. Never had he witnessed any kind of desertion of a post like this during his seven years in the military, or during his eight and a half years as a K-9 officer back in Kentucky for that matter. The eerie atmosphere transformed Jeff's walkabout into a wandering investigation.

Heading across the grounds to what looked like a P.T. area, Jeff saw a flash of movement about five o'clock. Turning fully around, there was nothing but buildings and vehicles with a lot of space between them. Pushing on to the P.T. ground Jeff noticed what looked like a command center, and he redirected his route. Everything was still deathly quiet as Jeff reached for the front door of the command center. Before he could touch the handle, a strong "pssst" broke the silence.

Quickly withdrawing his hand Jeff searched for the source of the noise and saw Mingo leaning against the side of the dormitory he just passed. Still wearing his khakis and blazer, Mingo was slowly shaking his head from side to side to indicate "No entrar por favor." Jeff sent Mingo his own signal, a military style communique that he felt sure would be understood. With his right hand, Jeff pointed to his own eyes using the index and middle fingers followed by sweeping those fingers across the installation grounds. Looking at Mingo, Jeff turned both palms up and raised his hands slightly to indicate "What gives?" with the emptiness. Using his right hand, Mingo made a fist and turned his thumb down, following that with clasped hands against one side of his face as he tilts his head. Jeff immediately blurted out "Siesta!" Mingo nodded his head up and down. Jeff responded under his breath this time, "Unbelievable! I thought they only did that in the movies!"

Turning for the exercise area again Jeff looked back to motion Mingo to come, but like an apparition he'd already vanished. Alone once more, Jeff moved along shaking his head thinking how differently the Ecuadorian government operated with its military posts completely shutting down for naps, its use of worn out pickup trucks and private guns for hire, not to mention cold hotdogs for breakfast. After forty-five minutes of calisthenics on the well-equipped P.T. course, Jeff felt better and was actually able to appreciate the region's unique mix of hot sun and cool, damp air. The good feelings along with the refreshing air turned his mind toward dogs, and how well they should be able to work in this climate. Every dog man knows, one of the quickest ways to shut down a working canine is turn up the heat. Hot and humid or hot and dry, when even the most driven dog heats up or dries out, he's done, period!

As Jeff's thoughts rolled around to his dogs and their possible whereabouts, the call for "cena" came screaming across the compound. Watching all the enlisted men scramble for the chow hall, Jeff got the picture and didn't need to be led to dinner this time. He was utterly famished. The smell coming from the "cocina" was distinctly different from that of the morning meal, and it definitely smelled appetizing. Approaching the serving table, Jeff could not believe his eyes: two cold hotdogs over white rice, alongside a bowl of disgusting cold soup, and a tall mug of bitter juice to wash it all down. Too hungry to pass it up this go-around, his only hope was that the G.I.R. post had to eventually run out of "tubed" meat by-products. Of course, the officers were subjected to no such torture. They were actually being waited on, and had their choice of several mouth-watering entrees with every imaginable side dish to go with it. Jeff could never get used to this inordinate disparity in food quality between men who fought side by side. He was aware of some differences between officers and enlisted men back home, but it was taken to an extreme in Ecuador. At least his belly was full of some kind of calories after the meal, and that hadn't been the case for a couple of days.

Franklin

Waking in the morning to reveille was a familiar call for Jeff. After a full tour as a Marine and his recent, several years stint with the Special Tactics Force, Jeff was quite comfortable with a military regimen. What he wasn't accustomed to was a full night sleep. By nature, he was a terrible sleeper, like his maternal grandmother who was such a strong influence on him, so four to five hours of down-time in one night was normal. That is why, although an innately happy individual, Jeff usually carries a tired expression in his eyes. His first night in Ecuador however, he crashed like a dead man, and he was not about to muster with the G.I.R. enlisted. In no hurry to eat more hotdogs, Jeff thought exercise and locating his canine charges would be the order for the day, provided that Hector didn't come for him. Fitness usually ranks high on a professional dog-trainer's priority list, especially with the caliber of dog and man Jeff works with. Conditioning canine athletes, as well as covering the instructional aspects of apprehension and scent detection work, is a very physical job. Vigorous exercise is a dog trainer's insurance plan against debilitating injuries. At heart Jeff is an athlete anyway, and he's always pushed his physical limits pursuing baseball and wrestling. Were it not for tearing his right A.C.L. just months after winning a "full ride" college scholarship, Franklin the dog trainer may have wound up playing shortstop for a professional baseball team. So, a little "P.T." seemed like the perfect medicine to mitigate the nagging headache he'd been carrying around since arriving at the high-altitude, G.I.R. stronghold.

Midway through his morning run around the installation, Jeff heard the sweetest sound in all of Ecuador, the powerful, staccato barking of stimulated dogs. Zeroing in on the familiar woofing in the distance, Jeff saw a small concrete-block building that was perched on a hill, away from everything else. Thinking that had to be the kennel in an animal shelter's typical juxtaposition to human living and working quarters, Jeff directed his run to the obscure building on the hill. When the cool Andean breeze shifted to the direction of the block structure, proof of the kennel hit the dog-man square in the face. Urine on concrete, wet canine hair and fresh stool, all those odors that make up the "kennel" smell which can be so offensive to non-animal people yet so comforting to dog trainers.

Unsure of whether it was the effects of the altitude or the anticipation of seeing his four- legged friends that was effecting him, Jeff was nearly dizzy with excitement by the time he reached the building. Rounding the front corner of the structure, he almost ran into the first outdoor pen which was attached to the building itself.

Bent over at the pen's gate to catch his breath, Jeff was jolted into a clear mind by the explosion of a ferocious German shepherd. From inside the kennel, a monstrous dog, violently charged into the outdoor pen to address the intruder. With a violent lunge the shepherd threw himself against the gate, hoping something might give way so he could unleash his fury on the trespasser. For a brief moment, Jeff and the snarling police dog were face to face, but within an instant the thunderous barking and violent lunging melted into wiggling and whining. Both Jeff and the giant canine recognized the other at the same time, bonded together during months of training, Jeff blurted out "Bosco" which triggered the dog to nearly climb out of his seven-foot-high pen.

Bosco was one of Jeff's all-time favorites. He was too fond of him as a matter of fact. Even though he already had two personal dogs, Jeff almost withheld this special shepherd from sale, just to hang on to him a little longer. Those are destructive feelings for a professional dog trainer to harbor. In a long career, there will be more outstanding dogs than one can justly keep. At the same time, there always seems to be a shortage of qualified or appreciative handlers, which can make the decision to sell a really nice animal more difficult. Bosco was this caliber of animal: high energy, physically assertive, courageous, and tenaciously determined. He was a relatively tight coated shepherd which meant he bulged with muscle definition, especially as conditioned as he was for his new commission with the G.I.R. Special Forces. Jeff has always given the same energy and attention to developing the canine soldier as he has their human counterparts. So, Bosco was fit and ready for duty when he arrived at the Quito airport. He was quite capable of working long days under the worst conditions for extended periods, just like the men he would be serving.

The kennel master, hearing the raucous cacophony, plowed through the back door of the kennel preparing to admonish one of his cohorts for irritating the new G.I.R. recruits. The care-taker lost his composure when he saw a stranger inside the pen bear-hugging the "man stopping" Bosco. "No! No! Ahy, ahy, ahy!" Jeff immediately tried to calm the very upset kennel master by explaining in English who he was, while Bosco jumped around and playfully chattered like a boy reuniting with his long-lost papa. The kennel master was so taken aback by Bosco's antics, Jeff's laughter, and the genuine affection between the obvious friends that he forgot what the emergency was about. When Jeff finally turned away from his wild canine friend and greeted the kennel master, the Ecuadorian smiled and asked, "Franklin?" Jeff smiled back as he stepped out of the pen and said "si, Franklin." With that the two dog men embraced one another, and the kennel master excitedly took Jeff by the arm while jabbering a mile-a-minute, to reunite him with rest of the four-legged students. What a relief it was to see his old friends so well cared for. Lobo, Blackjack, Sniper, and all the rest were vibrant, in good weight, and wearing happy expressions.

When Hector and the Vice President of Ecuador visited the United States the previous winter, Jeff advised the South American entourage during their dog selection process. After a few days of extensive testing, Jeff congratulated Captain Liano on securing eight canine "specimens", all of which were pre-selected and purchased in Europe by Franklin himself. The eight dogs ran the gamut of contemporary breeds typically trained in police work. In the group there were three pure bred Germanshepherds, two Belgian Malinois, two Dutch shepherds and a Malinois/Dutch shepherd mix. All were strong, upper-middle size animals except for Bosco, who was a leviathan! Seeing his canine troops after nearly two weeks of separation, Jeff agreed with his own assessment of a few monthsprior, "They were specimens!" Walking through the kennel facility dragging his fingers along the pen gates so that all of the dogs could lick his fingers, Jeff didn't feel alone anymore. Now he was in his element,with his familiar friends along with their familiar noises, and odors. The American dog trainer was at home at last in Ecuador.

Two

The G.I.R.

Jeff's mission in South America was relatively straight forward. Integrate the eight freshly trained police dogs with their new handlers, assess the G.I.R.'s overall canine training program and evaluate the utilization of the dog/handler teams. After the impromptu visit to the kennel, Jeff's training juices were flowing. He was more than ready to jump into the fundamental part of his mission, which was to prepare the eight four-legged students for their yet to be assigned human partners. Too excited to wait for Hector's return, Jeff raced back to the barracks to feast on some jerky and nuts (a gourmet meal in comparison to the chow hall) as he changed into his dog-training gear.

Jeff began refreshing all eight dogs in their tactical obedience and bomb-detection instruction that morning. The apprehension, or "bite-work" would have to wait until he received a little assistance in the way of designated handlers for the dogs, or an officer assigned to be a decoy (a "bad guy"). That way either Jeff would don the padded "bite suit" and direct the handlers while he was being savaged as the canine's target, or one of the G.I.R. soldiers would volunteer for the "decoy" job because their Captain insisted on a volunteer, and Jeff would orchestrate from the handler's position. Jeff was a very fit and experienced trainer, so either position would work for instruction purposes. Although a person will collect a variety of nasty bruises (through the protective suit) from hard biting dogs, the adrenaline rush and sheer excitement of being ferociously attacked by a combat ready canine makes the superficial wounds worthwhile for most enthusiastic dog-men. Franklin, an athlete, proudly displays the scars to prove he seldom hesitates to climb into a "bite suit" in hopes of catching a little adrenaline rush while training dogs.

With the assistance of the kennel master, Jeff used an unlocked storage building to set up a makeshift work area. He often used a pencil and paper to draw out for his G.I.R. helper all the items they needed for instruction, like obstacles for a tactical obedience course and odor aids for scent detection. The kennel man was one of the regular G.I.R. enlisted, but unlike the two men who picked him up at the airport, and all of the soldiers he'd met on base for that matter, this guy was on the opposite end of the scale when it came to amiability. He was always smiling, and he went out of his way to gather everything Jeff needed for the canine students. He would even check on Jeff throughout the day bringing him water and snacks from the cantina.

Although a relatively new dog-man, this Ecuadorian soldier who turned into a kennel manager was all about training the animals he'd already grown fond of. Jeff remembered how intently this fellow studied every move he made while working with the police dogs, and neither man took a siesta break that first day of training either. The Ecuadorian later told his superior officer that he saw Franklin as the master of a trade he had just taken up, and he intended to learn as much from the American dog trainer as he could during the short time they'd be together. As far as Jeff was concerned, he valued having the Ecuadorian's enthusiastic and helpful company. He did nothing but enhance the instruction for his canine corps and make day number two with the G.I.R. very satisfying. During the first practice rounds of explosive detection, Jeff was pleasantly surprised to see how sharp all of his dogs' noses were. The majority of them rested their nostrils less than twelve inches from a planted target, literally pointing out the explosives with the black of their nose. Not only that, but their indicating posture, "sitting", was overall crisp and confident. It was like they had not travelled or changed ownership at all. Of course, that's what Jeff had trained them to do, and that's what the Ecuadorian police force were counting on. However, Jeff expected that with such a drastic change in culture and climate that there would be a substantial adjustment period for the dogs. If nothing else, this first successful day of training inside the compound proved that his canine corps had been and were being well cared for. Jeff also concluded that with such outstanding detection responses from this newly trained group of dogs, the "fast progression" training protocol he developed for the U. S. Military yielded the same consistently, accurate results regardless of curing time. With the Special Tactics Force, Jeff had many months to prepare each dog for its tasks in combat. Comparatively, the Ecuadorian dogs only had one-third of the instruction and conditioning time.

The "fast progression" protocol challenges a canine student to absorb manageable bits of information in rapid succession over an extended period of time. Mild to moderate environmental stress is created by this "learning load" which in turn heightens the canine student's cognitive skills. After months of conditioning, the end results of this unique instruction approach for the Special Combat Group were fast and accurate bomb detection with dogs, who only moments before, were deployed to hostilely disable a human target.

Jeff developed a unique kind of soldier for the U.S. Military, a combat dog specifically groomed to work with a special group of fighting men. As a unit they were capable of stealthy, directed eruptions of face to face violence that ended in screams, gun shots and death. In no more than minutes, this extraordinary detachment of men and dogs could transition into a machine of energy control, quiet concentration, and pinpoint accurate odor detection despite the lingering taste of blood, the smell of death, and the ringing of gunshots.

The Ecuadorian government, more specifically the head of their National Police Task Force, sought Jeff Franklin out to enhance their existing canine program with the caliber of dog and instruction he provided for the U.S. Military. That all sounds straight forward enough, until real life gets in the way as it usually does. With a host of unpredictable obstacles, such as budget concerns, time restraints, and political games, the canine program that Jeff had originally proposed to the Vice President of Ecuador had to be pared down. Fewer dogs with less training, compounded by reduced instruction time for the handlers meant the Special Tactics Program that Jeff had originally planned for the G.I.R. operation had to be reduced to its skeleton form. "Streamline everything, yet expect the same results", sums up the South American project that still makes Jeff shake his head in frustration! On the flip side of that coin, the first day's performance of all the canine rookies is one of his best memories.

When training wrapped up, Jeff helped the kennel master feed and tuck all of the dogs away just in time to get in line at the chow hall. Sitting next to his training helper, Jeff learned the secret of eating cold hotdogs and rice. The "tubed meat" needs to be chopped up, and mixed with the rice. Stir that concoction into the cold soup, and you end up with a palatable meal. At least it seemed to help, or maybe Jeff was just that hungry. Either way, he was adjusting.

Very late that night, Jeff was awakened by a distinct "rap" on his door. Reaching into the personal bag he always kept at bed side, Jeff retrieved a Streamline Scorpion flashlight for one hand and a Timberline Tactical knife for the other. Out of habit, Jeff usually sleeps in his 5.11 BDUs when he's away from home, just in case there's an emergency. So, when such a rousting occurs in the wee hours of the night, there's no need to fumble with lamps or clothing. The combat veteran simply steps out of bed ready for action. Jeff purposefully kept all the lights off in the little room as he made his way to answer at the door. Confessing during one of our interviews that the rational, business side of his brain said, "Turn on the lights, you don't need a knife to answer the door here in the middle of a Special Forces compound! It's no doubt a friendly visitor in the off hours of the night," the seasoned Marine/K-9 Officer side of his mind assessed the situation entirely differently. "What does it hurt to be on guard? Maybe the whole camp sleeps as soundly at night as they do during their siesta. Maybe that's what happened to Hector, he was whisked away in the middle of the night after being turned over to the F.A.R.C. by a traitor." It really didn't matter which aspect of his character won the debate, because in only seconds he was easing the door open with his tactical light at the ready. As soon as a face could be discerned in the shadows, Jeff flooded the eyes with his Streamline. "Por favor Franklin mi amigo, soy Hector!" Making out the features of his familiar friend, Jeff couldn't keep himself from laughing as he turned on the room lights. With a quick embrace at the door, Jeff apologized for temporarily blinding his visitor as he invited Hector inside.

Accompanying Captain Liano was one of his First Lieutenants, as well as a professionally dressed woman who looked to be a civilian. The woman introduced herself right away with fairly correct English. "My name is Casandra and I do administrative work in the G.I.R. office. Captain Liano brought me along as a translator." Still carrying his tanto-blade Timberline, Jeff sang out "halleluiah" and hugged Hector's assistant. "Don't tell anyone, but I'm in love! No offence Hector, but

Casandra the interpreter hangs with me. I'm done with picture drawing and obtuse hand signals. It's time for Jeff Franklin to take part in
conversation!" Hector had a much better command of English than Jeff
did of Spanish, but he only understood bits and pieces of what was being
said in such an excited fashion. He simply smiled back with pleasure at
his obviously happy friend, and seemed to be genuinely amused that
Franklin was so elated. After brief pleasantries and a handshake with the
First Lieutenant, Captain Liano suggested that they all go over to the
Cantina for refreshments. He and Franklin had a lot of catching-up to
do, and much to discuss about dogs.

Jeff was living in a better world having Casandra along as an interpreter. Subconsciously, he had harbored some worries over his ability to
convey training details during this week of instruction for his Spanish
speaking handlers. Obviously, he wasn't concerned enough to arrange
for a translator ahead of time. He tackled the language barrier in typical
Jeff Franklin style, deal with it as it comes up. On this trip that meant
communicating through hand signals, body gestures and picture drawing until an interpreter appeared. Reminiscing about the experience,
Jeff felt that if Hector wouldn't have arranged for a translator he would
have, especially if the instruction program suffered at all. But, being
honest with himself as he thought back, "An interpreter may have been
like a television, if I never had the luxury, I wouldn't have missed it!"

When they stepped into the Cantina, Hector and the Lieutenant
went about gathering some refreshments for their party. Left alone
with Jeff at a table, Casandra asked him where he lived in the United
States, and how he ended up in South America fulfilling a police dog
contract. Jeff gave his pat response for the first part of Casandra's question. "I'm from Kentucky Derby Country, the world's tenth top sporting
event. Specifically, I call Louisville home. A beautiful city located on the
Ohio River, and whose basin is home to nearly ten percent of the U.S.
population." Although Jeff's reply is rehearsed, it thoroughly satisfies
the "Where are you from?" question for most people, and that's good for
business. Because, all too often when Mr. Franklin is pressed to answer
pinpointing, follow-up questions like; "Where is that?", or "Is that next

to the Grand Canyon?" his smart-ass side surfaces, and that's not good for business! To answer the second half of Casandra's inquiry, Jeff only needed two words, "Eduart Haghen!" Before she had a chance to ask the obvious, Jeff gave her the lowdown.

Mr. Haghen was a working-dog broker in Holland that Jeff met in 2006 while on a canine procuring trip. To say this man is successful at what he does is an understatement. Over the past two decades his Holland kennel has evolved into the international hub for "high performing" canines. Jeff had to seek out Mr. Haghen when the U.S. Military's Elite Canine Program ran into a serious glitch. In fact, the program under Jeff's supervision almost collapsed because of a dog-training malfunction in the heat of a top priority mission. Jeff determined the fix for the nearly catastrophic problem was a higher caliber dog that would better facilitate these Special Operations. The Covert Combat Group needed a dog as hard and driven as the Commandos themselves. Jeff found out the hard way that no amount of training could prepare a standard police-type dog for the tasks the Commandos were commissioned to carry out. So, it was actually a training mishap that launched Jeff into a world-wide search for the sharpest and toughest dogs that money could buy. The search began in the United States and ultimately ended in the Netherlands with Eduart Haghen, a self-made broker of the highest caliber working-dogs. Over the years, Mr. Haghen had acquired a unique reputation and had amassed considerable wealth by utilizing his canine-savvy in conjunction with an aggressive business strategy. Since the first successful trip to Holland, Jeff has visited Mr. Haghen's kennel numerous times. As their relationship developed, Eduart gradually grew into Jeff's business mentor and took it upon himself to set lofty goals for the young, American dog trainer. So, Eduart planted a seed in Jeff's mind; "Take what you've learned as a dog trainer from working with the U.S. Military, and develop similar canine programs for other governments." Jeff wrapped up his diatribe when he saw Hector and the Lieutenant returning to the table, "I'm sure, that's more information than you wanted, but this G.I.R. project represents my first attempt at thinking 'Haghen big', and that's the 'skinny' on why I'm in Ecuador talking with a translator!"

After a bite of food, Jeff asked Hector where in the world he'd been. He also added, "I hope the business that kept you from taking care of a friend was at least somewhat important, or my last surviving 'feeling' will be hurt!" Thinking back on this visit at the Cantina, Jeff recalled how satisfying it was to be able to fully communicate details and emotion with his friend Hector through an interpreter. Their friendship deepened tremendously in a single evening. Hector wasn't nearly the raconteur his American friend was; however, he did give the interpreter a workout when he explained where he'd been for the past three days. Given the nature of Captain Liano's specialized force, "The Group of Intervention and Rescue", the story of his whereabouts was not that unusual. However, the level of danger and risk of mortal harm that the G.I.R. soldiers operated under was mind-boggling to Jeff, who was an ex-police officer himself.

Hector relayed that three mornings ago their office received a hysterical phone call from the aid of a high-profile politician who reported a kidnapping. Only minutes before the call came in, the politician's daughter was abducted from her vehicle at gunpoint by unidentified guerillas. She was ripped from the car in broad daylight just outside of Quito's town square. The kidnappers orchestrated a commonly used two vehicle blockade in order to trap the young woman. In this part of the world, a vehicle trap is often the setup for an abduction, because it usually facilitates a speedy extraction and a clean getaway. With a hot lead like this, the G.I.R. leapt into immediate deployment. In Ecuador, as in the United States, time is of the essence in a kidnapping case. Few will argue over the correlation between early action with an abduction and the increased likelihood of a successful recovery. The politician's aide was left unscathed in the young woman's car, so he told the Quito Police and subsequently the G.I.R. that the kidnappers barreled out of town in a northwesterly direction. No surprise to anyone in Quito that the guerillas were on a direct course for the equatorial jungle, and quite possibly Columbia. Not only would the dense rain forest cloak any escape route, but the crossing of the Columbian border would stymie any pursuit by Ecuadorian law enforcement. At the time of Jeff's visit, Ecuador and

Columbia had been existing under strained relations for some time due to differences in political policy. To further compound their relationship problems, the Columbian government initiated a huge faux pas prior to the young woman's abduction. A Columbian military unit attacked a F.A.R.C. stronghold inside Ecuadorian territory without the knowledge or consent of the Ecuadorian government. Even though the siege on the guerilla encampment was highly successful (seventeen F.A.R.C. members were killed, including Raul Reyes who was the second in command of the organization.), the event led to a complete diplomatic breakdown between the two countries. Under those current conditions of non-cooperation between the two countries, Ecuador's pursuit of any captors into Columbia would be severely prohibited. With those considerations, interception of the kidnappers prior to them reaching the border would be crucial if the G.I.R. hoped to liberate the politician's daughter.

Without delay, Captain Liano and his First Lieutenant struck out in a lone vehicle to intercept the fleeing captors while a larger contingent of G.I.R. soldiers pursued from the point of abduction. Feeling certain that the kidnappers would want to take refuge across the border, Hector planned to make visual checks of the known drug houses and terrorists hideouts along the main routes leading into the Columbian jungle. This was a very dangerous plan for a number of reasons. Some of the drug manufacturing houses are well guarded and that's why they also serve as good hideouts for kidnappers. Since the late 1990s, the G.I.R. as well as the National Police have run into elaborate booby-traps and complex explosive devices during raids on these terrorists' strongholds. The F.A.R.C.'s education in explosives became international news in 2001 when three members of a Northern Ireland terrorist organization (IRA) were arrested on charges of teaching bomb-making to members of Columbia's Revolutionary Army. Following the arrest, the U.S. House of Representatives Committee on International Relations published its findings of IRA activity in Columbia. The report pointed to a long standing connection between the IRA and F.A.R.C. It was estimated that the IRA had received millions of dollars' worth of drug proceeds from F.A.R.C. over the years in return for their instructional services. So, began the serious business of bombs in Ecuador.

Hector couldn't stop thinking about the eight trained dogs back at the kennel, and how desperately the G.I.R. have needed their help. If only the politician's daughter would have been abducted a week later, there would be an altogether different strategy in place for her rescue. A highly skilled canine team could clear a drug-house or hideout of bombs in a fraction of the time it takes an entire Special Forces Unit without the help of a dog. The shock-and-awe effect of a trained combat dog leading the charge into a terrorist stronghold during a raid could seriously tip the scales in favor of the extraction team. Hector fully expected search and rescue protocols to change for the G.I.R. with the addition of Jeff's dogs. As far as their current situation was concerned, Hector realized he had placed himself, as well as his right-hand man, in substantial peril for the outside chance of a speedy interception. They were out manned, out gunned, and deep into F.A.R.C country with no canine support. In truth, without the help of more men or trained dogs, searching any of these drug-houses for a kidnapped victim would be a difficult and risky challenge at best.

Two days into the operation, Captain Liano and his Lieutenant ran into a small band of guerillas along a jungle roadway. The para-military group was masquerading as a contraband checkpoint, which is a common ploy used by such groups in the area to control the drug trade. Both the Captain and his Lieutenant were in plain clothes for this mission to help conceal their identities. When they were confronted by three armed guerillas, Captain Liano immediately stepped out to address the men, hoping to talk his way through and get on with the search. Before Hector had a chance to describe to Jeff (with Casandra's assistance) what happened next, the First Lieutenant begged to interrupt. For long minutes, while the Captain was calmly recounting the events thus far, Jeff and Casandra could feel the Lieutenant's buildup in emotion. Hector politely nodded, and allowed his Lieutenant to take command of the narration.

The Lieutenant admired Captain Liano, and he wanted to make sure that sufficient attention was given to the details of what he saw as a heroic story, so he picked up the tale from his perspective inside the truck. Almost instantly, the Lieutenant could feel the conversation between his Captain and the guerillas, who have identified themselves as soldiers of The Revolutionary Army (F.A.R.C.), turn sour. Tension grew like a wild fire in dry tinder as hostile words flew from the mouths of the guerillas, each of whom had a 9mm Uzi which was slung at the side. Listening from inside the truck, the Lieutenant felt his stomach twist as goose bumps covered his body, his own precursors of impending mortal combat. Careful not to call attention to himself, the Lieutenant was quietly and quickly trying to free his sidearm. He was a seasoned soldier who had been in many skirmishes with his "Capitan", and he could smell conflict coming!

Through the open driver's window, the Lieutenant watched the scene unfold. Tall and calm, Captain Liano stood close to the truck no more than three strides from the guerillas who were standing shoulder to shoulder. Two of the guerillas harshly directed accusations of "Policia" and "enemy" at the Captain, but Liano's blood pressure didn't seem to rise. He insisted on controlling the situation in a cool business-like manner, never deviating from his civilian story. The three F.A.R.C. soldiers were not to be placated, and their accusations abruptly turned into threats. The Lieutenant was easing open the passenger door, when he saw the closest of the three guerillas make a fatal move. Demanding that Captain Liano raise his hands because he was now being taken prisoner, the F.A.R.C. soldier reached to pull his Uzi around. The Lieutenant had clarity of the situation as if it was slow motion. His eyes were glued on the Captain, and his arms and legs seemed to move through "thick mud" while exiting the truck. As the Lieutenant's head passed through the doorway, he saw Liano's right hand pulling out a M1911 from under his shirt. By the time he'd leveled the handgun on the enemy, Liano's left hand had cleared a waist pouch with a full magazine of .45s. The guerillas scrambled to pull their sub-machine guns around to take aim on the bold Captain. But, before the nearest soldier reached his trigger, Liano slammed the magazine into its well and sent two bullets ripping through the man's center mass. Charging toward the front of the truck, the Lieutenant saw in simultaneous slow-motion, guerilla number one crumbling to the ground, and guerilla number two aligning his Uzi barrel toward the Captain. A couple of shots rang out, and guerilla number two moaned as he spun into the dirt road.

Plowing around the truck with his handgun extended, the Lieutenant was fully prepared to face 9mm machine gun fire to join the Captain. Two steps from Liano, the Lieutenant heard a few more reports as hot .45 casings hit him in the face. Still in slow motion, the Lieutenant witnessed an empty magazine fall from Liano's 1911, and before the last terror-ist's body settled into a heap, the Captain had completed a reload with machine-like accuracy.

While Surveying the carnage and considering Liano's deadly precision, the Lieutenant concluded that the Captain was as formidable as the handgun he carried. Hector stood face-to-face with three armed terrorists and dispatched them all at point-blank range, in the time it took the Lieutenant to exit the truck. After a quiet period of assessment, Liano broke the silence and suggested that he and the Lieutenant make haste in their departure and turn the search back toward Ecuador. With no complaint from the Lieutenant, and no more ceremony from the Captain than reloading his magazine, the two men climbed into the truck and drove off in a southerly direction toward Quito. "Without apologies," the Lieutenant said, the slain F.A.R.C. guerillas were left in the roadway, the place where they met justice.

Liano typically carried his sidearm empty. He believed that self-imposed stress helped him maintain an edge over the enemy. The Captain felt that knowing he had to execute three requisite loading movements before discharging his weapon, and the enemy didn't, forced him to be hyper alert. The acute concentration derived from an intensely alert state, combined with the accuracy acquired from continual practice created the edge. Captain Liano staked his life on that policy. Since their first meeting, Jeff felt that Hector was the same caliber of man as any Top Tier Operator he'd trained with over the past several years. Intelligent,cool and confident, Hector was always "squared away".

He perpetually worked at his tactical skills and physical fitness, and actually competed in Triathlons as a hobby. Hector Liano was the essence of a Captain in appearance, with broad shoulders, a well chiseled face, and piercing dark eyes. Over six feet tall, Hector was a large man among his fellow Ecuadorians. But he was never harsh or crude, when he spoke he commanded attention.

Captain Liano represented the entire package as far as Jeff was concerned. He was serious about his business, he was a devoted family man, and he was a trusted friend as well as the perpetual realist. The admiration from his First Lieutenant, and the details from the After-Action Report of that mission, only confirmed what Jeff felt about Hector all along.

After two hours of conversation about everything from dogs in law enforcement to personal hang-ups, the group called it a night and agreed to meet for breakfast post reveille. The "wake-up" call came early with only a few hours of sleep, but that suited Jeff fine. The short night seemed to have no negative effect on Hector, the quintessential soldier. He's always "ready" with a tight haircut and a clean, tucked-in uniform. All his comrades agree that there's no way to tell how he really feels inside. As for Casandra and the First Lieutenant, they looked like they had just returned from an all-night raid, so they were desperately looking for a calorie boost. Forgetting for a moment who he was going to breakfast with, Jeff was coaching Casandra on the culinary nuances of chopping and blending of certain foods to improve their palatability. Not only were Jeff and Casandra escorted by officers into the Chow Hall, they were with Captain Liano.

There was no waiting in line for cold rations, and there was no line for them at all. The entire party seated themselves at a well outfitted table, and were immediately attended to by a couple of servers. They were given full menus with their choice of many different breakfast foods including real bacon, eggs and pastries of all kinds. Jeff even had a selection of familiar juices. A heavenly breakfast! Everything was perfect except for the faces of the men across the room, the enlisted G.I.R. soldiers who had become Jeff's meal-time comrades. The working-class man from Kentucky, couldn't bear to watch those men choke down hotdogs and rice while he ate like a king. After that reality check, the meal lost all of its charm for Jeff. He had to turn his chair around and face the wall in order to swallow a mouthful of eggs he had just shoveled in.

Hector had a busy training day planned for Franklin and the canine recruits. Captain Liano wanted all of the dogs matched with their prospective handlers, and each canine team run through multiple bomb detection as well as apprehension scenarios. Jeff could definitely sense an air of "hurry-up" surrounding Hector and his officers. The push on the new handlers to function like experienced dog men was tough. The dogs were adjusting well to their human partners, but it wasn't possible for the newly formed canine teams to execute as a synchronized unit within a single day, or even a few days for that matter. Expectations were high for a quick deployment of these teams, and Hector's last mission drove home how desperately the small G.I.R. search detachments needed the assistance of canine noses and jaws.

Jeff was well aware of the G.I.R.'s dire need for canine back-up. After all, it was that desperate requirement that sparked the Commander of the Intervention Group to wrangle the Vice President of Ecuador, and to solicit eighty-five thousand dollars from the U.S. State Department in order to fund the project. However, Jeff Franklin's job was to insure to the best of his ability, that the dogs he worked so hard to prepare for the Special Operations in Ecuador were in the hands of competent men who were as ready as the dogs for combat. That's what the Ecuadorian government hired him to do, and that's what his respected friend Hector was counting on. So, Jeff had no intention of letting anyone down, regardless of how many feathers he had to ruffle to gain the appropriate time to execute training and deployment appropriately.

This "his way, the right way" mindset grew from years of answering to the U.S. Military Brass while working with the Special Tactics Force. From his earliest days in professional dog training, Jeff embraced the adage, "A quick fix almost always led to a quick ruin!" All the instruction took place within the compound on that first training day.

Captain Liano counted on Franklin to bring to the G.I.R. what he developed with the U.S. Military. With that priority in mind, Hector gave his American friend all the free rein he needed to accomplish the goals the two men envisioned months ago back in the States. At the end of theday, when all of the dogs had been secured in their kennels, Hector and Franklin shook hands and agreed "It was a good day!" Both men were on the same page in regard to training and deployment protocols. Both men had the same order of considerations as well; the first concern was the men, then came the dogs, and lastly the mission.

On training morning number two, Captain Liano surprised his friend Franklin with the day's agenda. He had scheduled a live sweep of the Presidential Palace, and an outing in a Vice-Presidential security detail. He felt sure that was more responsibility and environmental distraction than his brand new canine teams could manage, and even Hector seemed uptight about using the dogs in this real-world scenario. So, Franklin asked the Captain an obvious question, "Why in the world did you set up such an early challenge for the fledgling program if you're uncertain about our readiness?" Hector responded with "I had no choice! My commander who is very supportive of the canine program gave me the same, specific directive that he was given by the Vice President himself."

Captain Liano's response didn't surprise Jeff that much. He was use to people in higher positions telling people in lower positions to accomplish things they had not been prepared to accomplish, and expecting it to be done in an unrealistic time frame. That seemed to be the common Method of Operation for military and Law Enforcement structures. In this particular case, the Vice President whom Jeff had the displeasure of meeting a couple of months ago back in the States, would have no problem "bullying" the head of the National Police to accomplish even a menial task, if only to prove that he could.

Ecuador's second in charge fit the template of an arrogant, self-serving politician who could star as the arch-villain in an international spy movie. He instantly made it clear to everyone involved in any of his projects, that all living beings were expendable in pursuit of his ambitions.

Long after Jeff closed the books on this South American trip, he summed Ecuador's V.P. up in one statement, "He was a cheating, pernicious, political scoundrel that nearly bankrupted my new company, Cobra Canine!"

Since the canine squads were already committed to the task, Jeff prepared to guide each man and dog team, individually, through the day as a high-stakes training exercise. Already in dog-training mode, Jeff recalled approaching the perimeter security around the magnificent and ornate Presidential Palace in Captain Liano's motorcade. His initial thought was the "first line of defense" was lightly manned, but could be beefed-up sufficiently with the addition of a couple of dual purpose dogs patrolling with the regular soldiers. The motorcade easily rolled through the one and only guarded gate after a ceremonial check of identification. The next stop or "second line of defense" was the single armed soldier standing at the front door of the palace. As the men gradually exited their vehicles, Hector called for his First Lieutenant, Franklin and Casandra to follow him up the steps to the grand entrance.

On the way up the endless steps, Jeff relayed to Hector through Casandra, "This can't be all the security there is! Tell me there's nobody home!" Captain Liano really didn't understand what Jeff's concern was about. "This has always been the level of protection for El Presidente. No harm has come to him yet at the Palace, only when he leaves!" No X-Rays or pat-downs were required, just a salute from Captain Liano opened the front door for the canine corps. Five meters into the ostentatious structure they met the President's personal assistant. He led them down a royal hallway, and when they turned the first corner they ran into none other than Ecuador's Commander and Chief. Introductions were led by Liano, and they were fairly casual, "El Presidente, Senor Jeffrey Franklin del Estados Unidos." Jeff responded with, "Very good to meet you Sir!" while thinking the whole time how special is this, a dog trainer from Kentucky shaking hands with the actual President of Ecuador inside the Presidential Palace, and all of this because of eight dogs!

After light conversation about the canine recruits and life in general, through the interpreter, it was time for Jeff to get busy. Jeff filled Hector's head with suggestions on how he would use the dogs to strengthen security by routine explosives checks along the Palace's perimeter, and by placing the canine intimidation factor in full view throughout the residence. That would at least be the place to start by his estimation. In truth, Jeff was thinking it would take weeks of revamping the entire security system to even compare to what he was used to back home at the White House. However, that kind of project went way beyond the scope of his mission. So, Franklin spent the day concentrating on what he was hired to do, getting the canine teams to effectively carryout their tasks of clearing bombs and utilizing the dogs' aggressive potential against any potential hostile invaders.

Synchronizing the handlers with the dogs to effectively execute their duties could not have gone more smoothly. Factoring in the environmental stressors of a "real world" environment, Jeff summed up the mission as outstanding. He attributed the on-the-job training success to the high caliber of men and dogs that made up the K-9 teams. Curled up on his cot, after a long and tedious day of instruction, Jeff drifted off to sleep with the thoughts of "What a different country!"

Three

Ambush

In the early pre-dawn hours of the next morning, Jeff was jarred from sleep by heavy banging on his door and blaring Spanish chatter. "Franklin! Franklin! Una reunion de emergincia!" Shaking off the grogginess of deep sleep, Jeff slipped into his well-travelled Reef sandals and Patagonia vest to meet the disturbance. When he opened the door, there stood one of the G.I.R. soldiers responsible for the alarm, and his body guard Mingo. With a rush of excited gestures, they encouraged Jeff to follow them across the compound to the Command Center. Jeff was ushered through the front door of the Command Center and into the bustle of a crowded meeting room. The bright lights and harsh noise made it difficult for half-closed eyes to focus on anything. The intense, overlapping conversations competed with radios that were on fire with incoming communications. Everyone who was anyone was there, pouring over maps that were strewn across a long conference table. Once his eyes adjusted, Jeff scanned the room to see who was actually in attendance. It was no surprise to see Hector with his First and Second Lieutenants of course; but he wouldn't have expected to see the Commander over the entire G.I.R. operation along with his second in-charge attending a midnight briefing. Even "sleepy-eyed" Casandra was there, no doubt for his benefit. With the inclusion of two more G.I.R. officers and Mingo, the room was filled.

Excluding Jeff and Casandra, everyone was in full uniform, including sharply dressed Mingo who was wearing tactical, safari-like attire. Although no one gave Jeff's shirtless, sockless outfit a second look, he began to feel a little self-conscious being so underdressed for the event, but then it came to mind that he didn't crash their party, they invited him! The self-consciousness left as quickly as it came, with the aid of his sleepy head screaming for Starbucks or the closest substitute. Excusing himself from Mingo's side, Jeff made his way over to the coffee machine for a cup of "hot tar", then squeezed through a few people to get next to Casandra, his communication source. He really didn't need an interpreter to smell a "priority-mission" in the briefing, but he was curious as to why the Dog Trainer was invited to the strategic meeting.

The focus of any one conversation shifted so quickly from man to man it was very hard for Jeff to keep up even with Casandra's help. The Commander took charge of the floor when he leaned over a specific topography map. Before he could finish drawing an imaginary line, Hector interrupted as he placed markers on the same map. Casandra kept her mouth close to Jeff's ear repeating as much of the frantic conversation as she could capture. The Commander mentioned "intel" and politician's daughter; Hector talked about interception points; the Second Lieutenant shook his head and said something about the Columbian border in connection with the Republican Army. One of the lower officers described a fast route NNE to Ibarra then a shift of ENE to San Gabriel and across into Columbia. The Second in Command vehemently opposed the border crossing and alluded to the G.A.U.L.A. (Columbia's Unified Action Group for Personnel Rescue). The Commander shot the G.A.U.L.A. suggestion down immediately. Hector pointed out two specific locations on one of the maps, and referred several times to "un perro." The First Lieutenant seemed to agree.

Practicing the canine assisted take-down.

As the discussions became more heated, Casandra worked like a machine to absorb each man's input with one ear and relay the key points to Jeff, while at the same time processing his questions with the other ear. Hector and his First Lieutenant elaborated on the strike plan. During their presentation everyone was quiet, even the Commander. Jeff heard one of the Lieutenants mention his name, and Hector agreed. The Second in Command questioned with concern a couple of points, then everyone was silent. The Commander asked about an exit strategy, and one of the officers suggested the San Miguel River then WSW through Nueva Loja. Again, an absolute hush fell over the entire room, and all eyes were glued on the Commander. Looking down at the floor with heavy countenance, the Commander slowly shook his head from side to side. When he looked up, he pointed a finger at Captain Liano and iterated, "Confidencia?" The Captain responded "Si Commandante!" With that the Commander made his way across the room to address Jeff and Casandra.

Making absolutely certain that nothing was lost in translation, the Commander asked Jeff, "Franklin, do you understand the nature of what we are discussing?" Jeff replied, "Yes sir!" The Commander went on to summarize the situation. "Two hours ago, we received credible intelligence as to the whereabouts of an abducted woman, the daughter of a high profile, political leader. We tried a few days ago to liberate her from the F.A.R.C. contingent that kidnapped her, but we failed. Captain Liano and his Lieutenants are confident that with a couple of dogs and your help we can successfully retrieve her this time. The plan is to send two G.I.R. units to engage the guerillas at two possible hideouts and utilize the dogs to aid in the extraction. My officers would like you to manage the dogs because our handlers are not up to speed as yet. Our plan would be to strike immediately. The strike force will travel at high speed, execute, and exit with the same expediency. More than likely, the mission will cross into the jungles of Columbia where there is a possibility of heavy F.A.R.C occupation. I must stress the extreme danger associated with this action. Captain Liano assures me that you are very experienced in combat and are quite capable of handling this responsibility. I will ask you directly as a United States contractor, do you feel this mission could be considered within the scope of your commitment and your ability?" Jeff didn't hesitate, "Yes sir!" The Commander pushed the point further,

"Are you willing?" Feeling the excitement of impending combat, Jeff fired back just two words,

"Damn Skippy!" With his classic half-smile, he also nodded his head in approval. Even though the Commander didn't understand Jeff's verbal response, he couldn't misinterpret the smile and the nod. That said it all! Turning toward his officers, the Commander called out, "Vamos!", and the room exploded into a scramble.

On the way out of the room Jeff heard Hector hollering "Franklin! Franklin!" Jeff quickly grabbed Casandra's arm before she could get away from him. On fire from the high-energy briefing, Hector was reeling off Spanish so fast that Jeff could only nod and shake his head in return. The whole time Jeff knew what a disaster this briefing and mission would have been for him without a translator. The Captain quickly laid out the immediate plan. There will be three Hiluxes in the strike force, and Jeff was assigned to the second truck. Within fifteen minutes one of the G.I.R. officers would be by the barracks to pick him up. Cassandra was excluded from this mission because of its highly dangerous nature, and unfortunately, the Commander would not give approval for Jeff to carry any firearms. So, in the event of a firefight Jeff must maintain proximity to one of the officers assigned to his truck. Also, Liano wanted Jeff to select two dogs that were best suited for this mission, and load one dog in truck number one (Captain Liano's) and the other in truck number two. The Kennel Master would meet the Strike Force at the kennel and assist Jeff in loading the two dogs of his choice. The Force would then launch from the kennel at precisely 0500, which gave the men less than thirty minutes before they had to "rattle and roll". As Jeff started to break away and run for his quarters to gear-up, he heard Casandra call out, "Franklin!" The Captain needs to go over one more thing." Hector firmly grabbed Jeff's shoulder with his left hand and patted his 1911 with the other. "I hate that I can't give you some weapon to carry. It's wrong to send you out there without, at least, a sidearm!" Jeff didn't like the idea either, but he wanted to relieve his friend Liano from the obvious angst he was carrying over the issue. So now it was Jeff's turn; he grabbed Hector by both shoulders, and gave him a broad full smile, "You forgot,

I have Bosco! Even the devil is no match for him! You worry about the mission; Bosco and Franklin will take care of themselves!" Before they parted, Hector expressed how he would be unable to forgive himself if his American friend fell into terrorists' hands during this mission. So, he and his First Lieutenant devised an emergency exit strategy.

There is only one narrow corridor into and out of the Colombian, F.A.R.C. territory where the targeted hideouts are located. That means, if the Strike Force becomes overwhelmed at any point during the raid, Jeff and the Second Lieutenant, who was the designated driver of Hilux Number Two, would be directed to bail out of the vehicle and run south toward the San Miguel River. Utilizing a Global Positioning System, the Lieutenant would radio an extraction boat with the approximate coordinates for a rendezvous. The pilot of the boat would have been briefed, and would expedite transportation down river to a designated extraction point near Nueva Loja, Ecuador. There, an armed G.I.R. vehicle would be waiting to complete the safe return trip back to the G.I.R. compound. Liano stressed that the weakest link in the emergency strategy was at the exit-point from the jungle. The boat would be extremely vulnerable holding on the Columbian bank, so the rendezvous window would be very small, only a few minutes. Also, the rain forest itself would be a challenge. Unbroken, heavy vegetation covered the entire area from the road where the Hilux would be abandoned, all the way to the San Miguel River. Hector felt certain the plan was sound, as long as Franklin and the Lieutenant made fast time through the forest while maintaining a southerly direction. "You can't be serious!" was Jeff's visceral reaction to Hector's suggestion, but he kept that to himself. There was really nothing about the G.I.R. extraction plan that Jeff liked; least of all, running unarmed through a jungle which was occupied by the enemy. It was also very hard to imagine being able to quickly find a tiny boat in such a vast area, even with the help of a G.P.S. So, Franklin came up with his own exit strategy, "Pray that he wouldn't need Hector's!"

Back in his barrack, Jeff threw on his 5.11 pants, a moisture wicking T-shirt and a tactical vest. After pocketing a bottle of water and some nuts, he shoved the Timberline knife into his pants and clipped the Scorpion light to his vest. Regretfully, Jeff left his customary ball cap and jacket in his gear bag, so the last thing he secured to his body were his Salomon high-top running boots. Whether it be tactical boots or baseball cleats, Franklin always laces them all the way up, and pulls them tight enough to nearly cutoff circulation. He makes absolutely certain they aren't coming off his feet while he's moving! It only took Jeff a few minutes to gear-up, but when he stepped out of his quarters, the Lieutenant and truck were already waiting. Jeff and the Lieutenant pulled up to the kennel at the same time as the kennel master. When the kennel man turned on the lights, Jeff peered down a row of sleepy canine faces. Quiet as mice, and curled up on their cots, they locked on the men's faces with a burning question, "What's up?" Jeff squatted down in front of Bosco, and asked him like he would a human being, "You wanna go to work?" With that, Bosco jumped off his cot in full barking mode. It wasn't so much that he understood casual conversation as it was a conditioned response. Bosco recognized this familiar signal as an initial step in a ritual between him and Jeff that always led to stimulating interaction. Step two in the ritual was the attachment of the leash and slip collar which was hung on each dog's gate. After Jeff slid the collar over Bosco's massive skull, the kennel master handed over Bosco's tactical harness which was the next consecutive step in the ritual. By the time the harness was strapped on, Bosco was beside himself, he needed no further convincing that real work was on the horizon. While Jeff took Bosco out for a relief run in the elimination area, the kennel man loaded a plastic airline crate along with a three day supply of food and water for the dog in the back of the second truck. Approaching the bed of his designated truck, Jeff reached to unlatch the tail-gait when "Big Bosco" sprang from the ground into the truck-bed landing in front of his crate. Bosco was so energized over the prospect of work, Jeff recalls that this giant canine was as agile as a cat.

Now, inside the kennel, there were no longer any quiet, sleepy faces. All the dogs were "jacked-up". They could sense the unusually high energy in the air. There was never any doubt in Jeff's mind which two dogs were most fit for this mission. Bosco would have been the first pick for any task, and the strong second choice for this "Commando" type of mission was Sniper. Like most Belgian Malinois, Sniper was muscled like an Olympic athlete, and he possessed a serious, combative nature much like Bosco's. High in energy and strong in nerve, Sniper was cut-out for this mission. He would make an ideal dog for Hector's team because he was a little more compliant during handling than the more independent Bosco. Jeff squatted down in front of Sniper's pen just like he did Bosco's and asked the same question, "Wanna go to work?" Even though Sniper was already on his feet looking very alert, a canine's response to Jeff's ritualistic question gives him a feel for the dog's mental state. If he asked Sniper the question and the Malinois quietly stared back at Jeff with no demonstration of arousal that may be an indication of a psychological or physiological imbalance. Because of behavioral conditioning, the initial step in Jeff's working routine always elicits an excited response from his dogs. When it doesn't, something is off in the canine teammate, and he may have to sit out a mission while awaiting further investigation. There was nothing off with Sniper that morning. Jeff didn't quite get the word "work" out of his mouth before the Malinois turned into a fawn colored cyclone. Bouncing from halfway up the gate to his cot and back to the gate, Sniper's feet didn't touch the ground until Jeff was able to wrangle a collar on him. As physically challenging as harnessing that energy may be, Jeff is always pleased to see his working canines so eager to launch into a mission.

After giving Sniper a chance to eliminate, Jeff loaded him in the back of Hector's number one truck along with the three-day supply of food and water. Once the weapons and radio-check were complete, the squad went over their orders a final time. The search and extraction approach was discussed along with the squad's exit strategy. Without Casandra, Jeff was privy to very little of the discussion. He was once again back to hand signals and drawings. However, he was clear on what his job would be once the team reached a hideout. Much like an American Special Forces maneuver in the Middle East, Jeff and his dogs would clear bombs or booby-traps. This would be done in a stealthy fashion, affording the extraction team an advantage of surprise when they made entry into the hideout itself. Once "Flash-bangs" had been deployed inside the structure, Jeff's dogs would lead the charge to the interior, immediately followed by the G.I.R. entry unit that would be carrying long-guns. The designated dog handlers were Hector with Sniper in truck number one, and Jeff with Bosco in truck number two. Although Captain Liano had handling experience, Jeff intended to keep a close watch on him to make sure the canine rookie didn't create compromising troubles for Hector. Truck number three was the most heavily armed and set up to protect the first two trucks, especially Franklin's. It wasn't by accident that Liano had his American friend sandwiched between two trucks full of G.I.R. soldiers. Hector knew that on the battle-grounds of South America, he was Franklin's "Lifeline." So, he had arranged for yet another surprise that was waiting at Jeff's Hilux.

As the men broke from the meeting and headed for their trucks, Hector walked over to Jeff and extended his hand in an unusual display of emotional concern. Even the First Lieutenant could tell that his Captain was carrying a load of worry over the American dog trainer. Jeff firmly gripped his friend's hand, and shook with energy. Face to Face, he smiled to ease Hector's tension and said "Easy day Captain, easy day!" With that the two men parted for the waiting caravan.

Coming out of the lighted kennel into the dark, Jeff's eyes were not yet fully adjusted when he closed in on his Hilux. There, leaning against the back passenger door, Jeff could make-out a familiar silhouette. It was one of those moments when a warm feeling preceded full recognition, but in an instant, cognition caught-up. "Mingo!" The entire caravan heard Jeff's emphatic exclamation, but he didn't care. Jeff's excitement was genuine, he'd actually grown accustomed to the bodyguard idea, and Mingo in particular. Jeff admired Mingo for doing his own thing, and doing it so well. Given his middle age, bushy head of hair and mustache, no one would ever think of Mingo as military. However, there was no doubt in Jeff's mind that this guy was as tough, hard and disciplined as any soldier in the G.I.R. force. Outfitted in his "safari-like" tactical uniform with the sleeves rolled up to the elbows, his uniform was complete with a full vest of what must have been two hundred rounds of loaded magazines for both of his Sig Sauer P226s. Mingo had one of these fifteen round, 9mm pistols strapped on each hip. He also carried a full sized "Fairbairn-Sykes" style fighting knife which was sheathed at the small of his back.

Propped against the truck, Mingo was as calm and collected as if he were standing in line for an ice- cream cone. You could never tell by his demeanor that he was about to charge into close quartered combat with the odds stacked against him. Jeff patted his body guard on the shoulder as he ducked through the rear passenger door. When Mingo climbed in behind him, Jeff said to the entire crew "With this guy and Bosco in the back, the F.A.R.C. don't stand a chance!" Even though none of the men understood a word of what Jeff said, his raw excitement and confidence fired them up.

By the early, blue light of dawn, the G.I.R. caravan was careening down a narrow, washed-out mountain road. Pitching and bouncing over softball size stones, Jeff felt the breakneck pace of the vehicles that were flying down the mountain, was truly suicidal. Keeping to the back roads of the country, the caravan slid into the shadows of the dense Colombian jungle before the sun broke the horizon.

Within five kilometers of their first "target house," they had yet to run into even one para-military group. One kilometer from the initial hideout, Captain Liano directs the three trucks off the road and into the vegetation for cover. The remaining distance to the house would be covered on foot with the bomb detection dogs in the lead sweeping for booby-traps. Jeff and Bosco would cover the right side of the private trail that led directly to the hideout, while Liano and Sniper would cover the left.

Liberating Bosco from his crate in the back of the Hilux, Jeff clipped him onto a military-grade, retractable leash. Hector followed suit with Sniper. This style of leash afforded the dogs all the freedom they needed to range-out, and effectively search for anything explosive. Naturally, both dogs were energized and bouncing to get busy. But, they had to be contained with strict obedience commands in order to preserve the stealthy advantage the small G.I.R. contingent desperately needed when confronting the usually larger and better armed F.A.R.C. forces. After giving the dogs a brief elimination break, Jeff led the way up the trail calmly and quietly directing Bosco to search to the right. Hector fell in immediately behind, sending Sniper to search left. With ready fingers on sensitive triggers, both Captain Liano and Jeff had a soldier with a shouldered MP5 covering their flanks. By closely guarding the handlers, the dog-men were free to concentrate on their first priority, the canine team members. Mingo drew one of his Sig Sauers from its holster, chambered a round, and followed the flanking soldiers. The rest of the strike force silently spread out in a staggered line and covered the rear. Three soldiers remained with the vehicles to protect their only way out of the territory. A slow and methodical approach to the hideout turned up no bombs or guerillas, the house appeared devoid of activity. With a quick survey, Captain Liano determined that the hideout had only recently been evacuated, and he felt they were on a hot trail of some kind, hopefully the right one.

Back in the trucks, the strike force rolled over miles of jungle road, allowing the caravan to spread out; the squad leaders were keeping in contact by radios only. Jeff remembered covering the distance between the first and second guerilla hideouts as an endless, stressful journey through a labyrinth riddled with settings for potential ambush. Mile after mile the men wondered, "Are we going to encounter gunfire around this bend, or up ahead through the overhanging canopy, or maybe when we get mired in one of the countless, soggy wallows?" At midday, their wondering came to an end. The first truck carrying Captain Liano's squad, ran into what Jeff described as "hell-fire" from all directions. Large caliber, machine gun rounds ripped across the narrow jungle road from positions deep within the recesses of the forest. The enemy and return fire was so intense coming across the radio that Liano's communications officer could barely be heard calling out the "Mayday." The radio talk was frantic, back-and-forth Spanish that Jeff couldn't make out at all. He had been in similar situations during Middle Eastern combat, so he could imagine the G.I.R. soldier's exchange of coordinates and enemy assessments. Jeff found out later that Liano's truck had taken major hits passing through the ambuscade, but miraculously no men or dog went down. Return fire on the enemy was only minimally effective because of the heavy vegetative cover. The G.I.R. troops were nothing more than living targets for the guerilla shooters.

The Lieutenant who was driving the second truck had pushed the accelerator through the floor when he heard the radio transmission come through from his Captain's squad. Mingo racked the slide back far enough on both his handguns to visually check that rounds were chambered and ready. Then he tightened his vest, and double-tied his boots. At that time, there was no doubt in Jeff's mind that he and his squad were charging head-long into the eye of a storm. Two troubling conceptions consumed him in the long minutes it took to close the gap between him and Liano; first was his worry over the dog's dangerous exposure to enemy fire, and second was his concern over how to protect himself and Bosco without any kind of weapon. There wasn't even enough time to bristle over the matters before the Lieutenant, who was receiving and relaying orders via the radio, swerved sharply off the dirt road and buried the Hilux in the jungle bush at high speed. This was an intentional maneuver, albeit risky, to instantly camouflage the truck and give the squad a chance to evacuate undercover. Jeff remembered being taught to execute a very similar tactic in Tanker's School by burying an M60 A3 tank in the sand at high speed. With the pick-up severely listing against a tangle of vines on the driver's side, the squad had to scramble out the passenger windows. They shoved their gear out first, and then squeezed through one man at a time. Jeff was the final man out! Climbing to his feet after tumbling out of the truck, Jeff saw the last G.I.R. soldier running break-neck through the jungle leaves toward the gunfire which was nearly on top of them. As Jeff watched the soldier disappear into the green abyss, he realized that he was now in a "worst case scenario".

With no time to clear his head, Jeff climbed into the truck bed to free Bosco when he heard what sounded like "Franklin!" coming from the road. The vegetation was so thick around the pick-up Jeff couldn't see past the rear bumper. There was no way to visually identify the person from where he stood, and unfortunately, he didn't recognize the voice. So, Jeff chose to ignore the call while working to free Bosco from his capsized crate. Again, from the road Jeff heard "Franklin, apura!" Only that time the call came through the brush much clearer and distinctly harsher. Gunfire was closing in quickly on Jeff's location, the clamor of soldiers in battle seemed to be just on the other side of a thin green veil. Giving up precious time, Jeff lowered himself to the ground and crawled through the mud and debris to get a look at the voice without exposing himself. Separating some vines Jeff saw a figure rushing towards him. About ten yards out, the outline of a man stepped around the bole of a giant tree. Jeff saw instantly it was Mingo. Holding true to his duty, he had returned to the pickup to protect his charge. Upon seeing his body-guard, Jeff jumped up and waved Mingo over. Mingo stood fast however. In a gravelly voice befitting his rough countenance he shouted above the encroaching gunshots and screams, "Apura, vamos!" Jeff understood what Mingo was saying, but he wasn't about to leave Bosco behind for the F.A.R.C. to kill or torture. Jeff turned back for the truck and hollered out, "I'm going to get the dog!" The men were virtually out of evasion time, and it showed in Mingo's furious response, "No perro! Vamos, ahora!"

As desperate and frightening as that situation was, the decision to go back for Bosco was an easy one for the Marine-turned-dog-trainer. Jeff could clearly hear the call to charge to the aid of a fellow warrior from his Sergeant in the opening moments of Desert Storm nearly two decades prior. The warrior not being human didn't really factor into Jeff's decision. Jeff's mantra is, "No living teammate left behind." In Mingo's defense, being the hard, stoic, non-dog-man that he was, Jeff had no expectations of him understanding those feelings. He fully expected, without blame, for his bodyguard to exit the scene in self-preservation mode, and leave survival up to each individual. The opportunity to fall back and regroup was gone by the time Jeff reached the Hilux. Live rounds were cutting through the trees only feet from him and Bosco. No more than five feet nine inches tall, Jeff is a medium framed man, but he's powerful. A lifetime of athletics cultivated extraordinary strength for a man of his size. Reaching over the truck bed, Jeff grabbed the mid-connecting flange of Bosco's crate, and with a Herculean grunt pulled the giant dog (crate and all) over the side of the pick-up. The crate crashed to the ground as the truck's windshield blew out from machine gun fire. With his boots against the bottom edge of the toppled crate, Jeff put ten fingers through the grated gate and pulled with enough force to pop it open. Bosco burst from confinement looking to eradicate the source of the incoming bullets! He had been contained for a long while, patiently waiting for this opportunity to make things right!

A world away from the average family pet, working canines come from long breeding lines of dogs specifically selected for their solid nerves, unnatural courage, and unstoppable determination. Under the skillful, and meticulous direction of a master trainer, an animal possessing this superior genetic make-up can be shaped into a warrior like Bosco; a fearless dog who is turned on by gunfire, and the roar of helicopters; a canine soldier, who through careful rearing, and training has never met his match! When a dog like Bosco comes face to face with the enemy, he doesn't experience trepidation. He's not intimidated by the size of his opponent, or a thirty-round magazine extending from a submachinegun. When the eyes of a combat dog lock onto the adversary, there is only one thought rolling through his mind, "Destroy!"

Four

Run Through the Jungle

There was no time to clip Bosco onto the short bungee-leash attached to Jeff's tactical vest. The plan was to run. Evade the enemy and run! Reach the G.I.R. fire power, and join in the fight. Lunging into the suffocating biomass, Jeff called for his back-up, "Bosco, with me!" Now it was man and dog together pounding through dense bushes and climbing over unimaginable tangles of vines. A fast scramble was as close as Jeff and Bosco could get to a run. It was easy enough for Bosco to navigate around the flora with his shorter stature and four feet. Jeff, on the other hand, was in a struggle for his life. Seldom able to rise above a stoop, he battled against constant obstructed vision from mammoth sized leaves hanging in his face. Stiff, prickly branches were relentlessly ripping and tearing his exposed skin. His face was on fire from profuse sweat running over his lacerations and into his eyes. The vines seemed diabolical in the way they wrapped his feet and pulled at his legs, just like a linebacker trying to tackle a ball carrier. Jeff and Bosco were trapped in an endless nightmare with no end in sight. Progress was painfully slow, but a change in strategy wasn't possible; "keep moving" was the only option.

At each pause to catch his breath, Jeff would listen for movement and gunfire in order to establish his bearing. Jeff thought skirting south of the combat zone and keeping the road somewhere off to the right would be the most advantageous route. That way he could use the boundary of the road as a directional point, possibly work his way up to Liano's truck location, and hopefully rejoin the G.I.R. force there. As he moved closer to the action, Jeff clipped Bosco to his bungee-leash which only extended to about twenty-four inches. This way Bosco had enough radius for maneuvering, yet not enough to create a tangle. From the point of near visual contact with the enemy, Jeff and Bosco kept low to the ground, often crawling side-by-side. Stealth and synchronized movements were an absolute must if they hoped to pass by the guerillas. Meticulous training always pays off in these life or death moments. In the theater of war, there is no room for error or disagreement between handler and dog. Success would hinge on Jeff's clear, silent directives followed by Bosco's smooth and exact responses. As the two crawled toward the location of the last gunshots, Jeff could not believe his eyes when he turned and saw Mingo in a low-crawl bringing up the rear. Camaraderie formed in battle is a special bond that only those who have experienced it can rightly know. Belly-down in the dirt and leaf litter, clothes soaked through with sweat, covered in bugs and blood, nearly swallowed up by a jungle crawling with F.A.R.C. guerillas,

Jeff had a wave of calm pass over him. He momentarily felt invincible lying beside his dog with his bodyguard only meters behind him. Jeff had his left arm wrapped around Bosco's shoulders, so using his right hand he twisted around, and gave Mingo a salute with a half-smile. It was in that dire moment, under those dismal conditions that Mingo felt moved enough by one of Jeff's acknowledgements to actually respond. So, for the first time, Mingo answered back with a salute, and a half smile of his own.

Ready to crawl forward, Jeff heard "Psst!" from behind. Looking back, he saw Mingo hold up two fingers then point towards the northeast. Slowly breaking their way through the vegetation, two armed guerillas were cautiously moving due south. If they held to that trajectory they would pass about twenty meters in front of Jeff and Bosco. Any westward drift in their course would be bad news. Bosco had already caught wind of the two adversaries. His entire body began to vibrate under Jeff's arm. His eyes were locked on the two human targets. His ears were pricked up. His once panting mouth was now tightly closed. His nostrils flared as he sucked in oxygen. As the guerillas closed to within fifteen meters, Jeff noticed Bosco begin to grip the ground with his front feet by contracting his toes and digging in with his nails. With that Jeff whispered into his champion's ear, "Easy, Bosco. Hold my friend!" Jeff slowly looked back over his shoulder to check on Mingo's readiness. In a prone position, Mingo had one of his Sig Sauers in hand and sighted on the enemy, he was ready.

As slow as molasses, Jeff unclipped his leash from Bosco's harness. They were literally cheek to cheek as the soldiers closed to within ten meters. Bosco's vibration had escalated into twitching muscles while he patiently waited for the magic signal to "Take em!" Both handler and dog could feel that they were on the brink of an attack. Jeff's heart was nearly pounding out of his chest. He was afraid the guerillas would hear it if they advanced much closer. Unblinking eyes locked on target, jaws clinched tightly, breathing became rapid and shallow, and muscles vibrated. It was difficult to distinguish man from beast while both lay in ambush that morning. Making certain that he didn't miss a directive, Bosco cocked his right ear towards Jeff's lips which were only inches away. Again, Jeff whispered reassurances to his partner with "Easy! Hold!" Jeff knew he had to wait for the perfect moment to spring his canine warrior. Bosco would need the element of surprise to circumvent the enemies' advantage of automatic weapons. That perfect moment would occur when both guerillas were looking away at the shortest distance from his position of concealment. Jeff was counting on Mingo to act fast when Bosco was released. The two men had never trained together through scenarios like this, but for several days back at the Compound, Mingo had watched G.I.R. shooters working with combat dogs. Jeff knew that Mingo could figure out when to shoot, he was a sharp man. Besides, it was too late to worry about all that.

The guerillas were directly in front of Jeff and Bosco when Jeff slowly unsheathed his knife with his right hand. His left hand-held Bosco's harness in a death-grip, making certain there was no premature attack. Quiet as death, they waited. Although he was being eaten alive by mosquitoes, Jeff barely noticed. During those long moments of hiding on the jungle floor, life hung in a very precarious balance for all the combatants. Not much had gone right on that mission, but Jeff was hoping that maybe this time the soldiers would keep on walking, or maybe God might drop a fully loaded AR15 in his lap, or maybe reinforcements might storm in. In the event things turned sour and none of the "maybes" came true, Jeff would send Bosco's ninety pounds charging through the cover of the bush.

When a dog of Bosco's size and fury collides with a man at full speed, the shock of impact can jar the breath out of the unsuspecting target. At contact, Bosco's bone crushing bite would inflict mind numbing injury. Hopefully, the guerilla's gun would be knocked loose. The effects of "Shock and Awe" was what Jeff was banking on. It was up to Mingo to take out the soldier Bosco didn't. Regardless, three seconds after sending Bosco to obliterate one of those F.A.R.C. soldiers, Jeff would charge in with his knife to back up his teammate. He felt their best chance of survival was "Take em" by surprise!

God did smile on Franklin and his little squad that morning. The two F.A.R.C. soldiers kept to their original trajectory. They passed within ten meters of Jeff and Bosco, making their way due south. Giving the two guerillas ample time to move out of sight and earshot, Jeff sheathed his knife, clipped his leash onto Bosco, and waved Mingo to move out. The heat of the rainforest had become nothing short of stifling as the equatorial sun reached its midday zenith. Still carefully making their way through the nightmarish tangle toward the possible G.I.R. position, Jeff stopped for the first water break of the long morning. He had never been so happy to have sloshed along with a couple of bottles of water in his cargo pockets before. Although cumbersome through tactical maneuvers, the thirst quenching liquid was a life saver for him and Bosco that morning. Jeff held up a bottle as an offering to Mingo, but the bodyguard refused; Jeff thought for sure he was carrying his own. Hobbling along, shortly after the drink, Bosco froze in mid-step. With a high, inflexible tail, he was clearly alerting on some kind of odor. One of Bosco's front feet was still off the ground as he stretched his nose upward to cast from side to side. From reflex, Jeff dropped to the ground when his dog alerted. Mingo followed suit. Bosco was left standing, filling his olfactory system with the scent of whatever was yet out of sight. When Jeff noticed the hair on Bosco's withers begin to rise, he gave him a hand signal to lie down. Jeff knew that Bosco's bristle didn't lie. During training, Jeff made it clear to the other G.I.R. handlers, "If the hair rises on this dog's back, a target is confirmed!" With his eyes locked on a distant point, Bosco eased into a "down" position as a demonic grumble rolled from his viscera.

A few minutes passed before movement out of the East became apparent to Jeff and Mingo. Bosco's early alert gave the two men a chance to establish good cover under a very dense shrub. The shrub's short, broad canopy afforded Jeff and his squad an excellent vantage point for observation or ambush. Waiting for an advancing party to come into view, Jeff was peering through the split of two colossal leaves when he felt a nudge from Mingo. Looking back at his bodyguard, he saw a Sig Sauer in one of Mingo's hands and two full magazines in the other. There was no discernable expression on his friend's hardened face, just raised hands that were offering his only back-up weapon. Nodding his head, Jeff whispered "Gracias" as he accepted Mingo's generous gift. Tucking the magazines in his pockets, Jeff unclipped the bungee leash from Bosco, and put his left hand through the top harness strap. With 9mm in hand, both men were now ready. Bosco's toenails were dug-in for launch, and his gaze had not shifted from the original point of interest. Tightly flanked by his teammates, Bosco continued with his low growl which was aimed directly at the approaching menace; whatever drew closer was real.

Step by step the intruder's image became more apparent through the thick green veil. At first it appeared like too much mass to be a single man. Jeff thought it may be a couple of men that were moving closely together. Whoever it was, they were careful, stealthy, and advancing with a definite purpose. Jeff tapped Mingo in disbelief to take a look. As Mingo spied through the leaves, Jeff asked "Do you see some kind of dog coming towards us?" "Si, Sniper y Capitan Liano!" Sure enough, Jeff looked out again and saw Sniper at the end of a six-foot leash leading Hector, who was carrying a submachine gun. Liano and his canine partner were headed due west along the southern perimeter of the battle zone. Liano later reported that after thwarting the F.A.R.C.'s ambush plan, he immediately made his way toward the last reported position of Franklin's truck. Liano was coming for his friend, and he wasn't going to let a band of guerillas stand in his way. It was customary for Liano and his men to be grossly outnumbered and outgunned during a conflict.

That is a common combat condition for most Special Operatives Forces. They are used to having no back-up other than the teammates on their squad. To accomplish many of their tasks, the G.I.R. are solely responsible for getting themselves into and out of a theater of action. According to Jeff, a superior skill set is the one consistent advantage Top Tier Groups seem to have over their opponents.

Still a short distance away, Jeff saw Sniper lock up on an odor alert. All morning, the air currents had been in Jeff's favor coming from an easterly direction. The scents of "living beings," or explosives that may lie ahead of his party were carried on these currents. Those air borne odors were responsible for Bosco's targeting and early warning indications. Liano and Sniper were heading in a westerly direction, and moving with the wind which severely limited those canine skills. That's why Sniper's alert occurred long after Bosco's initial warnings of upcoming intruders. When Sniper indicated there was trouble ahead, he and Liano immediately dropped to the ground in combat ready positions. At that point, it was up to Jeff and Mingo to convey to Liano that they were "friendlies." Jeff needed to do that without the use of Spanish, or moving from cover, or announcing who he was to the entire region. Since he could not coordinate a signal with Mingo, Jeff decided to callout to Hector with mutually understood words. Considering the likelihood of enemy soldiers within earshot, Jeff restricted his communication to bursts of single familiar words, until Hector recognized the caller. This way he felt he could convince Hector of who he was, and minimize the stream of noise which would act as an audible beacon to his place of concealment. Jeff first hollered out "Sniper," then "Bosco," then "Casandra!" No more was needed for Liano, he hollered back "Franklin?" Hearing that, Jeff responded with "Si! Hector?"

Before climbing out from cover, Jeff told the battle-ready Bosco to "Stay" (which he did begrudgingly), and he motioned for Mingo to wait in concealment so as not to be exposed unnecessarily. Pushing the P226 into his waistband Jeff stepped forward to meet his friend. What a sight for sore eyes as Hector and Sniper came out from their cover. So elated to see the other unscathed, the two men hugged for a long moment with no words exchanged. It was good to see Sniper working with Hector as well. Jeff had feared the worst for him because of the gunfire that the squad endured during the earlier ambush. Liano smiled from ear to ear when Jeff called Bosco, and he signaled Mingo out from under the bush. No time to chat. After patting Mingo's shoulder for sticking with Franklin, Liano gave the bodyguard the current lowdown. Jeff found out after the fact that priority one was getting him out of the enemy infested Columbian jungle, and back into the safer regions of Ecuador. That was going to be Mingo's sole responsibility. An extraction boat had already been radioed with coordinates for a rendezvous on the northern bank of the San Miguel River. The arrangements were made with the assumption that Franklin was still alive, and well enough to travel. The boat was piloted by a river savvy indigenous man, who was deathly afraid of anything F.A.R.C., and would only hold at the designated point for a short time. This was the best possible extraction plan to get Jeff out of danger, and Liano promised his commander no harm would come to Franklin. Obviously, Jeff knew he was not officially part of the G.I.R. unit, but he couldn't stand the thought of leaving his friends and the battle. He tried to convince Hector to let him remain with the squad, but Liano was adamant, "El rio mi amigo!"

Mingo pulled a GPS from his vest pocket, and conferred with Captain Liano about the coordinates of the extraction point. After Jeff gave Sniper a once-over, he and Hector exchanged final well-wishes. Already moving south for the San Miguel River, Mingo hollered back towards the two men, "Franklin, andale!" Mingo was nearly out of sight when Jeff gave Bosco the "Heel" command. Although middle-aged, Mingo set a blistering pace through the oppressive tangle. The air under the tropical canopy, which was fully heated by the afternoon sun, was thick with bugs and one-hundred percent humidity. Mingo's pace was fast, and the vegetation was so thick that Jeff had to cut Bosco loose from his leash to allow themselves room to navigate independently in order to keep up. Gulping for air and smearing gnats from his eyes, Jeff found himself running through the jungle doing his best to execute the extraction plan.

After a grueling forty-minute scramble, Mingo stopped to look at his GPS. Jeff seized the opportunity to pour a little hydration down his and Bosco's throats. He also offered a drink to his bodyguard, and to Jeff's surprise the tough Ecuadorian accepted; the truth was Mingo had brought no water with him, and Jeff's offering was Mingo's first drink of the day. Comparing their present location to the designated waypoint, Mingo determined that they had drifted east in their progression, and precious time, not to mention energy reserves, would be required to correct the error. Since it wasn't possible to navigate through the underbrush in a straight line, Mingo committed to check coordinates every ten minutes to avoid any further drifts in trajectory. Jeff and Mingo were anxiously aware of the time sensitive nature of the riverboat extraction. The window of opportunity was small at best, and both men could feel it closing. They made their one mistake, and there was absolutely no room for any others.

Three coordinate checks later, the feeling of panic was difficult to stave off. Exhaustion was beginning to take hold of the party while the rainforest seemed to have no end. Even Bosco, the canine triathlete, was wearing down. The blistering pace that once marked the beginning of the scramble had reduced to steady trudging. Sixty meters beyond the fifth GPS stop, Bosco's head carriage raised higher than it had been for the past hour, and his ears were pricked on alert; even his pace increased to the point of taking the lead. Their canine scout was clearly alerting to something ahead, but owing to the physiologic effects of dehydration and exhaustion, Mingo and Jeff barely reacted. No communication was necessary as they pushed ahead in a drone-like pace. Each man pulled his handgun free and resigned to deal with the impending danger when they reached it. Shortly after the alert, Mingo, Jeff, and Bosco stepped from the suffocating vegetation into a large sphere of smoky emptiness, it was like entering a bubble inside the jungle. The squad had penetrated a camp of indigenous people. It was a scene straight out of National Geographic. Smoke hung over a handful of barely clad, dark-skinned people who were squatting on the dirt floor near the opening of a primitive shelter. Because of his desperate situation and the effects of depletion, Jeff was not able to appreciate the richness of the encounter, however. He only recalls the "out of body" experience of the event and remembers thinking how strange that moment must have been for the primitive family. They watched in silence as two city-dwelling men and a giant dog plodded right past the cooking fire, without so much as a hiccup in stride or a glance their way.

Not long out of the indigenous camp Jeff imagined he could smell the river. Hollering forward to Mingo, Jeff was looking for confirmation with his one-word question, "Rio?" However, there was no response from the Ecuadorian, just pushing on. Bosco's pace had carried him considerably out in front of Mingo, to a point where Jeff had to call him back. On Bosco's return Jeff could see the excitement in his face confirming that the river lie ahead. Jeff knew his dog well. He could instantly read that drinking and swimming were on his mind, not fighting. This time Jeff called out to Mingo with confidence, "El rio mi amigo!" Although there was no audible response from his bodyguard, when Mingo stopped and stood up straight, with his hands on his hips, Jeff knew they had arrived.As Jeff walked up beside his bodyguard he could see a stretch of muddyriver. Down on the river's bank, directly below where Mingo was standing, sat a small, flat boat with an indigenous man sitting at the rudder. Slowly shaking his head from side to side, Jeff looked at Mingo and exclaimed in disbelief, "I don't know how that is possible even with a GPS. Countless miles of river running through countless miles of Jungle,and you delivered us to the exact spot of extraction!" With that Jeff extended his hand, and Mingo returned a firm handshake before the two slid down to the river.

Bosco was the first to reach the muddy water, and he wasted no time before diving in. The boat pilot could not hide his uneasiness about the German shepherd swimming around his very flat vessel. The pilot was equally uncomfortable with Mingo, who by appearance could have been a member of the dreaded Revolutionary Army. Dressed only in an ill fitted, and badly worn pair of shorts, the meek indigenous boat captain would not make eye contact with Jeff's bodyguard. When Mingo introduced himself and confirmed instructions from G.I.R. headquarters, the pilot responded to Jeff. Probably because of his short blonde hair and blue eyes, Jeff came across to the captain of the little vessel as a neutral outsider. After witnessing how frightened the pilot was of Bosco and Mingo, Jeff thought it must have been divine intervention that kept the timid fellow waiting at the designated spot.

Once directions were confirmed, the flat-boat was ready to shove off. Well hydrated and cooled off from his drink and swim, Bosco rocked the boat when he jumped on from the bank after Jeff called him. No sooner than all four of his feet hit the deck, Bosco made a beeline for the pilot. It is the rare dog who is not inclined to greet a new member of a group, and the smaller the pack the more important the greeting is to a dog. Although Bosco meant nothing more than to say hello, that was considerably more attention than the timid captain could manage, especially from a dog of Bosco's stature. Before Jeff could give his companion a verbal cue to slow down, the pilot of the flat-boat had bailed out, and he was swimming for the opposite bank with the determination of an Olympic athlete. Mingo immediately took hold of the outboard's rudder. While he worked to start the engine, Jeff hopped onto the bank to untie the vessel. As soon as Mingo fired up the engine, Jeff jumped back on board and they were in quick pursuit of their river guide. Mingo guided the boat right alongside the pilot so Jeff could reach down and grab his arm to pull him in. Although it was much easier said than done, Jeff eventually wrangled the timid pilot back onto the boat. He and Mingo convinced him that Bosco would ride at the bow, and the stern would be for the pilot only. It took a while before the pilot actually settled in and concentrated on steering the boat. For the first half of a mile down river, the pilot would twitch to jump overboard every time Bosco turned his head; but once everyone settled in, Jeff remembered, the early part of the boat trip was very pleasant transportation.

On this leg of the journey Bosco had it made with all of the water he could drink, a nice breeze in his face to keep the bugs away, and a coat of hair to protect him from the equatorial sun. Jeff Franklin on the other hand wasn't quite so comfortable. He and Mingo shared the last swallows of water when they stepped onto the boat to begin their three-hour river journey. They were not well hydrated at that point. An hour and a half into the trip, Jeff was struggling to keep from drinking the organism laden river water. To compound the effects of not drinking, the hot sun was beating down on Jeff's white, unprotected skin. Unlike Mingo and the boat pilot, Jeff didn't carry the natural skin pigment to shield him from the harsh tropical sun. Jeff had no hat or shaggy head of hair to shade his face and neck. He had no long sleeves to roll down to protect his arms. Unfortunately, for the Kentucky dog trainer, he had just come out of winter back home, so he had no tan at all prior to this trip. Jeff ultimately resorted to hanging his arms over the side of the boat and submerging them while the boat meandered down the river. As far as his face and neck were concerned, Jeff alternated between pulling his tee shirt over his head while his back burned, and then pulling his shirt down to protect his torso. The river trip began as a pleasant transition from the jungle trek, but it ended in its own kind of misery.

The river boat pilot carried out his duty as planned. He safely delivered his living cargo to a G.I.R. patrol unit that was waiting inside the border of Ecuador north of Nueva Loja. Jeff had to be taken straight away to a pharmacist (a common medical practitioner of the region) due to his severe burns and dehydration.

One day after Jeff, Mingo and Bosco arrived back at the G.I.R. compound, Captain Liano and company rolled in with all men and one dog accounted for. They suffered no casualties and sustained only minimal injuries throughout the entire squad. Finding Jeff was the first thing on Hector's agenda. He couldn't wait to report how happy he was with the dogs' integration into their combat units. Both Sniper and Bosco performed under battle conditions as well as the men with whom they served. They seemed to have completely adjusted to the environmental demands of the region. Hector was most pleased with the dogs' olfactory ability, both in clearing bombs and scouting for the enemy. All of these excited thoughts were rolling through Liano's mind, and he wanted to talk to Jeff in detail about a number of items. On the way to the kennel where he expected to find Jeff, Liano stopped by the administration building to invite Casandra along. As Liano and Casandra approached the kennel they saw several men outside working dogs through tactical obedience drills, but there was no sign of Franklin. Captain Liano called out to the closest man, "Donde esta Franklin?" The man who was dressed in bite protection pants, a baggy uniform shirt, and a boonie hat turned around and said, "I'm right here!" Jeff was purposefully hiding beneath the wide brimmed hat and oversized G.I.R. shirt to protect himself from the sun. When Hector saw Jeff's severely sunburned face, he instantly forgot about all the pertinent ideas he wanted to discuss. After Hector's initial shock wore off, there was some careful shoulder pats over safe returns and lots of teasing about Jeff's skin not being Ecuadorian tough. The rest of the day was devoted to a stimulating discussion about the mission and the G.I.R.'s new canine soldiers.

The remainder of Jeff's time with the G.I.R. handlers and their canine recruits was spent peacefully mulling over training details and deployment procedures. With the exception of logistics, the Ecuadorian canine program closely modelled that of the U.S. Military's Special Tactics Forces. From the kennel set-up and veterinarian care, to the high caliber dogs and passionate handlers, the program possessed many of the major elements needed for success. While Jeff fulfilled his contract in South America, he couldn't help but notice that the G.I.R. operation generally lacked organization and resources. Whether it be men, supplies, weapons, or dogs, coordinating the expedient resource with the respective mission seemed to be beyond the abilities of the Ecuadorian Special Police at that time. Although Jeff offered suggestions on transportation readiness, he knew the actual designation of trucks, trailers, or drivers would be left to those higher up in the government who were far removed from the canine program. So, until the G.I.R. dog campaign made enough positive noise, they would have to limp along sharing their limited number of well used Hiluxes and plastic shipping crates.

Jeff ran into a financial snag himself with one of the higher-ups of the Ecuadorian government, namely, the Vice President. The United States State Department funded the entire G.I.R. canine project. The money for everything from the Royal Canin feed for the dogs to the pay-out for Jeff's contract, which included the purchase of all eight canines, came from the U.S. directly to the government of Ecuador. It was then left to the appropriate Ecuadorian officials to pay vendors and disburse funds as necessary. Jeff's contract was with the government of Ecuador not the United States, so there was little the State Department could do when Ecuador's Vice President refused to pay Jeff and kept the money instead. However, after nine months of negotiating through the U.S. State Department and the U.S. Embassy in Ecuador, Jeff was able (with the help of Captain Liano and his Commander) to procure half the value of his total G.I.R. canine contract. For a small upstart company like Jeff's Cobra Canine, the nine month wait for a half- payment was nearly devastating. The money he was awarded for the South American project didn't even cover expenses. When Jeff reminisces about the experience he laughs over his contract-bidding naivety, even though some bitter feelings remain.

The night before Jeff was scheduled to leave, Hector was called out on another priority mission. Good-byes came early for the two friends. Hector, his First Lieutenant and Cassandra stopped by Jeff's barrack around 2200 to wish him good travels. The visit was reminiscent of their greeting days ago, the same three people knocking on the door in the middle of the night delivering handshakes and hugs. Jeff teased Hector about being a superhero who slips into and out of places unseen. Hector apologized for not being able to accompany his friend to the airport. But he promised Mingo and two of his top soldiers would see him onto the plane. Jeff relayed through Casandra that he wasn't disappointed that his bodyguard would be sending him off in place of Hector; he'd grown to genuinely like Mingo and his ways. Besides, in Jeff's assessment, a mission would always trump an escort obligation between friends. Before Hector exited he passed on a side note to Jeff; he said that as of 2400 Mingo was officially discharged from his bodyguard duties, but Mingo insisted on volunteering to protect Franklin all the way to the plane for no pay. Mingo said that he had gotten accustomed to watching over his North American friend.

On the morning of his departure Jeff made an early visit to the kennel for a final look at his canine squad. In all likelihood they would never work together again, so he wanted the opportunity to pet each dog one last time. Weeks ago, when Jeff left his canine crew at the airport to be shipped to South America, the farewell was temporary and exciting; he knew that it wouldn't be long before he would follow them to their destination and be reunited. This time however, the parting was permanent, and the mood was somber. Jeff spent a couple of minutes with each dog in their kennel. He showered them with encouraging words while giving them their final rubdown and inspection. Bosco was the first to get his good-byes, and he was also the last. Walking away from Bosco's pen was emotionally painful for Jeff. It was hard to close the kennel door on all of those familiar whines and barks.

Five

Lady

I met Jeffrey Scott Franklin in June of 1991. He had just returned from Iraq after serving as a tank operator for the United States Marine Corps during the Desert Storm War. I was hired by a professional training kennel to teach Jeff the intricacies of canine aggression and higher forms of behavior shaping. Jeff was only 22 years old and all warrior, I thought then what I still tease him about today, "He was born 40 years old." From our initial handshake I genuinely liked Jeff. Albeit a serious young man he was full of life, quick to laugh, and usually smiling. His sharp blue eyes radiated energy when he was engaged in conversation. However, since the day I met him, Jeff has worn a tired countenance from too much work and not enough sleep.

Since he was fresh out of the Marines, I would have expected Jeff to be disciplined, confident, and determined. But there was no hiding the fact that with Jeff these characteristics were innate, and the military only bolstered these qualities. Just as inherent were Jeff's forgiving nature, amenability, and affection which balanced his personality and made him well suited for dog training.

During Private Franklin's stint "pounding sand" in Marine Corps boot camp on Paris Island, his mind had kept wandering back to 1984 and his 8th grade math teacher Mr. Richardson. Mr. Richardson's obsession with working German shepherds filled much of his class time as well as Jeff's imagination. Mr. Richardson was a retired D.C. Metro Police officer, and he owned a couple of German shepherds. Young Jeff Franklin could recall nearly every word of his math teacher's police K-9 stories. Jeff even went so far as to harass Mr. Richardson for an entire semester to bring one of his dogs to class. One cold winter morning Jeff's efforts paid off. Mr. Richardson, trying to appease Jeff, finally won approval from the principal to bring one of his shepherds to class. So instead of equations, the class studied Ralf. He was the real deal, straight from police working lines. Ralf was a large, solid black German shepherd with a serious attitude. He was the retired police officer's bodyguard, and he was Jeff Franklin's dream companion.

The experience of meeting Ralf ignited a passion within Jeff that has only intensified over the years. Jeff began selling his parents on the idea of a pet the moment he arrived home from school that day. He was determined to convince them that the family desperately needed a protection dog like Ralf. Being a modest working-class family with two teenage boys, not only did Jeff's parents not want the responsibility of a watch dog, they didn't have a spare dime to invest in one. In spite of weeks of persistent salesmanship, Jeff's dad pronounced, "We can't afford no damn German shepherd that I don't want anyhow!" That proclamation didn't deter Jeff in the least. He simply went to work looking for a free shepherd. Each day Jeff would scan the pet section of the newspaper. Whether he was on foot or on his bike, when Jeff saw someone with a German shepherd (no other breed was considered) he would stop and ask if they knew where he could get one. Days turned into months, but Jeff's enthusiasm never waned. On his way home from a friend's house one evening, Jeff struck "pay-dirt." There was an elderly man walking on the opposite side of the road trying to wrestle a shepherd mix into some kind of order. The older man was clearly exasperated with his four-legged companion; the dog demonstrated with every step that she had a mind of her own. Sticking to his plan, Jeff reluctantly approached the frustrated dog-walker and asked if he knew where a German shepherd could be obtained for a low price. Without hesitation, the man said, "Sure, her name is Lady. She is about twelve months old, her shots are up to date, and she's free." Before Jeff had a chance to respond, the man handed over Lady's leash and walked on down the road. To fourteen-year-old Franklin, who had been dreaming of nothing but shepherds for months, that moment was like winning the lottery.

Jeff and his new charge purposefully took the long route home that evening. Extra time was needed to construct a perfect, bomb-proof reason why Lady was meant to be a member of the Franklin family. Lucky for Jeff, his father was working out of town that week. Of his parents, Franklin senior was the most opposed to the idea of taking in a dog. Although Mrs. Franklin had never been a pushover for Jeff, she could be persuaded with a well-thought-out argument. The story that ultimately won Lady a place in the home centered on struggles in school, suffering self-esteem, and "man's best friend." Whether that argument really moved Jeff's mother is still up for debate. Everyone agrees that Jeff's pure excitement and abundant enthusiasm sold the entire family on Lady, even his Dad.

The morning after Lady was introduced to Jeff's dad, Franklin senior presented his son with a few conditions in regard to the new family dog. Franklin senior was a hardworking man from a simple background, and he never minced words. He told Jeff, "Lady is solely your responsibility. You feed her every day or she's gone. You clean up after her every day or she's gone. You work with her every day or she's gone. You treat that animal right, and take good care of her every day, or she's gone. You slack off one day and she's gone. Am I clear?"

From his first thoughts of owning a German shepherd, Jeff fully intended to perform every duty to care for his dog. But, hearing those severe words coming from his dad, and knowing that he was incapable of bluffing, the full weight of his serious responsibility hit home. Jeff gave his dad a very sober response, "Yes sir," and followed it with a partial smile revealing just a bit of a lip curl. Little did young Jeff Franklin know that one day this confident half-smile would become his classic response to any challenge.

Jeff grew up in the days before YouTube and Google, when research was done at the library. A library card was his access to knowledge, and Jeff quickly located two choice books on dog training. One was about obedience control, and the other was one of the few books at the time dealing with the subject of protection training. The librarian must have thought that book was a peculiar selection for a fourteen-year-old boy. Of course, she was unaware of the potential police dog in Jeff's backyard. Although Lady was not quite a Ralf, she was a dream come true for the neophyte dog trainer.

Over the following months of self-taught dog training, Lady's novelty never faded in Jeff's mind, as is often the case with teenage endeavors. During that period of time there was seldom a dinner without Lady updates. Most weekends involved some kind of training demonstration so the Franklin family could witness Lady's progress. Jeff's parents could tell that Lady and her training were more than just a young man's

passing fancy. This was a real passion for their son. Franklin senior actually became intrigued when Lady's instruction advanced into confidence
building as Jeff taught her how to traverse homemade agility obstacles.
But, it was the personal protection phase of Lady's training that really
piqued Franklin senior's interest. He was fascinated with the whole idea
of aggression development and control. In fact, Jeff's dad would routinely inquire about Lady's training during dinner, and he often roared
with laughter as his son described a bungled attempt at teaching Lady to
apprehend one of his friends who was wrapped in football pads to
shield himself from bite wounds. Jeff's mother and grandmother
(Nanny, as Jeff called her) on the other hand, thought the whole idea
of teaching a dog to bite people was wrong. They didn't want to hear
about their sweet Lady attacking Jeff's gullible friends who were
talked into pretending they were criminals, just so they could act as
"bite dummies."

At one dinner when Jeff was not much more than fifteen years
old, he saw a glimpse of his dad that was a portent of things to come.
Describing one of Lady's training escapades, Jeff's mother interrupted
with "enough dog talk." Immediately, Jeff's dad retorted with, "No
ma'am! I want to hear every detail. These aren't just dog tricks were talking about here. Jeff is doing wonderful things with this dog. I've never
seen such a trained animal. Our son has a real gift with dogs and I don't
care if anyone else is interested or not, I'm proud of our son, and I tell
everybody how impressive his ability is!" Jeff sat quietly at the table with
tears welling up in his eyes, he didn't know what to say after hearing his
dad come to his defense. Jeff had no idea that his dad had such a soft
spot for him and Lady. Young Mr. Franklin could have never imagined
that his greatest supporter was his papa.

After a high school basketball game, during the winter of Jeff's soph-
omore year, he and a friend went to an after-game party. Mr. and Mrs.
Franklin had rigid curfews in place for events such as that, and both
teenage boys took them seriously. On this particular frigid night, Jeff
was subject to the whims of his friend who drove them to the game and
a subsequent party. Long after the curfew time came and went, Jeff had
to become confrontational to get his chauffeur-friend to leave the party

Jeff's first companion, Lady.

long enough to take him home. When Jeff finally made it home, he was now a full two hours past the understood cut- off time, and until that moment he had never missed a curfew in his life. Jeff wasn't a partier, he didn't even drink. He wasn't one to push the limits, and in no way was he a trouble-maker. So, when he missed "lights out" time it was a big deal. An hour past curfew and no Jeff was a real worry. An hour and a half past the designated time and no young Franklin, his mother went into action. First, she called Franklin senior who was working late, then she called friends and family trying to locate her obedient, yet missing son. Coming up empty, she called the local police and filed a missing person's report. By the time Franklin senior made it home, panic was setting in. Just minutes before Jeff was actually dropped off, his mom and dad struck out on their own to search for Jeff.

Finally, at home, Jeff saw that the house was dark, and he feared the worst. No one was home because they're all out looking for him, and there was no way to communicate because this was 1987, years before the cell phone boom. Not only was the house dark, it was locked tighter than Fort Knox. Jeff left his house key in a dresser because his mother and Nanny were home, and he had no intention to be out late anyway. After trying every door and window hoping to make entry into the house, it was then stroking midnight, and the temperature had fallen below zero degrees. Wearing only a light jacket, Jeff had begun shivering uncontrollably when he realized he was in a drastic situation that was going to require drastic measures to remedy. He dare not leave the house to seek shelter in a neighbor or friend's home. Jeff couldn't take the chance on his parents coming home and the three of them crossing paths again. He could throw a lot of fuel on an already hot fire by breaking out a window to gain access to the warm abode. But he couldn't imagine the fury he would have to face from both of his parents for wrecking a window they couldn't afford to replace because he overshot a curfew by two hours. Freezing to death would have been much less painful.

Searching the garage for a solution, Jeff stumbled across an old pair of his dad's coveralls. Trembling as he zipped into the oversized jumpsuit, Jeff noticed Lady's incessant barking. When he stepped into the yard to investigate the curious behavior of his normally quiet Lady, he saw her standing in front of the dog house barking for all she was worth. Thinking maybe a possum or raccoon might have commandeered the cozy dog house that was stuffed full of fresh straw, Jeff wandered over to take a look. As he approached Lady and her accommodations, she quickly darted inside her little house. Jeff peeked into her warm little nest and got a face full of licks from his tail wagging companion. No possums or raccoons in there with Lady, just the warm, clean, new straw that he and his dad put in the day before preparing for the subzero temperatures. Jeff only began to ask his dog what she was barking about before the idea hit him like a hammer. Laughing out-loud, Jeff gave Lady credit where credit was due, "Thanks for the invitation girl. Tonight, I'll take my best friend up on the invite!" With that, much to Lady's delight, Jeff crawled into the warm quarters next to his trusted companion, who was nearly coming out of her skin with excitement over the in-house visit from Jeff. Albeit a little tight, the straw and shared body heat made for a comfortable arrangement. Curled up together, Jeff and Lady fell asleep almost instantly.

Meanwhile, the missing person search went on all night. Neighbors, friends, even a police helicopter were called in to help find young

Franklin. At daybreak, Jeff's dad was exhausted and distraught. He noticed that the backyard had appeared to be uncharacteristically empty all night during the search and Lady seemed to be missing. Hoping to gain some evidence as to her whereabouts, Franklin senior began looking around the backyard. Upon looking into the dog house, he was confronted with a growling dog and a miracle of all miracles, his son. Long feared abducted, or frozen to death, Jeff was rousted from sleep by his growling bodyguard and screams of shock and joy coming from his worried-sick father. Crawling out of Lady's house, Jeff was greeted by hugs from his dad that squeezed the breath out of him. There was no need for Jeff to explain himself in that moment. There was no anger or chastising to be dealt with, he was overwhelmed with hugs and kisses from Nanny and mom. Jeff was alive and well, that was all anyone cared about.

Over a jubilant breakfast, Jeff relived all of the night's details, especially the invitation from Lady to sleep in her warm, safe quarters. Franklin senior stepped way out of character that morning and personally delivered Lady a special breakfast. The family thought a lot of Lady before that night, but from then on, she was special. On any especially cold winter night, it's not unusual for someone in the Franklin family to kid about sleeping out in Lady's dog house where it's warm.

High school years represent an action-packed period for most of us. For talented or serious athletes, there's hardly a moment to catch a breath between school work and sports. So, it was for Jeff Franklin. A competitive wrestler for his school, he was also a scholarship recipient in baseball. Those evenings and weekends that weren't devoted to practice or competition, Jeff spent with Lady. This schedule left only a little room to squeeze in some homework (scholastics were never a focus for Jeff anyway). Arranging the classes for his junior year of high school, Jeff noticed a real stumbling block on the agenda, Spanish. At seventeen years old, Jeff viewed that class as an unacceptable disruption in his busy routine that revolved around those things that he loved, sports and Lady. The homework load from a foreign language class would have eaten away at either one of those, and Jeff wasn't having it. Desperately looking over the semester's schedule, he could only find one suitable replacement in regard to credits and class periods, Marine Corp ROTC. Jeff thought it over for less than a minute, Spanish class or the Marines and he told his supervisor, "I can do the Marines, but that Spanish thing scares me."

Jeff excelled as a baseball third baseman during high school, and somewhere around the close of his senior year baseball season he was offered a full scholarship to play for a college that he admired. It just so happened that same year during a wrestling match, Jeff severely tore the meniscus in his left knee. He kept the injury a secret so as not to taint his scholarship prospects. Knee wraps, anti- inflammatories, and compensation with his right leg allowed Jeff to continue playing his dream-sport without missing a beat. Jeff saw college ball for what it was, a gateway into the "big leagues," and nothing was going to keep him from passing through.

The baseball scholarship pushed the Marines, which Jeff had grown to appreciate through the ROTC program, to the "back burner." He devoted all his energy to perfecting his baseball skills and honing his physical condition. His sights were now set on an early draft into major league baseball. Jeff, as well as his coaches, felt confident that he was competitive and skilled enough to play professional ball. Always his own toughest critic (that whole "born forty years old" thing), Jeff didn't need anyone to push him harder in conditioning. Although just a teenager, Jeff was fully aware of what was on the line if he could step-up his game. Weight-lifting, ball practice, cycling, more ball practice, running, even more ball practice; that regimen became Jeff's entire life. He was determined to be one of the top baseball recruits of his class.

Scholastics suffered under such a rigid athletic routine, of course, but Lady remained a top priority. Jeff always made time for her. He loved that dog, and not one day did he break the agreement with his dad over her care. The family knew if Jeff was at home, he was with Lady. If Lady were alone in the backyard, they didn't have to wonder where Jeff was; he was either in school, or conditioning for baseball. Jeff and his dog were connected at the hip. In fact, the only thing young Mr. Franklin didn't like about baseball was the fact that Lady couldn't be there with him.

Roughly eighteen months after his scholarship offering, Jeff was playing third baseman on his college All-star team when he jumped to snag a high ball. Making the catch, Jeff fell back to the ground only to feel his dreams of professional ball shatter. Like a shock from a lightning bolt, nauseating pain shot through Jeff's right leg as his foot grabbed for purchase. Instantly he knew this was no benign knee strain, and in the same moment the real horror of the injury settled in; this was his good leg. Jeff did, in fact, completely sever the anterior cruciate ligament in his right knee during that last athletic catch of his young baseball career. His powerful right leg had carried a heavy load for over a year, compensating for the weakened left knee with the torn meniscus. His strong knee simply gave out. Hanging his head under the weight of such harsh reality, Jeff hobbled off the field on what used to be his bad leg. He couldn't even entertain the notion of a miraculous recovery. There were far too many talented, young players vying for the third baseman's spot for Jeff to think he had any real chance to compete after multiple surgeries, a long rehabilitation, and grueling reconditioning. Besides, he had given baseball his very best for a considerable portion of his life, and that was just enough to allow him to make the cut. Jeff couldn't see a time in the near future where he would be fit enough and young enough to get back on the roster; and that was assuming his repaired knees would be able to withstand the brutal training regimen again. Jeff's baseball dreams died with that last catch. He never again talked about the "big dance" or what could have been. He moved on and refused to revisit the painful departure from his cherished sport as if it never happened.At home, just weeks after tearing his ACL on the baseball field, Jeff was paid a visit by the United States Marine Corp. They were recruiting ROTC students for an up-coming class, and he was on their list. Jeff genuinely liked the Marine officers he was exposed to during his ROTC training and they liked him, so it wasn't a surprise when they came calling. Life without baseball was a depressing void for Jeff. For nearly a month he had languished around the house waiting for his upcoming knee surgery. He desperately needed something all-consuming like the Marines to focus on. If it were up to Jeff, he would have shipped-out the same day the recruiters came to visit. Since that wasn't possible he did the next best thing.

Without taking a single moment to ponder, or consult with his parents, Jeff signed up for the Marines first class of 1990. Excusing away his distinctive limp as an insignificant sprain in his right knee, Jeff assured the recruiters that he would be in shape and ready by the ship-out date which was a couple of months away. Jeff broke the news to his parents as soon as they got home that evening. Mr. and Mrs. Franklin wanted to be excited for their son, but they were a little perplexed about the proposed timeline. According to the recruiter's schedule, Jeff would be due to arrive at boot camp on Paris Island just a few weeks after his scheduled ACL surgery. Jeff's parents didn't understand how that would be possible given all the rehabilitation that would have to follow his knee repair. Young Mr. Franklin attempted to ease their minds by telling them that there would be no scheduling conflicts because he intended to cancel the surgery and attend boot camp with a gimpy leg. Franklin senior told Jeff that was craziness and the medical officers at his physical wouldn't pass him. Jeff replied, "They won't know because I won't limp or wince in front of them." Jeff's mom asked how he intended to make it through the physical demands of the toughest basic training program of the U.S. Military. Jeff simply replied, "I'm going to concentrate on keeping my knee straight during physical training. As long as I don't twist or turn too sharply it won't give out." After a brief moment of silence, both Mr. and Mrs. Franklin responded with their own frustrated versions of, "Well that's just brilliant."

The very instant he signed on the dotted line, Jeff's mind was set in motion and no amount of coercion was going to change his plan. Mr. and Mrs. Franklin tried of course, and they even convinced Jeff's surgeon to urge him to wait for a class later in the year. As far as Jeff was concerned, he had missed out on a baseball career, and he wasn't going to wait one hour longer than necessary to become a Marine. The impetus behind Jeff's obsessive drive to achieve is not altogether apparent. No one else in his family is quite like that, and he hasn't "taken after," or modeled anyone that he knows of. In truth, Jeff is as perplexed as

At the threshold of a sporting career

anyone over his seemingly instinctual need to succeed, win, or acquire the top placement at any cost. Jeff's motivating, psychological condition may have been born out of a need to keep one step ahead of Tommy, his domineering older brother.

Tommy's relationship with Jeff went beyond competitive sibling rivalry. Jeff has described his brother as actually ruthless at times when they were left unsupervised. Jeff felt that Tommy, being his mother's firstborn, was her favorite child, which afforded him more liberties in regard to his cruel behavior. Although, unsure of the reasons why he was tormented to accomplish; Jeff felt quite certain that postponing basic training allowed misfortune the opportunity to take control of his new life-plan, and he wasn't going to stand by for that.

Any time Jeff's mom and dad were desperate to make a point with their son, they would call in their "big gun," Nanny. She was the person Jeff respected more than anyone. Nanny had been Jeff's confidante for as long as he could remember. Since Jeff's birth, both of his parents had been committed to tough jobs with long hours in order to make financial ends meet. All through Jeff's childhood, Nanny acted as his caretaker. She groomed Jeff to be a self-sufficient man from the beginning. That's why she taught him to use a sewing machine, and iron his own clothes. Nanny and Jeff grew very close over the years.

When Nanny showed up to talk to young Mr. Franklin, he addressed her with confidence, "I love you like no one else, but come hell or high water I'm going to Paris Island. They may kick me out when I get there but I will be in that first class of the year." That's all Nanny had to hear. She reported back to her daughter that "Jeffrey was cut out to be a Marine, and he's man enough to know whether or not he can handle it with a bad knee. I think we should give him a good send-off." From that point on, there was no more talk in the Franklin house about ACLs or surgeries. Chatter about Marine Corps and what Lady was going to do for three months without Jeff, dominated dinner conversation.

On December 27th, 1989, Jeffrey Franklin left for Paris Island. Weeks prior to leaving for boot camp, Jeff concentrated on walking without a limp and building up his leg muscles, especially in his left leg. With the more recent and serious injury to his right knee, the left leg was going to be his workhorse for locomotion. The range of motion of the right knee was Jeff's biggest worry. He had to experiment with extremes of torque on the knee in order to judge what movements would throw it out of place during running and jumping exercises. They were very painful experiments. The only way to know how far he could push the envelope was to push the envelope too far. Jeff was so accustomed to the dull ache he carried around in that leg, at times, he almost forgot it was damaged. By the time he started boot camp Jeff had completely eliminated his limp. But the excruciating twinge of pain with excessive strain was impossible to mask. In preparation for basic training, Jeff drilled himself on launching from the left leg, landing on the left foot first, and keeping his knees straight regardless of the exercise he performed. The ultimate goal was to get through the rigors of basic training without further injuring his right knee and subsequently, having the torn ACL discovered. Jeff recognized what a tall order that was, but he was confident that he could pull it off. Jeff's family will tell you that he was actually high-spirited during his pre-boot camp conditioning. He was rejuvenated by having intense physical and mental training to fixate on once again. The Marines turned out to be the perfect replacement for baseball.

During the twelve weeks of basic training Jeff only exacerbated his right knee injury twice. On both occasions Jeff's weak knee gave-out, so he was transported to medical care for treatment. For each incident, "lucky" Jeff Franklin somehow escaped the diagnostic protocol of joint manipulation and X-rays that could have revealed his potentially dischargeable injury. Jeff was also fortunate that most of the original swelling associated with the torn ACL had dissipated before arriving at Paris Island. So, without obvious signs of injury, or complaints from the patient, the stolid doctor simply asked Jeff, "What happened to you?" Jeff's response each time was simple, "Nothing that an Ace Bandage and a few aspirin won't take care of." That was a good enough answer to send the young Marine right back into action. With his knee wrapped tightly and extra aspirin in his pocket, Jeff was none the worse for the wear; and according to the doctor that treated him, he was "the happiest injured man he has ever seen walk out of his hospital."

Three months away from home was an eternity to Jeff. Until the Marines, he had not spent more than a week away from his family at any given time. The days at camp gradually turned into weeks, and over time he fully acclimated himself to his new family. Letters from his parents kept him in touch with the neighborhood and family activity. Regular reports about Lady's good health and her quiet days in the backyard with nothing to do always made Jeff feel homesick. After two full months away from home, he still had dreams about training with her.

After graduating from boot camp, Jeff and his Marine class were granted a ten- day leave before they shipped out to their assigned schools. For Jeff, this meant he could return home to his dog and familiar faces in order to recharge his batteries. After a ten-day dose of good energy from family and friends, he would be ready for the rigors of his next two challenges; eight weeks of mandatory Infantry School, followed by twelve weeks of elected Tanker's School. Unknown to Jeff at the time,

Tanker's School was one of the most grueling and mentally challenging schools the Marine Corp had to offer. Had he known then what he knows now, Jeff may have spared his poor knees from that torture.

Back in Kentucky at last. The happy faces of his mother and father greeted him at the airport. Jeff felt exhilarated as he walked out of the airport into the damp morning air. He was now a bona fide Marine with proud parents at his side, he was home, and he felt "on top of his game." On the drive to the house, Jeff's dad was talking about Lady's peculiar behavior that morning. She turned up her nose at breakfast, and she opted to pace back and forth at the front gate with her favorite Kong toy in her mouth. Franklin Senior was convinced that Lady somehow knew her master was returning home, after a three-month separation. He said, "She hasn't missed a single meal since you've been gone. And she hasn't touched that Kong you two religiously played with in weeks. Now you tell me she doesn't know!" Jeff's mother even chimed in, "I just saw a documentary about dogs' uncanny ability to sense things like that, and how they can find their way back to loved ones despite hundreds of miles of separation. Lady is that kind of dog, and it makes me want to cry over how much she's missed you." Jeff wouldn't say in front of his mom and dad, but he felt a little emotional over Lady's devotion too. He couldn't wait to see her and pick-up with some remedial training, hiking, and their favorite Kong retrieve.

When Lady saw Jeff walk around the side of the house, she froze like a statue in disbelief. As Jeff drew within a handful of steps, she nearly lost her mind. Lady shrieked with emotion as she spun like a whirlwind throwing herself against the rickety backyard gate. Jeff couldn't get the gate open fast enough to suit her. One foot into the yard and Lady practically mauled him with affection. Just as explosively as she jumped on Jeff, Lady broke away, almost in a panic it seemed. She began racing around the yard, nose to the ground clearly searching for something. Bounding like a puppy from around her doghouse, Lady leapt towards Jeff with the treasure she had been looking for, her bright, red Kong. For twelve interminable weeks her favorite toy lay dormant, it held no value without Jeff. Compared to Jeff's company, even food had no meaning for Lady. Clearly, she lived for the young man who had finally returned home. Unfortunately, amid the hugs, barks, and laughter, Jeff had to break some bad news to his companion. Talking to her as if she were human, Jeff apologized for having to cut out prematurely, but he had committed to lunch with a couple of friends. He promised his greatest fan that he would return to her in a couple of hours for Kong retrieve and a long hike. Peeling himself away from Lady, Jeff could almost feel her heart break, since they had only been together for a few minutes. He had not even thrown the Kong, and he was already leaving. As Jeff latched the run-down gate, he reassured her that he would be back in two hours for me-and-you time. Obviously, not understanding a word of Jeff's soliloquy, Lady stood rigid in disappointment as young Franklin hurried away to meet his friends.

Jeff had just gotten on the road when a heavy feeling of guilt fell over him. He couldn't get Lady's image out of his mind. She had her front feet on the fence and the Kong in her mouth desperately watching as Jeff rounded the front of the house toward his truck. With every mile, Lady's image grew stronger and Jeff's guilt felt heavier. By the time he reached his destination he couldn't stand himself anymore. Jeff thought, how awful it was to just abandon Lady in that small, empty yard. She had waited patiently on him for three months, and he couldn't give her three minutes. He could have easily arranged to spend the first part of the day exercising Lady and met with his friends later for dinner. So, at the risk of looking sappy in front of his friends, the Marine walked into the café, gave his buddies a hug, and said he was going to pass on lunch because he had cheated on a very important obligation that he had to make right. Jeff told them straight-up, "I'm ashamed to say that I just walked away from a loyal friend. She was beside herself to see me after being gone so long at Boot camp, and I barely took the time to say hello before leaving again. The friend is my dog Lady, and I left her starving for my attention in the backyard. If she weren't totally dependent on me for social time and exercise, it would be a different issue. But outside of me, she has no one else in the world, except my parents who only feed her. Thank goodness, she is a tough German shepherd, or she would have died from let-down. So, I need to go back home and spend a little time with her, but I'd like to catch up with you guys for dinner if you all are game." After enduring a little razzing over his storybook boy-and-dog relationship, Jeff arranged to meet his friends later for pizza.

Although headed for home, Jeff still felt emotionally off balance, almost anxious over leaving Lady begging for company at the fence. He took a different route back home trying to save a little time, because his negative feeling seemed to worsen with each passing minute.

When Jeff rolled into the driveway, he was fidgeting from anxiety. He started calling-out for Lady as soon as he opened his truck door. Turning the corner for the backyard, Jeff fully expected to see Lady still attentively perched on the fence with the Kong in her mouth. Instead, he looked in alarm at a rusty, old gate swinging open with a broken latch. Jeff hollered for Lady at the top of his lungs as he turned to run for the road. There was no doubt in his mind where she had gone. He felt sure she had chased after him when he left to meet with his friends. Calling and whistling for Lady, Jeff ran right past his truck and out onto the road. Burning with a sense of urgency, he was moving at a full sprint down the busy suburban road hoping to get within earshot of Lady before she ran into misfortune.

Jeff didn't have to run very far. Nearly two miles from his driveway he saw what looked to be a discarded remnant of carpet just off the side of the road. Jeff's heart was pounding out of his shirt when he zeroed-in on the carpet. He picked up his pace, and as he closed the distance on the remnant, his bottom lip began to tremble. Through watery eyes, Jeff saw what might have been the striking hues of a familiar friend. The closer he got to the remnant the more it resembled someone he knew. Still twenty yards away, Jeff slowed his pace to a walk. Ten yards away, he stopped altogether, for now he could see clearly in all of its horror, the lifeless body of his beautiful Lady. Several yards up the shoulder of the road laid their bright, red Kong. His faithful companion couldn't bear another separation with so short a visit. She broke through the pitiful little gate that she had voluntarily respected for years. Lady chased after her only friend, with the Kong in her mouth, so that she and Jeff could surely play when she caught up to him.

Overwhelmed with emotion, Jeff knelt down beside his lifeless Lady. He soothed her with a few strokes like he'd always done, and then he removed her collar. Several kind people stopped to offer help, but Jeff refused their assistance by swallowing his sobs and shaking his head. For the longest time, he knelt on the shoulder of the road and stared at Lady, wrestling with a guilt that was nearly strangling him. Eventually, Jeff ran out of tears, staggered up the road to retrieve the Kong and started his long walk home to get his truck.

Jeff still has Lady's collar and Kong. He still carries the guilt of cheating her with too little attention when he first returned home. He still thinks about that rickety old fence that he and his family were too poor to fix. He thinks about how Lady should have been a house-dog. He thinks about how fond he was of her and how it was a shitty way for such a good dog to die.

Six

The Desert

Lance Corporal Jeffrey Scott Franklin aroused himself to peer into the tube of his thermal night-vision sights. He studied the small green-lit screen for temperature contrasted images that might indicate enemy movement, along the horizon. With the thermal night-vision, heat-producing bodies such as human beings and exhaust manifolds would stand-out in stark contrast to the non-heat- producing features of the landscape. For hours Franklin had been scanning the florescent landscape looking for irregularities while fighting off sleep. Inevitably he would find himself drowsily waking from an involuntary nap. After rubbing his eyes and slapping his face, Jeff would once again direct his attention to the monotony of the green screen. And so, it had been going all night. It was 0130 on the morning of February 24th, 1991. Jeff was one of a four-man tank crew. He and his crewmates had been restricted to their battle stations for the past six and a half hours. They were dressed in full Mission Oriented Protective Posture (MOPP) gear and were on high alert.

Jeff was in Alpha Company of the 8th Tank Battalion, which was attached to the 2nd Marine Division under the command of Major General William Keys. By February 7th, 1991, surrounded by the immense Saudi desert, General Keys had formed a strategic defensive position northwest of Al-Kibrit just south of the Kuwaiti border. Two months prior, in December of 1990, Lance Corporal Franklin and the men and women of the 8th Tank Battalion had been deployed to the Saudi port of Al Jubayl. There, the Marines were put to work off-loading many hundreds of tanks, armored vehicles and pieces of artillery. From the sheer number of assault vehicles and armaments that had been committed to this operation, there was little doubt in the minds of the military personnel that something very ominous awaited them in the not too distant future.

At the time of his deployment, Jeff was two months past his nineteenth birthday, and only sixteen weeks out of Tanker's School. He was young, green, excited, and standing in front of the proverbial fan moments before someone threw in the dung. Jeff was one of many thousands of Marines, Navy, Air Force, and Army personnel serving in the

Persian Gulf, and all of them were fully aware of the mounting tension surrounding their task at hand, Operation Desert Shield.

On August 2nd, 1990, Iraq's dictator, Saddam Hussein, directed his army to aggressively invade and occupy the peaceful country of Kuwait. This hostile invasion acted as an unsettling message to the surrounding Middle Eastern countries. Iraq's incursion was especially disturbing to Kuwait's closest neighbor, Saudi Arabia, who also happened to produce much of the world's oil supply. President George H. W. Bush, along with Prime Minister Margaret Thatcher, led a western alliance in an immediate response to Iraq's threat of Middle Eastern usurpation. In order to set-up effective defenses against Saddam Hussein, the western alliance needed a military staging and launching area inside the borders of Saudi Arabia. Gaining such approval from Saudi's King Fahd was no small arrangement at the time. After all, the western defensive maneuver would require the access of countless thousands of Christians into the homeland of Islam's two holiest sites, Mecca and Medina. However, King Fahd, didn't take the hostile invasion of their peaceful neighbor lightly. He was well aware of the likelihood that Iraq may further push into Saudi Arabia to seize control of the region's oil commodity. On August 7th, 1990, after only a few days of negotiations, Army General Norman Schwarzkopf, Commander in Chief of the U.S. Central Command, and Defense Secretary Richard Cheney reached an agreement with Saudi Arabia's King Fahd which allowed a western military build-up deep inside Saudi borders. The United States led the coalition of countries in this defensive operation that was labeled Desert Shield.

Within two weeks of Desert Shield's enactment, 15,248 marines were deployed to the desert of Saudi Arabia. Routine temperatures in excess of 110 degrees, and a ubiquitous, invasive sand greeted the U.S. Marines with the region's harsh hello. The climate was so hot and dry that the first formidable enemy the U.S. forces encountered in the Persian Gulf Theater was dehydration. Keeping thousands of American troops hydrated in such a parched environment amounted to a herculean task for those in charge of provisions. Virtual mountains of bottled water had to be dispersed over countless miles of arid and unforgiving territory.

The fine grain sand of the region infiltrated every piece of the marine's gear, regardless of meticulous packing. Special filters had to be fitted onto the air intake devices of all the tanks, trucks and gunships operating in the dirty environment. Due to the effects of equipment-fouling sand, personal weapons often needed to be cleaned twice a day to prevent malfunction. Maintenance on machinery was constant and never ending. This theater of conflict would come to be known by many of the men and women that served there as simply "the desert."

Jeff was sitting in the driver's seat of a M60 A3 Main Battle Tank, 6,888 miles from home. He and his crew, which included a commander, gunner, and loader, were ensconced within fifty-four tons of steel, and perched on a small sand dune. Although somewhat outdated, Jeff's tank had been upgraded with a thermal night sighting system, as well as partial reactive armor plates which increased the crew's protection against anti-tank rounds. With these improvements, Alpha Company would be better equipped to contend with the more advanced Russian built T72 tank that they would have to face in any confrontation with the Iraqi's elite Republican Guard. The Iraqi's T72s were three and a half tons lighter than the M60s, partially because they only needed to accommodate a three-man crew due to their state-of-the-art Auto Loading Mechanism. Considering the V12 diesel engine of the Iraqi's main battle tank produced eight hundred and forty horse power, almost a hundred more-horse power than Jeff's tank, the Republican Guard would possess a decisive advantage over the Marines in terms of speed. But the critical advantage the T72s had over M60s was the size of their main gun. The Russian built tanks were equipped with 125mm cannon as compared to the smaller 105mm main gun of the M60s. The disparity in the size of main guns amounted to a deadly difference of range in tank-on-tank combat. In theory, with their long-distance guns, the T72s could deliver a mortal blow to the approaching M60s before the Marines could maneuver close enough to strike back with their shorter ranged cannons. If conflict erupted with Iraq, the 8th Tank Battalion would have to rely on their extensive training in tank maneuvering and maximize the M60's top speed of 30 miles per hour in order to dominate the Republican Guard forces.

Once the Marines 2nd Division had been fully assembled it included over 20,500 personnel and 257 tanks. According to Major General William Keys, "It was probably the heaviest Marine division with the most combat power ever to take to the field." The 2nd Division was also reinforced by the Army's "Tiger Brigade," which accounted for 170 of the total tanks at Major General Key's disposal. The "Tiger Brigade" didn't just bring any armored vehicle to this fight; they brought the best battle tank the United States had to offer, the M1 Abrams. The M1 was the advancement of the M60. Its turbine jet engine could produce fifteen hundred horse power and propel the tank to a top speed of forty-two miles per hour. The M1 was also fitted with an updated thermal night vision system, as well as an additional mounted 7.62 M240 machinegun. Most importantly, the Abrams packed a larger main gun: a 120mm cannon that could match the T72's guns in range and destruction. Adding to the 2nd Division's combat power on Kuwait's western border, the 1st Division brought 19,500 troops and 123 of the older, not as powerful M-60 A1 battle tanks. With both divisions combined, plus the amphibious force in the Persian Gulf, the marines had over 90,000 troops deployed to the region, a greater commitment than the largest battles of World War Two.

Throughout November and December of 1990 both the Iraqi forces in Kuwait and the US forces within Saudi Arabia grew in number and potency. Once fully mobilized, Saddam Hussein had committed the majority of his 600,000-armed troops, 3100 pieces of artillery, 2800 armored vehicles, and 4200 battle tanks to the Kuwaiti theater. On the far western end of the Kuwaiti border, near the area known as the "elbow," seventy thousand United States Marines of Divisions One and Two with their air and ground support units were dug in. They were the first line of defense for the Saudis against the intimidating Iraqi menace, and the marines were outnumbered in personnel and armaments by a margin greater than two to one. Lt. General Walter Boomer was the overall commander for most of the marines' Gulf War contingent, and he wasn't content to just wait for the much larger Iraqi force to charge into his defensive position.

By mid-December, General Boomer, President Bush, General Schwarzkopf, along with other allied commanders were in the planning stages of an offensive to liberate Kuwait. Taking the fight to Hussein, and catching the Iraqi forces off-guard, could substantially reduce the advantage the Iraqi's possessed in fire power. In order to accomplish this bold plan, General Boomer's Marines would have to open several corridors from Saudi Arabia into southwest Kuwait by breaching what Hussein labeled his "impenetrable tank barrier." This barrier was comprised of two extensive minefields, barbed wire, and a fire-trench that was heavily protected by 1200 pieces of artillery concatenated along the southwestern front. By far, the minefields were the most serious concern. The Iraqi's had methodically planted about 3.5 million mines of eighteen different types. Many of the buried devices were designed to destroy tanks and armored vehicles. There were just as many mines planted specifically to target dismounted Human detectors. The minefields themselves ran in two bands that stretched from the coast of the Persian Gulf, along the southern border of Kuwait to the Wadi al-Batin, a broad valley running along the western border with Iraq. Each field varied in depth from sixty to one hundred and fifty meters. The cleared corridors through the minefields would have to be substantial enough to allow for the speedy passage of both U.S. Marine divisions so as not to create dangerous bottle-necks that would vulnerably expose the leading troops.

Just after midnight on January 16th, 1991, Operation Desert Shield was officially upgraded to Operation Desert Storm with allied air attacks into Kuwait and Iraq. The air strike campaign virtually destroyed the Iraqi air force, eliminating their reconnaissance ability, which in essence blinded Saddam's Army to the movements of the allied forces. By the time the air campaign had ended, all the bridges and supply lines leading to the north had been annihilated. The Kuwaiti theater of war had been effectively isolated from Iraq. The moment allied forces took control of the air-space above Kuwait, a massive movement of troops and supplies to the extreme western border of the warzone began. Like a dusty ribbon that stretched for seventy miles across the desert floor, hundreds of trucks carried thousands of tons of water, food, fuel, ammunition, spare parts, and mine-clearing equipment from the staging areas near Al Jubail to the newly designated offensive position northwest of Al Kibrit. The goal was to have enough supplies in place by mid-February to support the allied fighting troops for sixty days. The stage would be set for the Persian Gulf ground war.

Waiting on the offensive line in the desert.

This conflict has been referred to by many historians as the "Nintendo war," because of its highly mechanized and technological nature. The utilization of Light Armored Vehicles (LAVs), Super Cobras, TOW missiles, Armed Humvees, A-10 Warthogs, and Rocket Propelled Grenades (RPGs) was prolific, but battle tanks would dominate the ground conflict. Boomer's plan was to have both Marine Divisions simultaneously begin their assault from the Saudi desert, breach the two minefields and charge through the southwestern border of Kuwait. Twenty-four hours after the marines committed to their strike, the Army's Seventh Corp would launch the main attack in northern Kuwait at the southern Iraqi border. In essence, Jeff and his fellow "devil dogs" would spearhead the allied offensive against Saddam's enormous war machine. The Marines, along with the Tigger Brigade, would face the fury of Hussein's armed forces for the full first day and night all on their own.

From February 8th through the 11th, Jeff's 8th Tank Battalion conducted their breaching operations planning as an element of the 6th Marine Regiment. The consensus of the planning was that the 6th Marine Regiment would cut one lane through both minefields for each of the three battalions of Division Two. The mine clearing equipment needed for this strategy such as "MiCLiCs" (rocket propelled line charges), front-mounted clearing plows, rakes, and rollers would be provided by Israel and the Army's Tiger Brigade who would also be covering the 8th Battalion's flank. While the 6th Marines worked on clearing lanes, Jeff's 8th Battalion would be engaged in pre-offensive attacks up and down the Kuwaiti border. Their mission was to target specific enemy locations in order to soften the Iraqi's defenses. Jeff and his tank crew had been conducting fighting drills day and night for two months readying for battle, and they were eager to commence the hit-and-run tactics. Preparing for the pre-offensive mission felt no different to Jeff than preparing for a training exercise. It had yet to sink in that he was going to be on the front line of the first major tank battle since Vietnam, and he was going to skirt the perimeter of a legitimate minefield firing real 105mm rounds at authentic artillery pieces, bunkers, and armored vehicles. However, at that point in his young military career, Lance Corporal Franklin had not experienced the sobering and unnerving effects of incoming enemy rounds that define the difference between training and combat.

In preparation for the two division's minefield breachings, Marine Special Forces and the 6th Regiment would be sent out ahead of time to find choice routes through the double tank barrier. Following these reconnaissance teams would be the Marine Infantry troops who would have to march over thirty kilometers across the desert from Saudi Arabia into Kuwait. The troops would need to be self-sustained, carrying with them all they would need for a few days of war. The typical backpack for one of these troops weighed upwards of one hundred pounds. Some of the troops even pulled primitive four-wheeled carts that were laden with heavier artillery. Helping each other stand with such hefty loads, the troops would have to march through the damp, cool night. Once they reached their designated positions along the boundaries of the mine-fields, they would be required to dig a hole large enough to sit in with all of their gear. Cramped in their hastily dug quarters, and shivering in wet clothes that would be soaked through with sweat from the long hump, the Marines would wait throughout the dark, Cimmerian night. Quiet and alone, the warriors would wait for the ugly head of the monster to rise up from the north, and if it did, they would be expected to hold their ground.

General Boomer felt that this clandestine maneuver to pierce the tank barriers and guard the marked lanes was absolutely necessary to expedite the advance of his massive divisions. Exposing so many of his troops across the enemy line, without the protection of machinery, was a terribly disturbing thought. General Boomer would have both his divisions on ready alert long before the "Go" word came down from his superiors. Come hell or high water, as soon as General Boomer anticipated the "green light," he intended to send the full force of his tank battalions crashing through Hussein's "impenetrable barriers." He was adamant about not leaving one man vulnerable for one minute longer than necessary.

Vehicles hauling the MiCLiCs would lead the main penetrations. The rockets of the MiCLiCs would be propelled along the marked routes. Each rocket carried behind it a 110-yard-long cable, along which explosives were attached. Once the cable was outstretched, the line-charges would be detonated and subsequently explode the mines around it. Immediately after the detonations, tanks and armored vehicles fitted with front mounted plows and rollers would proof the newly cleared lanes by pushing away or triggering any live mines that remained. Once the cleared lanes were proofed and widened, the main battle tanks would roll through to engage the enemy with the rest of the division bringing up the rear. As the driver of a M60 A3 in the 8th Tank Battalion, Jeff would be one of the many men leading the charge.

By mid-February, Alpha Company had been stationed along the Kuwait border for months. Nearly all of that time, the troops had been under light and sound discipline, which meant no lights or noise of any kind was tolerated. Jeff recalls that the desert nights were as dark and quiet as the inside of a football. On certain nights, when Jeff climbed out of the tank to relieve himself, he felt like he had to duck under the stars. If there were no moon, only the light from an occasional gas-flare at a distant, sabotaged, Kuwaiti oil well could be seen. Most nights were cool, quiet, and so dark a person literally couldn't see their hand up against their nose. Between gunfire and explosions, the desert was the quietest place Jeff had ever experienced.

Daytime in the Saudi Desert is typically pleasant in February: mostly sunny with overcast skies, clouds and rain occurring less than one third of the days. February of 1991 was different. The noxious pillars of smoke from over six hundred burning oil wells routinely merged in the upper atmosphere to darken the entire sky. When the air currents were right, the dense, dark smoke from the burning wells in the southern Rumailia oil field would block-out the sun and turn high noon into an eerie dusk. For the tank crews of the 8th Battalion, some days the toxic fumes were impossible to escape. Merely exposing your head from the tank meant getting misted by a dry deposition of smoke residue. Choking on foul air and expelling black mucous from the nose was common. Mixing this nasty atmosphere with the earth-shaking explosions from the Navy ships' sixteen-inch guns out in the Persian Gulf, the missiles from fighter jets overhead, and cannon rounds from the tanks on land, the world around Jeff felt very apocalyptic.

Looking out from his driver's hatch, Jeff could usually see all five tanks in his platoon off either flank, or sometimes more of his company's nearly two dozen M60s. Maintaining a line of sight with one another was a battlefield requirement. Even with the mandatory line of sight rule, for the weeks approaching the Desert Storm conflict, Jeff's universe was very small on the Kuwaiti border. It mostly centered on his three other crew mates and their M60.

Life was slow for the tank crews when they weren't engaged in training exercises or real maneuvers during that period of time. Since maintenance of their firearms and the tank was constant in the desert environment, it worked out well that there was plenty of down time for the men to keep their equipment in battle ready condition. During down time after maintenance was caught up, Jeff and his crew would indulge themselves in one of two kinds of recreation. One of the crew would start-up their obsessive card game of "spades" on the front of the tank, or someone would restack the M60 size hill of discarded MRE components, climb to the top, throw off his shirt, and proclaim, "King!" With that the battle for king of MRE Hill would rage on until one of them hollered out, "Spades!" The four tank men would often get lost in the card game for hours, which worked wonders for keeping their minds off the highly touted Republican Guard or their own far away homes. Each night a member of the crew took their turn at "watch" while the other three pretended to get comfortable on top of the fifty-four tons of steel or slouched down in their constricted battle stations as they were required to do during combat periods. Either way, comfort wasn't part of the sleeping equation. During many of those long nights, Lance Corporal Jeff Franklin thought of Lady and dog training. He realized that nothing he had done in his life thus far was as fulfilling as working with Lady. The Marines and the tanks were stimulating, baseball was satisfying, but neither of those pursuits took his mind off of dogs. It was there in the desert, crouched down inside the M60 A3 that Jeff worked-out his life plan to become a professional dog trainer. Although he didn't know much about that profession then, Jeff believed dog training was his chosen path. He intended to seek-out schooling for dog trainers as soon as he finished his tour in the Middle East.

The M60 A3 was powered by a twelve-cylinder diesel engine, and it held three hundred and fifty-seven gallons of fuel not counting the surplus cans secured to the turret. The wheels rolled, the track turned, the turret spun, and the breech slid in that gritty desert environment because of grease, and lots of it. The M60 was a true war machine with one main purpose, delivering deadly projectiles to enemy targets. Jeff's tank was well equipped to do its job. The M60 carried sixty-three, fifty-pound rounds for its main 105mm cannon. It carried nine hundred rounds for the TC's (tank commander) 12.7mm heavy machinegun, and fifty-nine hundred rounds for the 7.62mm coaxial machinegun, not to mention twelve large smoke-screen grenades. The men trained with these weapons multiple times a week preparing for war. Any tanker will assure you, there is no reason to wonder what a tank and its crew smell like during wartime. They wear the fragrance of their environment, diesel fuel, grease, and gunpowder. Personally, Jeff was glad that the strong aroma of his steel environment permeated everything. He said, "Without it, we would have gagged smelling each other. Bathing wasn't an option in the desert, and four filthy men living in tight quarters wears on the nose."

It didn't take long for life in the desert to become tiresome for Jeff and his military family in the Middle East. Weeks of digging a hole in the sand so you can take a crap, rationing toilet paper, and having sand in every orifice can frustrate even the most tolerant person. The lack of hot food, showers, music, and other modern conveniences definitely worked to strain relationships and lower morale. Jeff was fortunate because he was assigned to an experienced and well-balanced tank crew.

As the youngest member of his crew, Jeff looked to the others, especially his platoon sergeant, for reality checks. Jeff marveled over Sarge's ability to rally the platoon when their overall mood became heavy from the trying conditions or separation from home. He was an excellent point man; he never let the others see him lacking in confidence or fortitude. Lance Corporal Franklin learned a great deal about combat and leadership from Sarge. The tank commander (TC) was the most experienced tanker in Jeff's crew. He wasn't known as "Mister Friendly," but he was a competent commander who was as cold as ice under pressure and guaranteed to get the job done. The gunner was the next in the line of seniority. He tended to be a little intense, too serious at times, but he was an excellent marksman. When it came to a hostile engagement he was all business and rarely failed to takeout the target. Having this gunner behind the sights of their 105mm cannon, Jeff felt they could out shoot the best of the Republican Guard's T72s. The loader was the closest to Jeff in age and experience. He was fairly quiet and a pleasant crewmate to share a tank with. During their extensive live-round training, this fellow turned into a machine. He became part of the "big gun," capable of loading a fifty-pound 105mm round every five seconds for long stretches. Jeff and his M60 crew were confident that, as a team, they could bring a real fight to the Iraqis and give them all they could handle.

On February 18th, Major General Keys, the immediate commander of the 2nd Division, received word from the overall Marine commander, General Boomer, to begin the clandestine movement of the 6th Regiment into the minefields. The ground war was officially set to begin on February 22nd. Both Keys and Boomer wanted their men well ensconced before then. The "war clock" was officially ticking, and from that moment on it would be difficult to reverse the plan. Soon there would be a substantial number of troops dangerously close to the Iraqi front without the protection of armaments.

Unfortunately, the weather leading up to "G" day wasn't very favorable for air support which all of the allied leaders were counting on for overhead protection. All concerned hoped that as dawn approached on the 22nd, the skies would clear and the "ceiling" would open up to allow for air support. The weather did not improve. In fact, it worsened, causing General Boomer to call for a twenty-four-hour delay to the start of the ground war.

By February 23rd, both Marine divisions were in attack positions along the Kuwaiti southwest border. Several thousand troops had secretly pierced through the tank barrier and were "dug in." Ironically, General Schwarzkopf, the commander of the entire allied initiative, was in a similarly precarious position to General Eisenhower on the eve of the Normandy invasion in 1944. In both conflicts, many months of exhaustive preparation had led up to the eve of decision. Tens of thousands of troops and armaments were in attack position, anxiously awaiting the "go" command. Desert Storm, like "D-Day," was constructed as a surprise offensive. This meant that every minute the plan was delayed, the risk of exposure was increased dramatically. For both commanders, the foul weather would not relent. Clouds and rain made vital air support impossible. General Schwarzkopf, like General Eisenhower, was left with the heavy decision of committing to the attack without the protective umbrella of air support, or abort the massive undertaking altogether. On the evening of February 23rd, 1991, this message made its way to the waiting Marines:

"Message to members of I Marine Expeditionary Force, 23 Feb 91
Lieutenant General Walter E. Boomer, USMC After months of preparation, we are on the eve of the liberation of Kuwait, a small, peaceful country that was brutally attacked and subsequently pillaged by Iraq. Now we will attack into Kuwait, not to conquer, but to drive out the invaders and restore the country to its citizens. In so doing, you not only return a nation to its people, but you will destroy the war machine of a ruthless dictator, who fully intended to control this part of the world, thereby endangering many other nations, including our own.

We will succeed in our mission because we are well-trained and well-equipped; because we are U.S. Marines, Sailors, Soldiers, and Airmen: and because our cause is just. Your children and grandchildren will read about your victory in the years to come and appreciate your sacrifice and courage. America will watch her sons and daughters and draw strength from your success.

May the spirit of your Marine forefathers ride with you and may God give you the strength to accomplish your mission.

Semper Fi.
Boomer."

With the last rays of sunlight on the 23rd of February, Jeff and his crew donned their cumbersome MOPP gear. The MOPP gear was essentially over-garments (hood, mask, gloves, jacket, etc.) which protected the men from potential chemical, biological, or radiation injury.

The platoon sergeant called for a huddle before his five tank crews climbed into their battle stations. It was an intuitive move on his part. None of the crews had voiced any dread or fear over their duty and impending battle. Nevertheless, Sarge, being an experienced team leader, addressed those hidden anxieties that most warriors have but don't usually express. Jeff will never forget the inspiring huddle before his first mortal combat. Many of Sarge's words have played through Jeff's mind prior to every lethal encounter he's faced since those days in the desert. Sarge cut to the chase with his opening comments, and he gave the men chills before he concluded: "We know the Republican Guard is made up of some bad dudes. Their tanks can out gun and out run us. We know the Iraqis have nearly three times the men and firepower that we do. Listen to me carefully; I don't give a single damn what they have or don't have. I don't give two shits what they, or anybody else says about how tough they are. We are the best trained and most disciplined military force in the world. We can whip anybody! We have night vision capabilities and they don't. So, we're going to knock the life out of them at 2,500 meters before the sun even comes up. By the time light hits the battlefield, our M60s are going to be right up their turrets. We'll be dueling at such close quarters their 125mm cannons will have no advantage. And don't forget, we have a tank full of 'Silver Bullets.' The crew is the M60 A3. The crew is the war machine. Our minds are the weapon. The tank is just the tool. The Republican Guard may have a better tool, but we have the superior weapon. Gentlemen, we are going to take them by surprise. We are going to strike early and strike hard. That's our biggest advantage. The truth is, we already have troops behind enemy lines, I intend to charge in and back them up no matter what. I'd rather die than leave my teammates to fight alone. We're Marines, and I promise you, the Republican Guard will rue the day we came calling." With that, the men butted helmets and cheered "Ooh-rah," then climbed into their hatches for a long wait.

At 0200 on February 24, 1991, a crackling message from the company commander came across the "all coms" channel in Jeff's helmet, "Let's get some Devil Dogs! Ooh-rah!" It was on. Jeff fired up the twelve-cylinder diesel engine, but before he put the 750 horses' worth of power in gear, TC gave his youngest crewmate one last bit of direction: "Franklin, it's your job to keep us moving, regardless of what happens. Those Iraqis aren't going to catch us shootin'." Ramped up with emotional energy, Jeff floored the fifty-four-ton M60 toward the Kuwaiti minefields and hollered back, "Sir, yes Sir!"

Cruising just ahead of Jeff's company were the tanks rigged with the mine-clearing plows. And in front of them were the vehicles carrying the MiCLiCs. They were all rolling across country in the direction of the dreaded tank barriers. As the group neared the perimeter of the first minefield, everyone held back a safe distance except for the trucks with the mine-clearing line-charges. The rockets towing the line- charges were launched in the direction of the yet-to-be-cleared lanes through the minefield that the 6th Regiment had marked the previous day. When the football-field length cables settled to the ground, the charges were detonated triggering hundreds of mines along the proposed corridor. Carefully, the tanks with the front-mounted plows and rollers moved in to clear away any remaining live explosive devices. Right on their tails were the tanks of Alpha Company. With the detonation of the line charges and the resulting explosions of so many mines, the announcement to the Iraqi army that the marines had arrived was undeniable. Their plan of attack was as exposed as the thousands of troops already inside of Kuwait. There was no turning back for the 2nd Division now.

Not long after the plows had begun moving sand, a few of them as well as some battle tanks ran into potent, disabling explosions that forced them to halt. The MiCLiCs failed to trigger a large number of mines. It was discovered later that the line-charges were ineffective on some of the hidden explosive devices designed to resist such a tactic. Now, committed to the minefield, Alpha Company was ordered to stand fast and wait for another clearing strategy. There was no time to analyze what exactly went wrong with the MiCLiCs. The enemy would surely be answering the knock at their southwest border any moment. The solution to the mine clearing conundrum came down from a seasoned higher-up. Although operating under layers of advanced technology, the virtual spearhead of a highly mechanized military force, the marines resorted to a proven, old-school clearing technique. Designated infantry troops were sent into the minefields on their hands and knees to probe for mines with their bayonets. Listening and feeling for contact with a mine, the men meticulously inserted their blades into the sand and slowly moved them about. The proposed corridor was cleared one meter at a time.

After hours that felt like days, the remaining explosives along the critical path through the first minefield were located and neutralized. The battle tanks were rolling once more, just as the Iraqi's artillery began to light up the black sky with 160mm mortar fire that were launching ninety-pound bombs into their vicinity. Arriving at the second minefield more MiCLiCs were deployed. The plows quickly moved in with the battle tanks on their heels. Again, more vehicles were disabled by live explosives. And once again, Alpha Company was ordered to stand fast inside the minefield, only this time the enemy's 155mm howitzers exponentially increased their peril by raining down highly explosive projectiles on top of their position. Due to the dense smoke from the sabotaged oil wells and the foul weather that day, air support would not be coming to assist the tank crews stranded in the barrier zone. Jeff and his crew openly prayed that their troops behind the lines would be able to stifle the Iraqi artillery. If not, the odds were against them ever getting out of the minefield. Although the world appeared to be breaking apart around them, the human mine clearers diligently and adroitly, on their hands and knees, worked to open the lane and allow their fighting machines to engage the Iraqi menace.

Finally, free of the second minefield, the handful of tanks in Jeff's platoon realigned with one another and struck-out toward the enemies' defensive line. Some distance past the tank barriers, the group of tanks paused to reconnoiter when heat emitting images were detected on one of the green screens of their thermal sighting systems. Jeff had his head and shoulders extended up through the open driver's hatch, which put his helmet just below the forward-pointing, cannon barrel. Looking northwesterly through the Night Vision Goggles (NVGs) that were attached to his helmet, Jeff could barely make out the ghostly representations of soldiers frantically tending to a trailer mounted weapon, followed by the blinding flash of a launching bomb. Jeff didn't need a directive for the next move. He dropped down into his driver's seat, closed the hatch and focused on tactical driving maneuvers while guiding their tank closer to the artillery line. Using the M60's laser rangefinder, TC called out the coordinates of an Iraqi artillery piece. The gunner confirmed, "Identified." Slamming the breech closed on a 105mm round, the loader responded "up," signifying the big gun was ready to fire. Without delay, TC shouted, "Fire!" "On the way," came from the gunner immediately, and before the men could draw another breath, a M43 mortar burst into fragments. Proficiency was no accident when it came to the performance of the Marine Corps tank crews. Their teamwork had been honed from countless hours of live-round training. Normally the all-powerful blasts from the main gun felt bone rattling to Jeff, but not on the opening morning of the ground war. Dodging exploding missiles and taking life from the human enemy was a real game-changer. The repeated rush of adrenaline kept his mind glued to his task. Jeff doesn't remember feeling much during the four days of combat, except that from the first unnerving moments in the minefield the war felt like one long grave experience.

After hours of fighting through the artillery front, Jeff's tank company pushed northward and entered a series of naturally-occurring waves of sand. Cresting the last of the waves, TC hollered, "Gunner, sabot, tank," then gave the coordinates for the target. A couple seconds after TC's announcement, two Iraqi T72s appeared on Jeff's greenscreen. The tanks were no more than 2000 meters away, and each was virtually buried in the sand. Little more than the topsides of the vehicles were exposed. Like funnel spiders cloaked in their traps, the Iraqi tanks were patiently waiting for their prey. Had it not been for the darkness of night and Alpha Company's thermal vision capabilities, which allowed Jeff's tank to stealthily close in on the enemy, the T72s with their larger 125mm cannons could have launched their lethal missiles at the oncoming marines well beyond the range of the M60's 105mm guns. The gunner shouted, "Identified." The loader followed, "Up." With no delay, "Fire" came from TC and "On the way" sounded from the gunner. The sabot round ("Silver Bullet") is virtually a twenty-pound dart comprised of depleted uranium. It can travel 2000 meters in one second and penetrate twenty-two inches of steel armor at that distance. Upon impact Jeff's crew witnessed an incredibly bright flash of light as the sabot pierced the deadly T72, instantly killing the occupants with overpressure. Allowing no time for a counter attack, TC ordered "Fire" on the second Iraqi tank. The projectile pierced the T72s turret which ignited the onboard ammunitions creating the effect of a giant Roman candle that blew the turret 150 feet in the air. The sabot round was the allies' tank-killing weapon of choice on the desert battle field for devastating reasons. The marine's stealthy, night-vision kills ruled in the pre-dawn hours of February 24th.

By sunrise, Jeff's platoon was deep into enemy territory and moving fast. Without the advantage of darkness, the marines had to rely on their speed of engagement and tactical maneuvers to survive. The desert floor rumbled from the non-stop cannon fire, while hour after hour their lives teetered in the balance of precision and fortune. The supply columns caught up with Jeff's company about midday. In the thick of the mortar rounds and missile explosions, the fearless infantrymen delivered the much-needed ammunition, fuel, water, and food no differently than a parcel service delivering a package to a neighborhood home. The sight of his brave countrymen bringing supplies to the forward tank crews brought a sense of comfort and relief that Jeff could not express to them in words. His tired, grease smudged, and sweat stained face told the entire story of their long battles. As one of the men handed up some fresh water, he grinned at Jeff and asked, "We're whoopin' 'em aren't we?" With a confident lip curl that turned into a half-smile, Jeff gave the infantryman his newly adopted warrior response, "Damn skippy!" During the fifteen minutes it took to refuel and restock the M60, Jeff almost forgot about their immediate life-threatening environment, a break he desperately needed.

On February 25th, the Second Division encountered their fiercest combat of the war. In two separate attacks from Iraqi mechanized, armored units, the troops of the Second Division fought toe to toe in what is considered the largest tank battle in Marine Corps history. In one conflict known as the "Reveille Engagement," Marine tank units were overwhelmed at dawn by a superior number of Iraqi T72s and T55s that assaulted from both flanks. When the dust settled, the remains of thirty-four Iraqi tanks and their crews littered the desert, just from that one engagement. The second day of the ground war proved to be one long battle for Jeff's crew. Their main gun had no break, as round after round TC hollered, "Fire!" Jeff performed as he was instructed. At full throttle, he maneuvered their M60 from one engagement to another while dodging incoming rounds by only meters and miracles. On numerous occasions, the Marines encountered the Iraqi's at dangerously close quarters of 1200 meters or less. At that range, superior training won the day, not bigger guns. The war raged on without remission all day. With no time to drink or eat, the Marines, although physically and mentally depleted, fought for all they were worth. The incessant ringing in Franklin's ears from the 105mm rounds, heavy machinegun fire, and the blaring communications in his helmet only exacerbated the stress of the longest day of his life. As Jeff drove through the immense scene of carnage that was strewn across the battlefield, the gruesome images of smoldering vehicle fragments, charred corpses, and oozing body parts, left an indelible mark on his psyche.

During a refueling on February 26th, Jeff's tank crew received word that their loader would need to replace another loader in their platoon who had been severely injured by a main-gun breech. As a consequence, Lance Corporal Franklin moved into the loader's position, and a recruit from the supply columns took over his driver's seat. With little time for adjustment between engagements, Jeff had to transition into the most challenging position on their tank crew. As the loader, Jeff had to heave fifty-pound cartridges into the breach of the main gun, lock the mechanism, avoid the action of the breach during firing, toss the spent casings out his top hatch and reload, all within seconds. Jeff had received training for the position during Tanker's School, but his real practice and proficiency would occur during battle. By the end of the third day of the ground war, Jeff had morphed into seasoned loader, capable of loading more than nine 105mm rounds a minute.

It was nearly dusk on the 26th and the Marine 2nd Division was sweeping west of Kuwait City to cut off the highways leading out of the capital.

The steady stream of Iraqi deserters coming out of Kuwait had turned into a river of prisoners trying to surrender to the allied tank units. Jeff and his company were still actively fighting the remaining Republican Guard while maneuvering around the congestion of enemy combatants waving white rags. With live artillery fire and cannon rounds coming in on them, there was no possible way to process the thousands of deserters. The tank crews were forced to wave the surrendering Iraqis to march to the rear where the supply columns would deal with them. Often, Jeff's M60 would nearly come to a halt trying to avoid running over the desperate Iraqis. On one such occasion, Jeff and his crew were on top of their tank directing the deserters, when an RPG (Rocket Propelled Grenade)was launched from a nearby berm. The grenade passed right between Jeff and TC, just a few feet above the turret. There was no time to put the M60 in gear, so TC turned the .50 caliber heavy-machine gun on the berm and opened up. With more return fire from the combatants, Jeff sent another 500 rounds from the coaxial machine gun into the hidden bunker. Silenced at last, a few of the marine infantry accompanying Jeff'stank approached the bunker to clear it of any remaining threat. Behind the berm, the infantry found one wounded Iraqi soldier sprawled in the bloody sand next to his discharged RPG. According to the humane rules of engagement, the marines were obligated to care for the Iraqi that only moments ago did his best to annihilate them. To add insult to injury, this wounded man had to be placed on the very tank he nearly destroyed in order to be transported to a rear supply truck. Lance Corporal Franklin rode on top of the M60 with the wounded soldier until they reached the supply column. One word captured the moment for the nineteen-year-old, battle weary Marine as he and his enemy glared at one another, "Unnatural."

By February 27th, the allied forces had broken through Iraq's defensive lines and all but crushed Saddam's entire army. Before nightfall, the 2nd Division occupied the northwest ridge of Kuwait City and sealed off the capital. The following day Arab troops were allowed to pass through the Marines lines and officially liberate the city.

On February 28th, President Bush ordered all units to cease their offensive action. When it was all said and done, the Marines had driven nearly one hundred miles in as many hours. They had defeated seven Iraqi divisions, destroyed 1,040 tanks, 608 armored vehicles and 432 artillery pieces. They had taken 22,308 prisoners at a cost of five casualties and forty-eight wounded. At a press briefing in Riyadh, General Schwarzkopf praised the Marines: "It was a classic, absolutely classic military breaching of a very, very tough minefield….and I think it will be studied for many, many years to come as the way to do it."

A few months later, Lance Corporal Franklin returned home to Kentucky with his company to receive a heroes' welcome. Hundreds of people were waiting at the airport to cheer-on the Marines. Alpha Company was even honored with an official parade at Fort Knox. Shortly after returning home, Jeff was invited to the Babe Ruth All Star game as a special guest. He was celebrated as a war hero and got to throw out the game-ball. Of course, Jeff didn't simply toss the ball like a regular honoree; he fired it into the catcher's mitt with real heat like a legitimate third baseman. Lance Corporal Jeffrey Scott Franklin had come full circle, back to the sport he left when he signed on as a Marine. The homecoming marked a point on Jeff's timeline when he shifted all of his creative energy to his dream of training dogs.

Seven

PROFESSIONAL TRAINER

By June of 1991, Jeff was back in Kentucky and had located a professional dog training kennel. As soon as he had enrolled in a professional dog training course, the kennel owner contracted me to guide the new student through the full spectrum of canine instruction that extended beyond basic obedience. Specifically, I worked with Jeff on developing handling techniques for the management of canine hostility: stratagems in which every professional dog trainer should be proficient. It is a rare day in a busy trainer's life when a canine tyrant doesn't need to have his assertive behavior curbed. My equally important responsibility in regard to Jeff's education was helping him develop the necessary skills to shape canine aggression into a serviceable trait. Channeled hostility is the mechanism that drives a police K-9 to clear a dark and hazardous building of potentially dangerous perpetrators. Directed aggression propels a combat dog into battle against the enemy of his fellow soldiers. If Jeff really intended to reach the heights of a master dog trainer, he would have to become proficient with all the nuances of both suppressing and amplifying canine aggression.

Every professional dog trainer can remember their first humbling encounter with a strong canine personality. For Jeff, that ego destroyer was named O'Leary. He was an eighteen-month-old Irish terrier who was a match for any Marine. I selected this dog specifically for Jeff's instruction because O'Leary demonstrated enough hostility to challenge someone trying to gain control in their partnership with a dog. But, at the same time, the feisty terrier didn't possess the extremes in stature or character to be a real threat to a novice trainer's welfare. O'Leary was a medium sized terrier about nineteen inches tall and thirty pounds in weight. He was psychologically stable, but he was also a legitimate bully to most people he encountered. The four-legged Irishman already had several injurious bites under his belt by the time he checked into training. So, when it came to conflict, O'Leary was considerably more than bark.

The catalyst for much of O'Leary's discord was his instinctual intolerance of leadership that was exacerbated by a real distaste for being physically managed. Our training task was complicated. We needed to get O'Leary in the habit of deferring to his handlers before springing into action, while at the same time charge him with the responsibility of capping his drive and energy. We intended to reach our goals by teaching, then reinforcing, five basic canine self-control responsibilities: composure, relinquishing treasures, visitor manners, door way control, and loose leash walking. However, the real challenge for Mr. Franklin was the practice of calm, but decisive responses to correct the scrappy Irishman. He wasn't at war with the enemy any longer. Jeff would learn from me and the hundreds of dogs we would train together that negative emotion had no place in successful dog training. Although countering the adversary with rage may win the day on the battlefield, it seldom if ever brought about positive results on the dog-training grounds.

The little brown terrier pranced alongside of me when I first walked him into the instruction room to meet his very "green" handler. No sooner than we entered, Jeff Franklin, the youthful reflection of the man he is today, sized up his first aggressive behavior case with a cocky, partial grin (including a slight lip curl) and a comment, "He doesn't look like much of a handful." To this day that erroneous, lightning-fast assessment of canine behavior rolls around in Jeff's mind as a rookie mistake that won't ever be repeated. Every dog that has since passed through Franklin's hands receives ample evaluation time and the due attention of a Master Trainer before any instruction begins. O'Leary proved to be enough challenge for the two of us that we've remembered him over thousands of dogs and two decades worth of training.

On the long road to becoming a professional dog trainer, Jeff gradually developed the discipline to deflect canine hostility that was directed his way without expressing negative emotion or retaliation. In the dog-training world, when a handler projects anger or frustration in reaction to an undesirable canine behavior, a dog's trust in the trainer disintegrates leading to a breakdown in communication. The dog's concern about the handler's emotional volatility leads to worries for self-preservation. In that anxious mental state, the dog is preoccupied with the strained relations with his handler and is unable to make appropriate decisions based on the consequences of his actions. When that situation arises, the training process is all but stifled.

After giving Jeff a brief tutorial on this subject, I had him record the first axiom in his trainer's log: "Register no personal offense when a dog uses his intrinsic behavioral tool of hostility against you." The second postulate reads something like this: "Punishment for a canine student is nothing more than an emotion-free, negative consequence which is purposefully attached to an undesirable behavior." The third truth I had Jeff commit to memory was: "A dog will not perform to his fullest potential without genuine praise and meaningful reward. All dogs quickly discern a liar." Since young Mr. Franklin was aspiring to be the best at canine behavior shaping, he would need to evolve into a master of emotional control, as well as an exemplar of steady nerve. O'Leary was the perfect catalyst to galvanize those qualities.

O'Leary challenged his new handler right out of the gate. On the second day of instruction Jeff attempted to take a ball from the terrier's mouth and wound up with thirty pounds of rebellious fury backing him off. Even as a neophyte trainer, Jeff immediately recognized O'Leary's excitement over the challenge and was a little taken aback by how much the little fellow seemed to enjoy combat. That was Jeff's first experience with a highly aggressive dog from a lineage purposefully bred to be feisty. In fact, the word terrier is derived from the Latin word terra, which means earth or land. Terrier therefore refers to a large and varied group of dogs specifically bred to engage or drive-out quarry that dwell underground.

As a professional dog trainer, Jeff needed to cultivate an appreciation for canine characteristics, like independence, tenacity, courage, and combativeness.

These were the purposefully, enhanced qualities that a healthy Irish terrier should exhibit. Unbeknownst to Jeff, O'Leary was not unlike the many police and military dogs he would work with in the future. The German shepherd, Belgian Malinois, and the Dutch shepherd are three breeds of dogs most commonly selected by police departments and the Armed Forces for combat related tasks. These three breeds come from a herding background, and they share an ancestry that has been selectively bred for fearlessness and pugnacity over many generations. It would be unfair to label a police dog that is aggressively responding to passersby from the back of his cruiser as "bad," or unstable. A more accurate assessment of the stimulated crime-fighter might be "misguided" or "out-of-control". The police dog should not be faulted for possessing a hostile potential that his breeders virtually ensured he would inherit. Nor should the assertive dog be debased for the very trait that the police department particularly selected him for. Jeff Franklin's goal was to develop into a well-rounded dog trainer who could not only appreciate the overly zealous police dog's misdirected energy, but also know how to properly channel all of that potential.

In the case of O'Leary, there was nothing inherently wrong with the terrier, he was happy and healthy in every regard. He was simply tough and willing to fight over issues he deemed worthy. Our goal as O'Leary's trainers was not to change his character, but to channel his natural potential in the appropriate directions. Obviously, confronting his handler was not a desirable behavior. Therefore, I instructed Jeff to deliver a sufficiently strong leash and collar correction in order to extinguish the terrier's possessiveness over the ball. I also put Jeff on alert to look for O'Leary's slightest behavioral movement in relinquishing the ball so that we could shower him with praise. With a feisty personality like O'Leary, we needed to maintain an appropriate balance between strong corrections and worthwhile rewards. Too much or too little on either the positive or negative side of the handler/dog relationship would throw O'Leary into his natural default behavior of combat. Walking a fine-line like this is a challenge for any trainer, however, the difficult task at hand for Mr. Franklin was not so much gaining control of the ball as it was gaining control of his own anger in the face of the terrier's assertive action.

Over the next twelve days, O'Leary ran both of us through the gauntlet. Jeff was actually working about six hostile dogs of various types within the group of canine students he was assigned. But, hands down, the Irish terrier was our toughest challenge. At one point in the second half of O'Leary's training, Jeff was assisting the terrier during a down placement exercise, when I noticed the dog's posture dramatically change. Jeff had yet to place his hands-on O'Leary in order to work on the "down" command, when without consent, the terrier decisively rose from a sit into a rigid stand. All four of his feet were spread well apart for balance. His mouth was tightly closed, but his nostrils were flared taking in an abundance of oxygen. O'Leary's tail was vibrating, not wagging, at a stiff, ninety-degree angle from his back. The Irish canine's head was high and rigid. Every aspect of his posture was screaming at Jeff, "I'm not tolerating any placement today!"

For nearly a week, Mr. Franklin and O'Leary had been working well as a team, with very little disagreement between them. As a consequence, Jeff's handling confidence rose (as one would expect) while his safety consciousness fell (which seems inevitable with new trainers). The shift in Jeff's demeanor led to casual hand placement on the dog's body while allowing too much leash freedom at the same time. Going into this exercise, I cautioned Jeff to be careful because placing a strong-willed canine into a down posture could be misconstrued by the dog as forced submission, which might be violently resisted. Unfortunately, the confident and very assertive terrier had no mercy to offer my "green" handler. As Jeff was pressing down on O'Leary's hips with the left hand and extending his two front feet with the right hand, I cautioned him to shorten the leash and proceed more slowly. Before Jeff had a chance to adjust his leash, I could see from my vantage point the terrier's upper lips wrinkling and exposing German shepherd sized fangs. Moving toward O'Leary, I shouted for Jeff to get his face back. I didn't get a full step in their direction when that Irish "snake" sprung on his handler. Because of athletic reflexes, Jeff was able to pull his head back before O'Leary could strike that first target. Instinctively, Jeff reached for the furious terrier to wrestle him to the floor, but his hands didn't make it to the wiry body before O'Leary sunk four huge teeth into a forearm. With one free hand, Jeff grabbed the terrier's muzzle and attempted to pry open the attacker's mouth in order to relieve the unbelievable pressure. Like a badger, O'Leary thrashed Jeff's arm and bared down with the concentration of an experienced biter, oblivious to anything but the grip itself. By the time I reached the combatants, the leash, which had been dropped during the scuffle, was wrapped around Jeff's legs. With no other option, I grabbed O'Leary's collar and twisted with both hands in order to restrict air flow (not unlike a wrestler's "sleeper hold"). As the terrier struggled I tried to console Jeff, "I've got him now, Mr. Franklin. You can release his muzzle. O'Leary is going to come off your arm like a snapping turtle, so watch your hands." I realized I was expecting a

Taking the "Hits" as a decoy.

lot from Jeff given that we hadn't known each other very long. In essence I was asking him to relinquish the fight and trust me with his welfare. That was a tall order for a young Marine in the throes of combat. However, without much hesitation, Jeff released the terrier, and I was able to remove him from the bloody arm.

Until that day, Jeff Franklin had never experienced a legitimate dog bite, or the subsequent medical treatment. I've often relayed that the vigorous brushing, irrigating, and trimming of the ragged puncture wounds is more horrifying than the bite itself. I felt terrible that Jeff got injured on my watch, and I was the one responsible for putting a dent in his infectious enthusiasm. The next morning, I reported to the kennel owner that I fully expected the new student to hang up his leash and never return, due to the walloping bite he received the previous afternoon. I had not yet left the kennel owner's office when in walked Jeff Franklin, right on time, ready for training and grinning from ear to ear over his very sore "badge of courage." I had to ask, "Are you back for more?" Jeff's confident response said it all: "Yes sir!"

I also needed to get a feel for his comfort level with the terrier. So, there was no beating around the bush: "Are you up for another round with Mr. O'Leary?" Grinning back, Jeff gave me his pat response to a challenge that I had yet to hear: "Damn skippy!" I said, "I'm not sure I've ever heard that reply before, but I know how to translate it."

Jeff stuck with the little terrier and completed his training. All things considered, they worked pretty well as an obedience team. Although the Irish canine was never going to transform into a lap-dog, we did reach our overall goals. Jeff and I were able to groom O'Leary. We could direct him to drop items from his mouth. He would also respond to five obedience commands in the midst of distractions. To top it off, these exercises could be accomplished with no leash in our hands. However, the most impressive accomplishment in regards to O'Leary's training was the fact that Jeff could get the combative student to follow through on all of these tasks without hostile protest. I liked Mr. Franklin when I first met him, but I genuinely respected him after the O'Leary project. Jeff demonstrated incredible resilience by maintaining his dog-training enthusiasm after suffering a nearly debilitating bite. Even that early in our teacher/student relationship, I felt that he possessed an extraordinary grasp of the "big dog-training picture."

There was little doubt in my mind that combining Jeff's natural rapport with dogs, his obsessive interest in canine behavior and professional guidance, he was destined to mature into an exceptional dog-man.

Some weeks after finishing O'Leary's training, I overheard Jeff advising a client, "Aggressive dogs aren't 'bad,' they just require more attention and quicker reflexes than the passive types do." Within a month's time, young Mr. Franklin had truly fostered a professional's attitude of respect and admiration toward tough canine students. The many hours of managing hostile dogs significantly altered Jeff's view of canine aggression. Jeff was ready for the next step in his professional education, which was learning how to shape aggressive canine drive into something positive and useful.

For a fledgling dog trainer like Mr. Franklin, the flip side of the O'Leary coin was Brutus, a muscular, middle-sized German shepherd who was enrolled in our training school to prepare for his first Schutzhund title. Schutzhund means "Protection Dog" in German. This sport was first developed in Germany around 1900 as a suitability test for the German shepherd. A dog competing in the three phases of a Schutzhund Trial, (Tracking, Obedience, and Protection) will be challenged to demonstrate the basic skills of a police-style working canine.

At a typical Schutzhund trial, the tracking test usually begins at sun-up and demands that the dog use his olfactory ability to follow a human-laid track to locate the track-layer's intentionally placed articles along the trail. Immediately following tracking is the obedience phase of the trial. The obedience test requires that a handler and dog team work through a series of formal command executions, including jumps and retrieves. The protection test is the final challenge of the trial, and it closes out the day. During this "bite work" phase, each dog is directed by his handler to search six blinds which are strategically placed in an open field. When the dog locates the hidden decoy (a designated sparring partner or pseudo"Bad Guy") behind one of the blinds, he is required to bark and guard the man who is dressed in padded, bite-protection gear. Several times during this test, each dog is encouraged to engage the decoy under varying combat scenarios and actually bite the decoy in order to subdue the human target.

Brutus was a high caliber dog who came from police canine background, and he had also been raised as an uninhibited competition dog. This meant when we began Brutus' instruction, he was the bouncing expression of raw potential and quite the handful for his family. Brutus' owners were newcomers to the world of working Shepherds and Schutzhund, so they needed significant help in managing a working shepherd. Brutus was fifteen months old when he was enrolled into our program, and he came with a decent skill-set. The handsome bi-colored dog was comfortable in his formal command responses. He already, at that young age, followed a human track pretty well although he wouldn't indicate articles at the time. Brutus was a natural athlete, so jumping on command came easily for him. I was hired to complete the abilities that Brutus lacked in order to achieve his first Schutzhund title. The exercises I needed to concentrate on were the Dumbbell Retrieve, Article Indication, and most of his Bite-Work requirements: the Blind Search, the Hold and Bark, the Escape and Courage Bites, the Cease Aggression command, and the Escort of the decoy. These were many of the skills that Jeff had yet to be taught as a trainer. This made Brutus a choice canine student to finish out Mr. Franklin's instructor's course.

Brutus was a spirited animal who loved to put a wincing bite on any man he sparred with. Jeff was equally as spirited, and he enjoyed any kind of physical competition, especially if it involved dogs. So, the training challenge for me was to orchestrate numerous sparring matches between Jeff and Brutus. During these structured matches, Jeff worked as the agitator/decoy and I served as the controller/handler. Over weeks of training, Brutus learned to optimize his bite-timing and placement, while Jeff steadily improved in canine-wrestling finesse. Unlike the O'Leary case where the goal was to extinguish aggressive behavior, the mission for Brutus was to build confidence in combat. My game-plan was to develop both Jeff and Brutus into adept sparring partners, who looked forward to a match on the Schutzhund field. Combining physicality with a bruising grip, Brutus was quite capable of compelling Jeff to forge the skills of a competent decoy. As a novice agitator, Jeff needed to develop the balance and bite placement techniques necessary to control a powerful shepherd like Brutus. Without these talents, Jeff's dream of training police dogs would be out of reach.

Because of his working dog background, Brutus was naturally inclined to subdue a hostile enemy, or a mock aggressor, with his teeth. Brutus loved skirmishes because he was genetically predisposed for this kind of work, no different from a Border collie obsessing over herding sheep, or a Labrador drooling over retrieving ducks. During Brutus' bite-work development, however, eagerness to engage was always balanced with energy-control and deference to the handler. Appropriate target focus, a bomb-proof "Hold" before an attack, and an immediate bite-release as directed by the handler are critical for effective protection training. Brutus wasn't the only one learning how to channel energy in preparation for the Schutzhund field. Jeff was also practicing how to mete out force like a good wrestling coach. As a professional decoy, he needed to become proficient at sending canine opponents away from combative encounters with fighting experience and a feeling of success.

More than anyone else, a skilled decoy develops a strong canine fighter.

Occasionally, Brutus was muzzled before a confrontation in order to capitalize on his physicality. By having his teeth removed from play, the athletic shepherd was compelled to adopt a head-butting maneuver that was powerful enough to actually stun Jeff when the opportunity arose. Without a biting option, Brutus also learned how to tackle Franklin, the "Bad Guy," not unlike how an NFL linebacker would take out a running back. The muzzle work proved to be the highlight of Jeff's Instruction

Course. Wrestling in the dirt for an advantage, while being pommeled by a wild, seventy-five-pound, German shepherd was usually more exhilaration than Jeff could handle without exploding into laughter. Even though the muzzle-fighting sessions were serious encounters, Jeff made it very difficult not to laugh along with him. As for Brutus, he didn't care whether the decoy laughed or cried; he was all in. The muzzle work seemed to be the favorite part of his training as well. It's hard to describe the exhilaration that accompanies decoying for biting dogs. In Brutus' case, he brought intensity to the sparring match. The average bite force from a middle-size German shepherd is measured at about 1060 newtons or 238 lbs. Even with the protection of a padded bite-suit, a goodgrip from Brutus would send actual chills up the spine, not to mention the mild hematomas left behind. Like most new decoys or agitators, Jeff remembers vividly the startling pressure and snake-like speed of the first intentional bites from a working shepherd. He described his first bite experience to new trainees as "fighting to maintain ground purchase and nerve composure, while being thrashed about in the jaws of a shark."

When I sent Brutus to engage Jeff on his initial blind search, he strained against the ten meters longline I was holding, like a horse wrenching against the plow rigging. He was hungry for an altercation with the "Bad Guy," and he intended to drag me right into the blind with him. Brutus' chest was nearly skimming the ground as his powerful hips and shoulders rippled under his glossy coat. He was digging in so fiercely that all four of his feet were churning up sod. Jeff, who was hidden behind a portable blind (which resembles a small half-tepee) that was placed in the open training yard, waited tensely in his hiding spot as the barking and panting closed in. Jeff could hear my heavy footsteps trying to slow Brutus as we thundered toward the blind. Mentally bracing himself for the fury headed his way, Jeff didn't need a visual to imagine his sparring partner's hungry expression and gaping mouthful of teeth.

Brutus' chest was heaving, and his chin dripped with saliva when he slid into the blind only millimeters from his quarry. Although his head was at belt level, Brutus' eyes were locked onto Jeff's. Like most human beings, before decoy instruction, Jeff had never experienced the cold, lifeless stare of a predator. He remembers vividly, "That dog looked right through my eyes and into my mind. It was the strangest experience, I couldn't break eye-contact with him. Brutus could feel my next move." Except for his snarling upper lip, Brutus' black face was motionless. His dark eyes were unflinching, while an ominous, guttural growl rumbled, "I gotcha now!" Without an inch, or a second of wiggle room, Jeff had no time to look at me for instruction or adjust his feet for impact before Brutus launched into the protection-suit. The seventy-five-pound German shepherd slammed into Jeff's right shoulder with a deep, bruising bite that dislodged the "weapon" (a padded baton). He exploded with such force that both man and dog crashed through the blind and landed hard on the ground. Brutus' full-mouth grip never slipped from Jeff's armpit as the two tumbled over top of one another. Immediately, I leaned back on the long line that was attached to Brutus' collar in an attempt to dampen the clash and help stabilize the situation. While Jeff strained to recover a foothold by righting himself, his ferocious adversary fought with his entire body in an attempt to keep his sparring partner off balance.

Throughout the two-minute skirmish, Brutus never eased up on the painful hold he had on Mr. Franklin. However, much like an experienced decoy, Jeff maintained his composure as he recovered his padded baton and vigorously acted out the role of "Bad Guy." Jeff not only protected Brutus from accidental injury, he also remembered to guard his own exposed body parts against a debilitating bite as he carried the battle back to the safety of the reset blind. After assisting Brutus on the bite release, I escorted him and Jeff off of the training field. Both man and dog were "sucking wind," and both were wearing the satisfied countenance of a battle well fought. This dynamic match between a Marine and a working shepherd was quite a spectacle for those standing around the Training Center. The fellow kennel workers even offered the titans a small round of applause as we setup for the next match. Both, Jeff and Brutus smiled at the onlookers in appreciation.

During the process of teaching Brutus how to subdue assailants, Jeff was also acquiring the techniques of a good sparring partner. In the same manner as his high school wrestling coach, Jeff built Brutus' confidence during battle by initially affording him the upper hand. But just like his coaches back in the high school gym, Jeff gradually and intentionally transformed into a more formidable opponent as training progressed. With this style of instruction, Brutus, like Jeff in his wrestling days, had to work harder with each battle in order to gain the victory he had become accustomed to earning. Given that other decoys weren't going to hand Brutus an advantage, no differently than a genuine perpetrator in the police-dog world may not easily submit, Brutus needed to be ready for tough encounters. Over weeks of training, Brutus' bite force increased as did his comfort level in the use of his legs to tie up the opponent. Learning to direct full pressure into his initial grip without adjusting his mouth placement guaranteed him victory with each engagement. Whether it be for sport or police work, graduation day for a combat dog will be on the trial field with a strange decoy, or on the street with a potentially dangerous felon. The proof of proper instruction for any canine trained to bite lies in the natural environment with all of its adverse conditions. That is precisely the environment that Jeff and I had in mind as we schooled Brutus.

The author (left) and Franklin leading a K-9 seminar.

Brutus' training acted as a real "eye opener" for Jeff. He realized there was little difference in preparing a canine warrior or the human counterpart for combat. It became clear that whether coaching a human being or a domesticated animal through the development of a skill, performance correlated directly to the quality of practice. Jeff learned in the Marine Corps that precision, along with effectiveness came from supervised repetition. "Shortcuts seldom produced the desired results": Jeff adopted this aphorism that he lived by in "The Desert," and he religiously applied it to his dog training regimen. As both a student of mine and an instructor for dog/handler teams during his trainer's course, Jeff recorded five guidelines in his trainer's log that would accompany him for the rest of his career: 1. Work side-by-side with a student in order to convey a clear image of the task at hand. 2. Build confidence in the student by moving quickly past the failures and focusing on the successes. 3. Support a student throughout the process, without hesitating to correct when necessary. 4. Allow a student's performance to dictate the length of an instruction program whenever possible. 5. Hurried training is almost always faulty training. With study, effort, and diligence Jeff grew into an exceptional dog-man. He was so talented; in fact, I hired him to work with me as soon as his professional trainer's course was completed.

Eight

Cobra

"Impossible to Replace"
Fin Hradni Sklep
July 27, 1991 – December 22, 2004

By the spring of 1993, Jeff and I had been training dogs together for eighteen months. Though I paid Jeff to work dogs for me, we had become good friends and actually interacted with one another much like brothers. My role was similar to that of an older sibling who had already established an active training kennel. Jeff represented the quintessential younger brother who was jumping on board with enthusiasm, ideas, and a hunger for knowledge. Since a great deal of our dog and handler instruction involved teamwork, Jeff and I grew to understand each other very well. Talking and listening between us came easily.

That same spring, my young protégé imported his first working dog. Jeff didn't actually inform me of this until a few days after he had sent the twenty-two-hundred-dollar money order to the Czech Republic. In fact, he wasn't going to tell me at all. His original intention was to walk into the kennel one morning showing off his new sidekick. However, after four days with no word from his European contact, Jeff could barely hold in his concern. Over the months of working together, Mr. Franklin had come to know me as considerably more conservative and frugal than he was. I had been open with him about some of the financial struggles I had experienced while supporting a family on a modest dog trainer's salary. Jeff had correctly surmised that I could no more send my hard-earned money to a non- English-speaking man in Europe (for a dog I had never seen) than I could flush it down the toilet. Jeff's angst over whether or not to tell me about his first import deal gone-wrong, stemmed from our close friendship. He wanted to garner some comfort from his older dog-training brother, but at the same time, he had no desire to feel the shameful effects of my disapproving head shake. On day five with no word from Europe, my friend spilled the beans. I couldn't keep myself from the disappointed head shaking. I tried to keep my mouth shut so as not to rub salt in the gaping psychological wound, but the obvious and unhelpful observation slipped out anyway: "That was one expensive lesson."

A couple of days later, Jeff was able to make contact with someone in Europe who was privy to the situation. In very broken English, the man convinced Jeff that they were putting his dog on a plane the next day.

Sure enough, thirty-six hours after the overseas conversation, we received a call at the training kennel from Louisville's Standiford Field Airport informing us that Mr. Franklin's shipment had arrived. With guarded excitement, Jeff hung-up his training gear and headed to the airport. On his way out the door, I prepared both of us for a very possible outcome: "Little Brother, don't be shocked when you peek into the shipping crate and see a pigmy goat instead of a German shepherd. You know that European dog broker probably spent your money on beer a week ago." Within an hour Jeff rolled back into the kennel parking lot. I watched as he stepped out of his truck wearing the biggest smile I had ever seen on his face. Following Jeff on a leash was a strong, above average sized, black-sable German shepherd. This dog glided across the parking lot with perfect working form and function. He was a handsome, magnificent animal. As Jeff walked through the front door, he said: "Meet Cobra, I named him after the Super Cobra Gunships that saved our butts so many times in the desert. What do you think?" To this day, Mr. Franklin recalls, my response verbatim: "You better enjoy this one, he'll be impossible to replace."

Jeff's introduction into the world of high-end, working canines began in earnest with Cobra. This canine version of a Marine possessed energy without hysteria, and confidence without defiance. He was intelligent and courageous, but never a bully. He was happy, but not silly. Cobra was as close to the ideal working shepherd as money could buy, and lucky Jeff Franklin bought him sight-unseen from a man in Europe he could barely understand. With that risky investment, Jeff was officially launching into the dog acquisition business, and he was doing it in style. Cobra represented the perpetual good fortune that seemed to follow Jeff throughout his professional career. Being bold, daring, and lucky has always paid Mr. Franklin with high dividends.

With a little assistance from me, Jeff and Cobra dove headlong into the sport of Schutzhund. In six months he accomplished a year's worth of training with his new companion. Cobra earned all three of the progressively more-demanding titles of Schutzhund 1, 2 and 3, back-to-back. By proving Cobra's worth on the Schutzhund field, Jeff was ensuring an increase in his dog's breeding value while expanding his expertise as a dog trainer all at the same time. As far as Jeff was concerned, Cobra's stellar performance in competition was the perfect segue into police work, his longtime dream. Finally, Jeff Franklin had the knowledge, skill, and the German shepherd to pursue a path he had thought about since Mr. Richardson's 8th grade math class. The spring of '93 marked a galvanizing point for the next two steps in Jeff's dog-training career. His immediate sights were set on joining a police department as a K9 officer. As soon as he secured that position, he intended to start his own working-dog breeding program. Just two years out of the Marines, Jeff had already laid the foundation for his role in the canine industry as a professional trainer, K9 officer, and importer/breeder of working German shepherds. Whether or not that precise plan was configured in Jeff's young mind is open for debate. Nevertheless, he was rolling somewhere at high speed.

Generally speaking, a K-9 officer position is difficult to secure with any police department. With that in mind, Jeff and I thought there would be many months available to shape him and Cobra into a functioning K-9 unit. But, as I eventually came to expect with lucky Jeff Franklin, he had no trouble locating a department that was eager to hire him and Cobra. We had planned on Jeff and his European partner to be proficient in the fundamentals that most departments would count on, even before he interviewed for a position. The skills list can be exhaustive for a working K-9 unit. The bare minimum would include basic obedience with bite-work that is tested under gunfire; locating, apprehending, and cuffing unruly perpetrators; discarded article location; and illicit drug searches. In February of 1994, only weeks after announcing his decision to go into law enforcement, Jeff signed on with his first department. When Officer Franklin shipped out to the Police Academy in Richmond Kentucky, he and Cobra were still a short distance from being a test-ready K-9 team. Although Jeff lived close enough to the Academy to come home on the weekends, a substantial portion of Cobra's training would have to wait until after graduation. Much to Jeff's surprise, the small-town department that hired him was short enough on manpower that they wasted no time putting their new K-9 unit on the street. Immediately following his graduation from the academy, Jeff, along with his partner Cobra, were assigned to a car and patrolling the country roads at night. Jeff's superiors on the department left it up to him to figure out how to expedite Cobra's preparation for duty.

Thankfully, owing to the previous months of Schutzhund training, Cobra's tactical obedience and bite development were efficient and only needed more practice under gunfire and emergency distractions in order to function in a natural rural environment. Shortly after acquiring Cobra's Schutzhund 3 title, Jeff jumped into his first attempt at scent detection training. He was able to imprint Cobra on a couple of pseudo drug odors and partially shape an indication-posture before leaving for the academy. Cobra's underdeveloped skills in combat tracking and area/building searches would be the top priorities when his instruction resumed. In those areas of police work, a K-9 team would often be deployed to hunt down criminals well in advance of other backup officers. For Jeff and Cobra, this meant that they would not only be the first to confront a possibly armed perpetrator, but they would be theonly officers on the scene at the moment of contact. For anyone in law enforcement, the real and present danger of ambush always seems to be looming around the corner. For a K-9 unit who typically leads the charge into areas of concealment after criminals, the threat of ambush is nearly constant. Given that neither Jeff nor Cobra had ever encountered a dangerous adversary on the controlled and predictable Schutzhund field,they had yet to accumulate any practical experience in such a hazardous realm. It was also likely that a scenario of that nature could arise within the first weeks of service.

For Officer Franklin and Cobra, transitioning from sporting work to police duty specifically meant cultivating the mindset, as well as the tactics, necessary for safe and effective action in a life-threatening confrontation. In order to acquire this expertise, Jeff threw away the Schutzhund rule book with prescribed decoy procedures and padded weapon regulations. He permanently filed away the guidelines for structured canine competition and sterile field requirements. In their place, he used law enforcement procedures, intimidating decoys with legitimate weapons, military scout-dog protocols from the U.S. Air force, and unpredictable environmental conditions for training grounds. Once Jeff and Cobra shifted into combat training, they never looked back.

Within the first weeks of duty, Officer Franklin befriended a couple of other patrolmen on nightshift and immediately recruited them into Cobra's training program. They all worked as a group to lay tracks, setup ambushes, don the "Bad Guy" role, and support as backup officers. Because of the other officers' involvement, the word about Cobra's abilities quickly spread throughout the P.D. Jeff's prized European import was fast becoming the official mascot of the entire department. Jeff appreciated all of the attention and acceptance, but it was difficult for him not to feel stress under the weight of lofty expectations. The Chief was bragging to other departments about their new secret weapon, even before Jeff and Cobra had a chance to prove themselves on the street. However, the wait for "El momento de verdad" wasn't long.

The official K-9 decals had not yet been placed on Jeff's cruiser when he and Cobra responded to their first serious call. Around midnight on a warm Friday night, Jeff heard the dispatch call out a request for a K-9 unit on the radio. The call was an urgent 10-39A signal (a stabbing), so Jeff did an emergency three-point-turn-around in the middle of a dark country road and screamed toward the address in a Code 3 (running with blue lights and siren). When Jeff arrived, one of his officer friends (Nate) was already on the scene. Nate had parked at an angle on the driveway in order to shine his headlights on the front of the house. There was also an ambulance already on location attending to the victim. Jeff parked on the street close to the other cruiser, but positioned his vehicle so that he could drench the back side of the house in light. Nate was one of the men who helped with Cobra's training, so he and Jeff knew each other pretty well. The two friends met at the roadside where Nate briefed Jeff on the domestic violence situation. The suspect was a large man, armed with a hunting knife. He assaulted his girlfriend and ran out the front door headed for an extensive wooded area that lay behind the residence. As Jeff headed for the trunk of his car to get Cobra's tracking line and harness, Nate hollered: "Franklin, this isn't the first time we've been called to this address. This dude has a history of violence and he's always hostile toward authority. He's even attacked police officers in the past. So caution and backup officers are a must in this case." Jeff heard Nate, and he believed everything that his friend had to say about proper protocol. But Jeff also knew that waiting for reinforcements would allow the perpetrator's track to grow older and colder, making it more difficult to follow with each passing minute.

Jeff was a young, green K-9 Officer in that summer of 1994. And on this particular call he felt nauseous because he was so excited and nervous at the same time. This was the moment he had dreamt about since Mr. Richardson's 8th grade math class. This was the very night that he and Cobra had worked so hard to prepare for. Tracking down and bringing into custody this violent suspect carried with it the full weight of expectation that the Chief had placed on his new K-9 Unit. Jeff wanted to wait, he wanted to defer to his more experienced friend, but listening to Cobra's whining and pacing in the back of the vehicle was more than he could stand. Years of police dog dreams, and months of K-9 training pushed Jeff to the trunk of his car where he pulled out Cobra's gear. As Officer Franklin was reaching through the back door of the cruiser to leash-up his eager K-9, he told Nate that he would take his time getting ready in order to give reinforcements a chance to arrive. However, Jeff also told his friend that he wasn't letting that track age too long. He wasn't going to set Cobra up for a loss, and he wasn't letting a slimy suspect slip away in the dark woods because of a dangerous reputation.

It took all of Jeff's self-control to wait for another officer to show up before he launched his dog on a track. The moment the strobing, blue lights of reinforcements could be seen rounding the bend a mile and a half down the road, Officer Franklin tightened the straps on Cobra's tracking harness. Jeff attempted to quietly walk Cobra for a bathroom break, but the four-legged police officer was too stimulated from the emergency conditions to relieve himself. In the weeks leading up to that night, Jeff and his training partners had executed a number of scenarios that began from a code-3 run. As a consequence, the lights, sirens, and gathering of vehicles all signaled to Cobra that fun was waiting in the dark, and he wanted to get to it.

By the time the third officer had parked his car next to the ambulance, Jeff had finished with Cobra's pre-tracking elimination ritual, so the K-9 Unit was geared up and ready to roll. While Nate was briefing the third officer, who was suiting up for an encounter, Jeff strategically walked Cobra along the back-property fence that was well lit by his car's headlights. His immediate plan was to locate a solid track starting point based on the suspect's escape route and the given terrain.

Jeff was working Cobra at close quarters on a six-foot leash, and he was watching for any indication that his sniffing companion might express over fresh human odor encountered on the ground. Jeff gave Cobra the tracking command, "Such" (pronounced "zook") as they made their way down the long fence that paralleled the road and bordered fifteen acres of wooded ground. If Cobra were to indicate on any odor that might possibly be the suspect, Jeff intended to call for back-up who were still at their vehicles waiting for more support. As the search approached the outer edge of available light, Cobra became agitated and reluctant to press forward. Jeff encouraged his partner to search on, but rather than moving into the darkness Cobra reared back on his hindquarters with his nose pointing high over the fence.

Feeling confident that his courageous dog wasn't unnerved by the dark, Jeff was a little perplexed why Cobra was reluctant to continue the ground search for odor. So, he knelt down with his arm around Cobra's neck and talked to him like he was a human being; "There's no time for delays my friend. You and I are going to catch this scumbag in spite of the dark, and his head start. I agree with Mr. Duffy; police dogs don't get better than you. Let's go get that piece of trash!" With that, Jeff removed Cobra's leash to afford him more working freedom, hoping the autonomy would excite him enough to resume his ground search. When Jeff stood up, he gave his aroused K-9 another command to "Such." Still refusing to move forward, Cobra reared back a second time with his nose in the air and his left front foot on the fence. With no more than a quick glance back at Jeff, Cobra leapt over the tall fence and into the darkness with one

Olympic bound. This was a maneuver that young Officer Franklin did not anticipate. In a rush to look for a track, Jeff left his flash light back at his vehicle, so he was forced to leave Cobra on his own and go back for a light.

The moment Cobra cleared the fence, Jeff called out for Nate. Running toward each other, the two men met halfway between the fence and their cars. Jeff grabbed Nate's flashlight and told him that Cobra hit on the perp's scent and went over the fence after him. As Jeff raced back toward Cobra, he heard Nate shout, "Franklin, you can't go after this guy alone! You have to wait for us!" Jeff ignored his friend's advice and hollered back, "I'm not alone, I have Cobra! My flashlight is on the console!" Jeff scrambled over the fence, and when he dropped on the other side he pulled his Sig-Sauer pistol from the holster. The brush was thick where Jeff entered the woods, and traversing through that terrain was noisy and slow. Cobra, on the other hand, was able to follow his nose and glide under or around the heavy vegetation. Realizing that his dog must have a substantial lead on him, Jeff periodically stood still, turned off his light so as not to be a lighted target for an ambush, and called for Cobra. Jeff listened for crashing or barking, then pushed on trying to close the distance between the two of them. Few situations are more unsettling for a police officer than searching for an armed criminal in the dark, but Jeff has no recollection of worries over self-preservation on that night. Not unlike a parent charging into danger to rescue their child, Jeff's thoughts were not on himself; they were on protecting his canine partner.

Jeff was just about to stop and call out when he heard Cobra's explosive barking echo through the trees. He recognized his partner's barking instantly and could hear the seriousness in his voice. There was no doubt Cobra was holding a human being at bay. Instantly breaking into a run, Jeff charged through the brush straight toward his companion's call. The briars raking across his face nearly blinded Jeff as he frantically made his way to Cobra. In the moment, Jeff felt no pain. The only sensation he had was the distance closing between him and the barking. Jeff remembers praying that the person held at bay remained still until he got there. Especially if it were the suspect with the hunting knife.

No more than a dozen steps from the action, Jeff's flashlight beam broke through the trees and shone on his beautiful sable shepherd. Cobra was on high alert, bouncing on his front feet and barking with full fury. Just above him, in the fork of a mature Sycamore tree, was a large man slashing at Cobra with a Bowie style knife. The man's long blonde hair, ragged T-shirt, and hunting knife all matched the perpetrator's description. The rush and excitement in that moment felt like a training exercise on steroids to Jeff. With no thought or hesitation, the rote of practice kicked in. Jeff called his K-9 off guarding with the cease-aggression command, "Aus!" Like a machine, Cobra sat perfectly still, staring holes through the prey he had treed. Jeff then called his partner back to his side, "Fuss" (pronounced "Foos")! Again, with the precision of a Schutzhund dog, Cobra raced to Jeff's left side.

For a moment, Jeff studied the situation. He was nearly mesmerized by the surreal, midnight scene of a savage-like man, hunched in the crook of a massive tree. With his chest heaving from exertion, the man's wild gaze appeared to be more animal than human. His exposed skin glistened with sweat in the light beam as he clung to the Sycamore and his Bowie. There was no doubt in Jeff's mind that this was the dangerous suspect he'd been looking for. With his Sig-Sauer leveled on the sweating man, Jeff announced that he was a police officer and ordered him to drop the weapon. The suspect jumped from the tree, clinging to his knife without responding. Jeff ordered him to drop the weapon once more. That time the big man shouted back, "Screw you and your shitty mutt!" Before Jeff could respond, the hostile suspect bolted into the dark woods. With no thought, Jeff patted Cobra on the shoulder and commanded him to stop the fleeing criminal, "Packen!" Tearing into the brush like an eighty-pound, sable missile, struck the man with bone crushing force just outside of Jeff's light beam. Virtually on Cobra's tail, Jeff heard a blood curdling scream as he nearly ran on top of the two combatants. Cobra had grabbed the suspect by the back of his upper, right arm and had driven the big man face down into the mud. While Cobra took control of the battle, Jeff frantically searched for the Bowie knife with his light, but the suspect's hands were empty. The knife had been jarred free by Cobra's powerful, full-mouth grip around the knife-wielding arm.

Even with the advantage of his large stature, the man was no match against the ferocity of Jeff's police dog. Repeatedly, Cobra violently shook the criminal to the ground, driving his horror-stricken face to the dirt. Once satisfied the weapon was clear of the suspect, Jeff ordered the man to lie still, so that he could call off his dog. The man continued to struggle in vain, as Jeff repeated his order. Finally, the suspect settled into sobbing, and Jeff commanded Cobra, "Aus!" With only a little reluctance, Cobra released his grip of the big man's mangled arm. As Cobra stepped off the suspect's back, Jeff called his police dog back to his side, "Fuss!" Once more, Jeff ordered the hostile criminal to lie still so that he could be cuffed and searched. With the newly acquired confidence of a proven K-9 unit, Jeff added to his order, "If you don't fully cooperate, I'll send my 'shitty mutt' in to change your mind." The criminal only moaned while he waited to be cuffed.

After placing the suspect under arrest, Jeff sat him against the base of a small tree while he and Cobra looked for the discarded hunting knife. New to article searching, Jeff didn't expect much from Cobra, but he had to try because locating the weapon was critical and Jeff had only a slim chance of finding it in the dark without Cobra's nose. Pointing his finger to the ground, Jeff told Cobra to "Such Verloren," just like they had practiced. Following his dog's nose with the light, on the second pass through the area, Jeff watched as Cobra's nose penetrated some dense poison ivy, not three feet from the seated prisoner. Encouraging his companion again, "Such Verloren," Jeff swept through the ivy with his foot as Cobra's tail began to wag. Cobra was not lying down as he should have to indicate an article, but he stood frozen, wagging his tail. Using his light for a closer look, Jeff spied the shimmer of stainless steel. Reaching in with a gloved hand, Jeff pulled out a full-size Bowie knife. "Son of a bitch," came from the mouth of the arrested culprit as Jeff smiled and pet his police dog. Escorting the prisoner out of the brush was no easy task. Nonetheless, it was a victory walk for Jeff and Cobra, for they were now a genuine K-9 Unit. Approaching the fence, Jeff saw the lights of his fellow officers closing in to assist. When Nate saw Jeff holding the left arm of the bloody culprit and Cobra guarding his right, he summed up the entire experience, "Now that's what I'm talkin' about!"

Nine

One Hundred Bomb-Dogs

In the summer of 2002, two men, two dogs and a Ranger pickup truck rolled south down Interstate 75. Franklin Senior had volunteered his truck and services to transport his son, along with two of Cobra's prodigy, to one of the world's busiest working dog sites, Neue Welt Kennels in Eastern Tennessee. Jeff had an appointment to demonstrate his two young shepherds executing their rudimentary scent detection skills to the kennel's head trainer. For months, Neue Welt had been sending communiques to regional police departments announcing that they were in the market to purchase "green" working dogs possessing bomb location potential. After picking up a fax from Neue Welt one night, Jeff was struck by the offer as an ideal opportunity to promote his Cobra line of shepherds that he had been breeding for several years. Jeff selected two of his best kennel dogs for this first trip to Tennessee, and he gave them six weeks of self-taught scent detection training in order to prepare them for a presentation. Having no access to bomb components, Jeff used odor training aids to develop basic search and indication abilities with the two shepherds. He felt certain that once Cobra's offspring demonstrated the genetic ability to be professional detection dogs, he could easily sell every pup from his breeding program to Neue Welt. Although a novice at scent detection instruction, Jeff was proud of the fact that he was one of only a few police-dog trainers in his geographic area that could actually accomplish the task. He looked forward to showing his wares at such a prestigious kennel.

When Jeff and his dad made their trek south, the September 11th, 2001 terrorist attacks on the World Trade Center were still weighing heavily on the hearts and minds of most of the "Free World." Airports and government facilities across the globe were operating under heightened security restrictions like never before. The frightening possibility of an onslaught of terrorist strikes in the post 9/11 era fueled a demand for bomb detection dogs that skyrocketed throughout developed countries. In 2002 there were only a few canine training facilities in all of Europe and the United States that were capable of high volume scent detection work. Of those special kennels, there was none more prominent in the international police and military dog scene than Neue Welt.

A short distance from their destination, the Franklins pulled into a final rest area to give their canine passengers one last bathroom break. As Jeff unloaded the two shepherds he appeared to be somewhat unsure of himself. Franklin Senior noticed a strained expression on his son's face. He watched as Jeff uncharacteristically fumbled with equipment and repeatedly tripped over the dogs. Jeff's mind, which was normally acutely focused, was absent from his tasks. In the weeks leading up to this trip, there had been no hiding the fact that Jeff considered the Neue Welt demonstration a career-changer and therefore stressfully signifi-cant. Franklin Senior could see the negative effects of expectation- pres-sure and an all-night shift work taking their toll on his son. Like all good fathers, he desperately wanted to ease his son's stress-load, but he had nothing in business skills or dog training advice to offer. Leaving the rest stop, Franklin senior didn't get a mile down the road before he pulled the Ranger over and parked along the shoulder.

When Jeff asked what was wrong, his dad said, "Nothing. In fact, I pulled over to tell you what's right. No man at this Neue Welt Kennel could have more natural dog ability than you. They may have more experience, but they aren't more gifted. Just show 'em what you and your shepherds can do. I feel sure that they'll want all of them that you can breed and train."

Without waiting for a response, Franklin Senior goosed the little pickup back onto the highway. Those fatherly words instantly worked their magic on Jeff. His nerves calmed and a confident half-smile returned as he leaned toward his dad and said, "Thanks Pop. That's just what I needed."

Pulling into the busy canine hub, the Franklins were startled to see the facility grounds in such disarray. A number of large buildings in need of repair were scattered over multiple acres. Spread out through the open areas between the buildings were several groups of handlers with dogs. All of the canine teams were very involved in following their instructor's directions. Franklin Senior slowly drove the little pickup through the commotion, looking for a parking place. Bringing the Ranger to a halt next to an SUV and the longest dog trailer the Franklins had ever seen, the two men stepped out of their vehicle amidst the training activity. Belgian Malinois, Labradors, German and Dutch shepherds all outfitted in working attire were being managed by handlers wearing various types of uniforms. Some men were clad in military gear while others wore class B police uniforms. All of the handlers-in-training had neatly cut hair to go along with their sharp uniforms and professions. Jeff found it curious that the only people on the property that didn't come across as "squared away" were the instructors. They actually appeared to be the antithesis of the men they were teaching. All of the instructors, seemingly from the same "biker" fraternity, sported tattoos, a head full of shaggy hair and they wore a hodgepodge of sloppy garments that conveyed an unprofessionalism that bordered on the stereotypical redneck. This wasn't at all the instructor-image Jeff had anticipated at a world-renowned kennel. He was so accustomed to uniforms and short haircuts from his twelve years of military and police service that Jeff expected "tight and neat," especially with ranking superiors.

As they wandered across the compound, the Franklins picked up on one of the instructors guiding his group in broken Spanish, while another was giving directions in a poorly articulated Middle Eastern dialect. Despite the initial impression of the facility and instructors Jeff was amazed by the high energy and busyness of the place. Although there was no visible signage identifying their location, the sheer number and variety of working dogs, along with the international mix of law enforcement personnel scattered about the complex, confirmed that the Franklins had arrived at Neue Welt. The only other places Jeff had seen such a display of handlers and dogs was at the largest kennel club competitions.

Looking for someone who might be in charge of the operation, Jeff and his dad walked into the closest building which appeared to be a retrofitted barn. The front door opened into a large open area. In the center of this substantial room was a row of five evenly spaced wooden boxes, each constructed as a twelve-inch cube. Standing in proximity to the boxes was a frumpy, middle aged man who was dressed in worn-out fatigues. He had tattoos on both of his upper arms and had obviously not frequented a barber in some time. When the Franklins paused to assess the situation, Jeff's dad facetiously whispered, "I'd say by that man's sharp appearance, he must be one of the instructors." The man wore a large leather pouch at the small of his back, and he was busy directing a very energetic Dutch shepherd toward the row of wooden cubes. The Franklins later found out that one of the five boxes contained bomb components which created an odor bouquet that dogs were being trained to detect. The other four boxes contained various examples of real-world distractors (human and animal food, critter representations, toys, etc.) that working canines have to ignore in order to locate the designated target odor. There were a couple of helpers assisting the man as one dog after another was being directed in turn through a series of detection exercises.

The musty training area was poorly lit and somewhat depressing, especially since no one was talking except the man in fatigues. The Franklins heard the man mesmerize each canine with "Such Sprengkorper! Gut Hund!" Handling one dog at a time, the man used a leash and training collar to direct the canine's attention toward the circular opening in the top of each cube as he worked from one end of the row to the other. With the finesse of a professional dancer, the dog trainer in fatigues had created his own modified "hop-step" technique to deliver every dog-in-hand smoothly to the box of interest. At the designated box containing the target odor, the trainer used his hands to deftly place each dog in a sitting position right up against the wooden container itself. Tickling the top of that particular box with his right-hand fingers, the man enticed each canine student to lower his nose into the round opening and investigate the distinctive bomb odor. At the moment when the dog's eyes and mind were focused on the odor rising into his nostrils from the hole in the wooden cube, the stealthy trainer delivered a ball from his pouch with such speed and accuracy it went undetected by the concentrating dog until it actually made contact with the box. Seizing the ball as it bounced off the top of the container, every dog in turn was convinced that the round, rubber prize exploded from the box itself. The trainer was intentionally building a precise association between the targeted odor and the canine's much desired treasure (the ball). Over a short period of time, the designated bomb odor and the bouncing ball would become a linked mental image for each successfully trained dog. Therefore, when one of these "bomb sniffing" canines are directed to seek-out an explosive device, they are in essence enthusiastically searching for one of their bouncing treasures which happens to smell like a bomb.

Jeff had never witnessed such precision and finesse in scent detection instruction. As the Franklins watched the seasoned instructor guide a long string of dogs through the "box dance," a spark ignited inside of Jeff as he declared to his dad, "This is where I need to be. I want to work bomb dogs at this intensity. There are buyers here from different parts of the world because this guy knows how to teach scent detection."

That very afternoon inside the old Tennessee barn, the course of Jeff's professional career changed forever. He made numerous trips to Neue Welt in the following twelve months, selling all of his available Cobra offspring as well as dogs he had purchased from professionals and families that were scattered throughout the Midwest. With each successive trip to the busy kennel, Jeff's canine students demonstrated better and better skill development, due in part to the training knowledge he was gleaning from each visit with the detection specialists. Jeff easily developed friendships with the Neue Welt trainers, and they were more than willing to share instruction secrets with a young man who was quickly becoming an insider. Although Jeff didn't look much like a "biker" with his "high and tight" haircut and tucked-in uniform, he naturally fit in when it came to dog handling.

It wasn't until his third business trip to Neue Welt that Jeff was informed that the unkempt, tattooed man in fatigues was actually the owner and operator of Neue Welt. His name was Jim Buckley, and he initially learned how to handle dogs in the U.S. Military. Like Jeff, as a young man, Jim was consumed with the idea of training dogs for a living, and he earned that opportunity during a full career of police K-9 work in the armed forces. As an active handler and instructor in the military, Jim was schooled in the canine instruction fundamentals of criminal apprehension, narcotics detection and explosives location. Through numerous joint operations with domestic and foreign law enforcement agencies during his military service, Jim became aware of professional dog training opportunities that could be cultivated in the civilian world. So, without delay, following an honorable discharge from the military, Jim established Neue Welt kennels and directed its operation toward the demands of law enforcement. Being as savvy in business as he was in canine handling, young Mr. Buckley reached out to K-9 departments he had been exposed to while in the military to initiate his first sales. Jim's mission statement was simple. He intended to sell, at a bargain price, fully trained multi-purpose police dogs that could locate and apprehend criminals as well as effectively seek-out drugs or explosives. Jim's ambitious business plan was to make his trained dogs available to any law enforcement department in need, both in the United States and abroad. By September of 2001 (the time of the terrorist attack on the World Trade Center in New York), Jim Buckley had already reached a "high bar" of success in his industry. In a single decade, Neue Welt had become well established in the domestic and foreign police- dog markets, and Jim's kennel had become known as the premier "go to" place for "street ready" canines.

In the wake of the 9/11 attacks when much of the world was feeling vulnerable and adopting a "red alert" security status against terrorism, Jim Buckley positioned himself on the forefront of a new bomb-dog detection movement. He expanded his network of working dog suppliers, and retrofitted Neue Welt's kennel buildings to accommodate as many as one hundred and fifty dogs. That was twice the number of canines they were accustomed to housing. Instruction protocols also changed at Neue Welt. In order to meet the rising international demand for explosives/bomb dogs, the development of single purpose detection dogs took top priority over the dual-purpose canines that were once thekennel's mainstay. Sparked by U.S. President George W. Bush's declaration of a "war on terror," police departments, military units, and security companies geared up to safeguard airports, government buildings, and utility installations. Clearing critical areas of explosives and potential bombers became the focus of law enforcement around the globe. The war on terrorism had legitimately begun by 2002, and Jim Buckley wanted his kennel right in the thick of it by being a high-volume supplier of detection dogs.

Jeff Franklin happened to forge a relationship with Jim Buckley at a fortuitous time. By 2003 Jim had secured several lucrative government contracts for explosives detection dogs with the United States and a couple of foreign countries. Jim Buckley and his trainers believed that Officer Franklin was not just an ordinary K-9 Officer, but also a talented dog trainer with excellent handler-instruction skills. Roughly twelve months after the Franklins delivered their first dogs to Neue Welt, Jim offered Jeff a job as one of the lead dog trainers. Although much was on the line, uprooting his family, walking away from a law enforcement career, and saying goodbye to me and other friends, Jeff didn't hesitate to accept Mr. Buckley's offer. Jeff had one condition to be met before the two men shook hands on the deal. Jim Buckley had to agree to personally teach Jeff everything he knew about selecting and developing scent detection canines, specifically for locating bombs and explosives. There was no indecision on Jim's part to shake hands, and passing on to Jeff all that he had learned from the military and ten years of professional scent detection instruction. Unbeknownst to Officer Franklin at the time, Jim Buckley had lofty expectations for Jeff. Neue Welt needed a capable man to specifically head up the bomb detection facet of the business that was growing at an alarming rate. Jim and his two other lead instructors already had their hands full trying to manage their existing business.

With both Jim and Jeff ecstatic over the new proposition, the wheels turned quickly to get Mr. Franklin on board and immersed in Neue Welt's expanding global presence. In the autumn of 2003, Jeff and his family left Kentucky and relocated to Tennessee. Jim Buckley held true to his word. Starting with the first week of on-the-job training, he worked side by side with Jeff through long strings of German shepherds, Malinois, and Labradors in explosives detection. Together the two men developed single and multipurpose bomb detection teams with handlers that came from around the world.

Within a few months, Jeff was escorting Jim on working-dog buying trips to Europe to learn how to select top detection prospects out of hundreds of canines being offered. In true Mr. Buckley style, the two men from Neue Welt only visited the highest quality breeding/working kennels in Holland, Germany, the Czech Republic, and Hungary. Jim introduced Jeff as one of his right-hand men to the most prolific dog brokers in Europe. The founder of Neue Welt fully intended to turn the canine procuring aspect of his operation over to young Mr. Franklin sooner rather than later. From their initial days of tandem training, Jim could tell that Jeff understood working dogs like few other people, and his new protégé was quickly filling the role that only he had been able to manage in the past. Jeff intently studied every nuance of Jim's dog handling and instruction manner until he mastered the art of detection training. No different than Jeff's tutelage under me in the foundation training of civilian dogs, Jeff became as skilled in police and military dog work as Jim Buckley himself.

Much like Jim, Jeff was a workaholic, so the two men were comfortable with long days and limitless canines and handlers to instruct. Neither one took advantage of the other in regard to workload. They both seemed to trudge along together naturally. The other trainers also labored hard, but Jeff and Jim just seemed to set no limits which fit perfectly with the fast-growing business. Welcoming all comers, at Neue Welt Jeff was routinely exposed to law enforcement and military handlers from other countries. Maneuvering around language barriers presented a training frustration that he quickly grew accustomed to. Jeff came up with his own sign-language when necessary, and he mastered just enough broken dialect to become a favorite instructor for some of the foreign visitors at the international kennel. One small squad of Nicaraguan police officers in particular clung to Jeff during their visit to acquire several multipurpose K-9s. The Central American handlers had been exposed to very little English prior to that trip, and they had little or no experience with police dogs. Devising a rudimentary pictorial system, Jeff was able to communicate with the Nicaraguans well enough to not only aid them in selecting the appropriate dogs for their needs, but also guide them through basic handling skills. The Central American police officers so trusted Jeff because of his extra effort to convey critical information, that they refused to deal with anyone else at Neue Welt during their visit.

The months flew past for Jeff at Neue Welt. The summer of 2004 stands out in his mind as the time he became proficient at canine selection, explosives and drug detection, as well as the combined purpose of criminal apprehension. By Jeff's calculation, he had trained nearly a hundred single and dual-purpose bomb detection dogs before the end of that season. The summer of 2004 stands out in Jeff's career for another reason also.

Nighttime instruction for K-9 units that are in law enforcement and military service is necessary protocol. Much of a K-9 team's function is carried out at night. Therefore, dogs and handlers must practice their skills in the dark in order to acclimate to the limited sight conditions while operating as a cohesive squad. On one such training excursion, Jeff was instructing a class of K-9 officers from various police departments on the nocturnal tactics of search and criminal apprehension. In essence, Jeff was recreating the experience that he and Cobra tackled back in Kentucky when they apprehended the "Bowie knife man." Jeff had planted a human decoy with a 38-caliber revolver loaded with fully charged blanks in the dark, quiet woods. Each officer would operate only with his canine companion as backup. Jeff had labeled that nocturnal course, "Worse Case Scenario," but he wisely attached a caveat, "Only a fool or young Officer Franklin would venture into this pursuit alone. Don't leave home without your backup. The capture isn't worth the risk.

However, if you happened to find yourself in this situation, I'll teach you how to manage the dangerous variables."

For that night's venue, Jeff had secured three fallow fields, each comprising about eight acres. The three fields lay side by side, and although they were separated by fairly dense wood-lines, the fields had been recently bush-hogged and were accessible along a dirt roadway. Jeff and his class arrived at the training location just before dark to ensure everyone found their way. The three fields were located in the heart of

Tennessee farm country with virtually no neighbors, no signage, and no lights of any kind. A few of the K-9 Officers in the class were from urban environments, and they joked about Jeff's selection of a venue out in the middle of nowhere. Jeff and his co-instructors loved the aspect of backcountry seclusion for some disciplines of their canine program, like the "escaped felon" scenario they would be working on that night. Jim Buckley touted Neue Welt's isolated, woodsy setting as one of the perks to working there. He frequently boasted, "We can be very hard to find if we want to be. This makes it difficult for unwanted guests to interfere with our training process."

By 2100, Jeff had worked his way through half the K-9 units. Each team was afforded the opportunity to experience the life changing shock of the 38-caliber blast while trying to apprehend the hostile decoy that lay in ambush, hidden in the pitch black woods. Standing in the beam of his truck headlights, Jeff had the class gathered around him as he critiqued the search efforts of one of the K-9 teams. At that moment the cool night air was violently disturbed by a powerful rumble. Jeff recognized the disturbance right away as the unmistakable roar of a helicopter gunship. Larger and more potent than the rescue helicopters most of the men were accustomed to, this rotorcraft seemed to split the tree tops as it approached.

Flying in at high speed and low altitude, the lights of the helicopter appeared instantly as it crested the ridge line bordering the farm fields. The gunship slowed to a hover in a low-light, stealth mode no more than fifty meters from Jeff and his class. Some of the dogs were stimulated into hysteria as the craft lowered to a landing, and most of the students thought it must be part of the night's training scenario. When one of the K-9 handlers asked Jeff what he had in store with the helicopter, Jeff said that he had absolutely no clue who those people were or what they wanted. Immediately after settling on the ground, with the rotor blades still whirling, several men unloaded from the gunship and walked in a straight line directly toward the group illuminated by the headlights. As the two lead men from the craft entered the fringe of light, Jeff identified their uniforms as high-ranking U.S. Military Officers that he was accustomed to seeing as a Marine. Without the courtesies or ceremony of a common greeting, the first uniformed man approaching the class announced, "I'm looking for Jeffrey Scott Franklin." Making his way from the center of the training group, Jeff cautiously responded, "That would be me."

Face to face with Jeff now, the lead man introduced himself, "My name is Colonel Paul Edward. I direct an elite force of Commandos that few people are familiar with. Come with me for a moment so I can explain who we are and why we're here."

Once Colonel Edward had Jeff away from the group, he continued, "My Special Task Force executes our nation's top priority 'Capture and Kill' missions. We carry out covert operations in every corner of the world, and we answer only to the highest departments in the United States government. The warriors under my command are the absolute best of the Special Forces world. They are selected from highly trained tactical units from all branches of the U.S. Military, and once these operators have been inducted into my clandestine community they learn the critical skills to become truly elite. The high-risk missions that we execute require weapons and equipment that have been developed just for us. What you see behind me is a UH-60 Black Hawk modified to fit my demands with a maximum speed, ferry range, and weapons system that out performs anything in its class."

Jeff listened attentively as the Colonel went on to say, "My access to intel is unlimited. How else could we have pinpointed your location this far out in the dark countryside of Tennessee? I actually know quite a bit about you Mr. Franklin. For example, I'm fully aware of the bum knee you try to hide and the botched ACL surgery you had a few years ago trying to fix it. I have copies of the incident and engagement reports from your war experiences as a Marine Tanker, and I know how many arrests you made as a K-9 Officer back in Kentucky. I'm also savvy to your dog training skills. Two months ago, you instructed a couple of my men in the art of bomb detection. Their take-away from your training initiated a plan I intend to carry out. I want, and I need multipurpose war dogs that can fully integrate into our small, intimate Special Tactics Units. I'm talkin' about a unique canine that can be trained to function in the same covert theaters of operation as my Commandos. These highly skilled war dogs need to be able to seek out and destroy the enemy in one moment and search for explosives among the dead bodies in the next, with very little time for transition. They need to be able to work for extended periods of time in high risk situations, and always under the cloak of stealth and secrecy. They need to be accustomed to deploying from helicopters, C-130s, water craft, and armored vehicles. We need hardy canine specimens that can perform in severe environmental conditions. My unit needs the 'whole enchilada.'"

The colonel continued, "All of my teams are combat specialists, and like me, they will not tolerate mediocrity, excuses, or failure. These men under my command are of superior character, and with no hint of exaggeration I can tell you that they are the best trained and best equipped combatants in the world. I want a canine counterpart that's capable of working side by side with them. I want the first-of-their-kind commando dogs. I flew all the way from Virginia for the sole purpose of recruiting you to accomplish this objective. Franklin, I think you have the character, the background, and the talent to help us reach this goal. If you accept my offer, you will be in charge of procuring the caliber of canines that can live up to this challenge. You alone will be responsible for developing the training protocols for the dogs, and only you will instruct the handlers through the multifarious applications of canine teamwork. In essence, Jeffrey Scott Franklin will build our Commando K-9 Teams from the ground up. I know I've thrown a lot at you with no forewarning, but is what I'm asking for possible? If so, are you able and willing to take on the project? I'll see to it that you're well compensated for your time and effort. Also, when it comes to an operating budget, you'll get whatever you need without questions. I probably don't have to tell you that this is a historically significant opportunity. You have a chance to develop a unique War Dog program for the United States Military and put your stamp on it. What do you say Mr. Franklin?"

Jeff's mind was spinning from the barrage of information that Colonel Edward dumped upon him. He wanted to tell the Colonel that he would have to think on it. With a life changing decision like this, Jeff felt that it would only be fair to confer with his family before giving an answer. And what about Jim Buckley, Jeff's new advisor and employer who placed so much trust and responsibility on him in the past year. He should at least give Jim a heads-up. Jeff processed all of these thoughts in a nanosecond while he was looking across the field at the blinking lights on the Black Hawk. Prudence proved to be no match for excitement on that summer night in Tennessee. In that brief moment of consideration, Jeff resigned to dealing with his family, Jim Buckley and all the fallout from a snap decision after the fact. Turning back toward the Colonel Jeff gave his reply; "I think your objective is attainable, and I also believe that I'm the man for the job. When would the project begin?"

Extending his hand in a gesture of good faith, Colonel Edward responded with a confident nod, "Just as soon as you get your house in order and I arrange your clearances." After the physical manifestation of their agreement, the Colonel hollered back as he and his party marched into the darkness toward the waiting helicopter, "We'll be in touch Franklin!"

Making his way back to the class, Jeff racked his brain over which past students may have been Colonel Edward's men, but he couldn't recall any unique personnel from that year. He had worked with too many U.S. Military handlers to remember any one or two, especially if those men happened to be operating incognito and presenting themselves as regular military. Jeff was genuinely curious as to what Colonel Edward's men may have experienced that would convince their elite unit to select him as their instructor over all of the other professional trainers in the country. Jeff didn't feel that special. He barely made it through high school. He left the Marine Corps as an enlisted grunt. He was only a K-9 Officer for a small county department in Kentucky, and he was the low man on Neue Welt's totem pole when it came to seniority. After a quick self-examination of his personal criteria, Jeff reasoned that it must have been the influence of luck that landed such a colossal invitation.

The K-9 Officers swarmed Jeff as he approached their group. They were all hungry for the details that they couldn't pick up from the distant conversation between Jeff and the Colonel. Unsure of how much information he should divulge from what had to be some level of a secret meeting, and given that the whole story seemed too far-fetched to be believed anyway, Jeff told the class that the midnight encounter was high ranking military brass wanting to exercise his influence in order to cut in line and get some soldiers into handler school early.

A Malinois grabbing his reward after a successful box exercise.

In the days following the face-to-face meeting with Colonel Edward, Jeff busied himself in silence preparing for a possible long-term adventure. He didn't intend to share any information about his secret offer until there was some kind of tangible commitment from the Colonel. Jeff replaced worn-out pieces of training gear and purchased all manner of working garments (not knowing where in the world he might be instructing if the Colonel's offer came through). Because of the immediate future's uncertainty, Jeff also pared down the family's less essential belongings. He sold two brood bitches that he had recently purchased to enhance Cobra's breeding line, an old Jeep Cherokee he used for hauling, a dog trailer, portable pens, and anything else that might complicate relocation. Jeff went about his activities with no offer of an explanation to his family or Jim Buckley as to what he was preparing for.

Three long months passed with no word from Colonel Edward or the U.S. Military. By October of 2004, Jeff had nearly forgotten about the clandestine midnight meeting. His feelings of disappointment over the fantasy opportunity that never materialized had all but dissipated. However, he still bore a stigma of foolishness for selling off his dogs and breeding equipment and spending money that he didn't have on gear that would never be used. All in all, Jeff was happy though. He had evolved into a premier bomb-dog instructor at a prestigious, international, police K-9 kennel. This was a dream come true in itself. I know this because Jeff called me periodically to pass along stories of government agencies and foreign police departments he had worked with. We talked about the richness of his experiences and the quality of dogs he was fortunate to train. We would sometimes chat for an hour and a half and never tire of our favorite subject, Canis familiaris. Jeff was living the dream that he began chasing when he was 14 years old.

On an ordinary Thursday afternoon at my training center in mid-October of 2004, one of my colleagues informed me that Franklin was on the phone and he gave the following message, "Relay to Mr. Duffy 'Pants on fire,' and I'll wait right here." Jeff's phrase was a code that he and I use when we absolutely need to talk to one another. We agreed from the beginning to never abuse our emergency code, so I was a little anxious when I handed over the dog I was training to one of my instructors and headed for the office.

"JSF, this is Mr. Duffy, are you OK?"

"I'm more than OK. I have incredibly good news! There is so much I want to tell you, but I can only give you a summary right now. I'm leaving Neue Welt for a special project with the United States Military. You can't believe who I'll be living and working with. I hate that I'm going to be out of touch with friends and family for a while, but this is truly a historical opportunity that was just dropped on me. I'm moving my family as we speak, and I'm going to do my best to swing by your place on our way to the military base. This is a high security project which means all my correspondences are censored, so I want to stop in and give you the details that I can't pass along over the phone. Will you be around tomorrow?"

"Absolutely!" Come by anytime, and we'll grab something to eat while you bring me up to speed. Jeff, if for some reason you can't make it up here, watch out for your 'top knot.'"

"Roger that."

Jeff never made it to my training center that next day. No visits, no messages, and no word on his whereabouts. He virtually vanished. Up to the time of his phone call, Jeff hadn't breathed a word of Colonel Paul Edward, stealthy Black Hawk helicopters, or U.S. Commandos to me. He kept that summer night's meeting exclusively to himself. I didn't find out until years later that the Commander of the United States most elite Task Force personally flew in to recruit him. Jeff also relayed to me, years past the cryptic phone call, that Colonel Edward contacted him with the news of approved security clearances and a "green light" for the program only three weeks before the ship out date. The Colonel's short notice gave Jeff only a small window of opportunity to explain his position to Jim Buckley, family, and friends. The consequence of such shocking news (albeit fortuitous) with very little adjustment time, left strained relationships in the wake, most notably with Jim Buckley and some of Jeff's family members. Unfortunately, Jeff expected everyone to process the life-changing information in stride, just like he did.

Jim Buckley especially didn't take Jeff's announcement well. Jim was hurt, and he felt betrayed because he had invested more coaching, energy, and trust in Jeff than anyone in his career. Jim was counting on Jeff Franklin to take over a substantial portion of Neue Welt's operation. That's why he personally guided Jeff through the nuances of scent detection training like the innovative "hop-step" and extended focus development. Jim also invested heavily in Jeff's ability to locate superior working dogs. Only a small percentage of professional trainers are capable of identifying the indispensable genetic qualities in a dog that make him police or military worthy. Jim Buckley was one of these men.

He introduced his young protégé to the top dog brokers in Europe, a list that Jim was years in the making. He also helped Jeff customize a selection test for working dogs that Jeff later refined into the screening process for all of the canines designated to be special task-f...

A German shepherd displaying outstanding focus on his indication.

Two and a half weeks before Jeff was due on the military base, the dreaded moment to inform his employer of the sudden career change presented itself. It was Tuesday morning and Jim's first day back from conducting a police K-9 seminar when Jeff seized the opportunity to coral Jim in the main office. The conversation between the two men began on a usual high note as Jeff and Jim discussed the progress of the latest bomb-dog class. After only a couple of minutes of strategizing, Jeff gave his friend and employer the shocking news of his fast approaching departure. In typical Jeff Franklin style, there was no candy coating on the hard news that Jim had to swallow. Jeff presented the bare essentials of an "offer too good to refuse," a couple of final dates, and an appreciation for the education he had received there. Jim sat stoically at his desk and offered nothing in response to Jeff's announcement. He was deeply upset over the prospect of losing such a pivotal member of his Neue Welt team, not to mention a friend. When Jeff extended his hand for a parting shake, Jim quietly reciprocated without comment or well-wishes. Walking out of Jim's office Jeff realized that he'd underestimated the effect of his departure on his one-time mentor. Jeff understood why Neue Welt's founder took the news seriously; he just couldn't understand why his friend Jim Buckley took the news so personally. The last days of training dogs at Neue Welt were awkward for Jeff. Although Jim Buckley busied himself around the kennel, he found little occasion to talk with Mr. Franklin. In fact, Jim seemed to avoid Jeff altogether whenever they found themselves in the same space, which created an uncomfortable atmosphere for everyone. Jeff never imagined when he began working at Neue Welt that he would one day be painfully counting down his final hours of employment there. On Jeff's last evening at the world-renowned kennel, Jim Buckley came through as a true friend and made things right. He put together a last minute "going away" party for his up-and-coming protégé. Jim had invited all of their favorite clients and supplied enough food, drink, and music to last late into the night. He even presented Jeff with a farewell plaque. After the party, Franklin exchanged some heavy "Good byes" with his Neue Welt comrades, then quietly drove away from his dream job.

On the home front, Jeff's parents were overtly gloomy during their "fair well" dinner. They weren't looking forward to the restricted contact with their son because of his clandestine working environment. Jeff's friends were simply disappointed that he wouldn't be around for the occasional bourbon and sushi any more. Franklin would not allow himself to think anything other than the heartache, strained relations, and burned bridges were all worth the opportunity to make history. And that's exactly what he intended to do.

In the fall of 2006, a full two years after Jeff's last succinct phone conversation with me, I had a very lucid dream one night. I was actually shaken into wakefulness over the dream's palpable nature, so I used the opportunity to get a drink of water. When I returned to bed, I immediately fell back into the same sleepy movie which was an unusual occurrence for me. The next morning at the training center, I stood in the back training room with David, my lead instructor, and described the dream to him. I told Dave that in this incredibly real vision, Jeff Franklin comes walking into our center unannounced with his son and daughter. I remember being surprised at how tall his kids were in the dream. I recall telling Dave how stout Jeff looked compared to the last time I saw him, and the three Franklins all appeared genuinely happy. I wasn't upset by the dream as much as curious about its intensity.

Trying to make sense of my experience, Dave responded with the same thought that had passed through my mind, "I wonder if this means Franklin is dead." Before I had a chance to comment, Dave and I heard, "Mr. Duffy!" The man's voice came from the front of the building. As we looked through the forward training room toward the waiting area and entrance to our building, we saw three silhouettes (outlined by the bright morning light shining through the front door) walking towards us. Again, we hear, "Is that Mr. Duffy I'm lookin' at?" Dave and I are both dumbfounded watching the three shadowed visitors move closer to us,because the slightly raspy voice we heard sounded just like Franklin's.As the three silhouettes came into full view, the man says, "Why Mr. Duffy, you look like you've just seen a ghost." There, standing before me was the robust, living and breathing Jeffrey Scott Franklin with his two teenage kids. I stood in disbelief for one long moment, then Jeff and I grabbed each other in a genuine bear hug. More than two years had passed since we had any contact; now here Jeff was on the heels of my dream. Once I described what Dave and I had been talking about when they made their entrance, the Franklins took their turn looking like they had encountered an apparition. It was truly a surreal moment.We laughed over the similarities between the dream images and the realthing, then all five of us chatted lightly about life in general. The small talk didn't get far before Jeff took me aside and said, "Come with me,and I'll tell you where I've been."

Ten

THE COMPOUND

Franklin

Six months after Jeff's visit, the stories of developing K-9 commando units carrying out top- secret operations were still tumbling through my mind. The concept of men and dogs intricately working together during covert missions intrigued me, so I decided to accept my friend's invitation to observe training operations while he was stationed in Virginia. His last words to me, as he departed from the previous fall's surprise visit, were, "Come out and see me. I can always arrange for a consulting clearance so that you can train with us. I know I'm hard to get ahold of, but you'll find me."

When my twenty-five-year-old daughter (Heidi) and my twenty-one year old son (Zachary) arranged for a break in their work and school obligations in the early summer of 2007, we packed our bags for a trip to Virginia. Jeff and I traded phone messages a few times in the weeks leading up to our trip, but he only gave me his general home-site location and not a definite address or destination. Jeff seemed legitimately excited that we were coming. I found it odd, however, that he didn't elaborate on the exact location of our final destination. Nonetheless, the missing direction details didn't dampen my enthusiasm or confidence in the least. I had two bright sidekicks with me and the latest in computer technology. Our plan was to target Jeff's location by using the general information he had already given me and cross-referencing that with the sparse information on his business website. After selecting the most likely addresses for a dog training kennel, we would use Google Maps to guide us to each location, and through a process of elimination eventually find Jeff's operation.

Seven hundred miles from home and nearly in view of the Atlantic Ocean, we were now only a short distance from Jeff Franklin. Our first stop on the east coast was a coffee house, where we indulged in some Wi-Fi and caffeine. While we sipped our coffee, Heidi perused the internet for commercial/industrial parks in the area that correlated to our meager information about Jeff's location. As she came up with possibilities, Zachary plotted routes to the likely spots via Maps so that we could investigate potential dog training facilities. Having owned or operated dog training kennels all of my working career, I had a good internal sense about zoning approval for that type of industry. Dog kennels tend to be the noisy, smelly "step children" that no business district wants. Undoubtedly, my friend has real clout with the U.S. military. However, I ventured to guess that his civilian canine headquarters would have little chance to locate in a new, high-end, commercial development like the first park we quickly drove through. But, when we approached the third site we struck "pay dirt." As we entered the park, all three of us agreed that this was a perfect run-down and forgotten area where someone could operate an "under-the-radar" dog training kennel. Narrow gravel roads riddled with mud holes led from one faded and dented steel building to the next. What was once a cluster of thriving businesses was now just a well-used, low-rent district for small upstarts.

Slowly making our way through the park, Zachary noticed several large, "blacked-out" SUVs that were haphazardly parked in front of a drab, monochrome building. The brand-new SUVs jumped out from their surroundings because they screamed modern and expensive while nothing else in the entire park did. There was only one entrance door and a single, small window in the front of the building that sat on a lot that was badly in need of gravel. Even though there was no human activity, this was as close to success as we had come on our search for Jeff thus far. I decided to drive around to the back of the building where it butted up against an acre of brush. Tucked between the building and the briars, out of the site of any passersby, were two long, low-riding trailers that were securely wrapped in tarps. Acting on a hunch that was too strong to ignore, I stepped out of my truck to peek under one of the tarps. Lifting a flap covering the end of one of the trailers I found the evidence we'd been looking for, a current government license plate that was attached to a multi-compartment dog trailer.

Standing outside the rear of the building, I tried to reach Jeff one more time from my cell phone. After leaving a message informing Jeff that we had arrived, Heidi, Zachary, and I walked around to the front of the building and knocked on the entrance door. A young man with a magnificent Dutch shepherd at his side opened the door. There was no greeting from the handler so I offered a suggestion, "Please tell Jeff Franklin that he has a friend here who has come a long way to see him."

With a stone-like expression the young man responded, "Who are you looking for?" Smiling, I replied, "Tell Franklin that he makes way too much noise to hide from me." As the door was closing I added, "Dog Handler, tell Jeff that I said something about 'pants on fire.'" No more than one long minute passed before Jeff barreled out the door. Laughing hysterically, he said, "I knew you'd find me."

Heidi chimed in right away, "You sure didn't make it easy on us. There are no signs or real directions posted anywhere."

Jeff responded, "Welcome to my new low-profile life. Everything I do now is done incognito." As soon as Jeff released his hug with Zachary, he demonstrated his uncanny awareness for details, "You're wearing your dad's K-9 ring from his sheriff's department days." Jeff seemed to notice and hang on to particulars like few people I've ever met. He hadn't seen that ring, or Zachary for that matter, in many years, yet the minute change jumped out at him. Jeff even commented on his tendency, "I think my weirdness about subtleties has really helped me in dog training, especially with this Special Tactics Group."

Once inside the dull gray building, we were introduced to six energetic young men who were busily handling dogs. Without mincing words, Jeff told us that all of those men were operators with the special tactics unit for which he had developed the canine program. These commandos did not look the part. They were all dressed in some form of cargo short and sport sandal. To a man they were youthful, mannerly, and intelligent. Most of them needed to shave, and their hair length varied from cut-off to shaggy. It was difficult to keep in mind that these amiable dog handlers were actually specialized warriors that had either just returned from, or were preparing to ship out to a combat zone. Once Jeff had introduced me as his friend and first training instructor, the young dog-men were eager to show off their handling skills. Heidi, Zachary and I were treated to all manner of war-dog demonstrations.

It was obvious as we moved about the building that the interior had been recently remodeled to meet Jeff's demands for processing new canine recruits. Well outfitted with high-tech training equipment, it stood in bright contrast to the worn-out exterior. At one end of the building there was a modest office that joined two large storage spaces filled to the brim with every conceivable piece of handler and K-9 gear. Hanging on the walls in Jeff's cluttered office were combat accommodations, numerous photos of Jeff "in-country" with his handling teams, and a commemorative Colt M16 rifle that had been presented to Jeff and his canine corps for outstanding service. Gauging by the respect and loyalty of his commando handlers, along with the accolades on the wall, it was apparent that Jeff Franklin had become the hub of a successful canine task force.

Jeff's undercover training kennel not only served as a preparation facility for the unique war-dogs, it was also his home where he ate and slept much of the time. If Jeff wasn't at the military base integrating canines into the task force, he divided his time between the kennel and his family that were anonymously tucked away in a house across town. When Jeff first signed on with Colonel Edward's group, he was advised to maintain a low profile in his personal life. The anonymity would help safeguard his family against possible retaliation from some of the terrorist elements that his dogs would be deployed against. Jeff took the Colonel's advice and enemy requital seriously, so he established a separate residence for his loved ones as a precaution. As challenging as it was, Jeff committed to living the double life of a full-time, elite-force contractor and a part-time family man.

While my kids and I were admiring dog training techniques and listening to combat adventures, Jeff made arrangements for us to have dinner with his family that night. He also confirmed the clearances to get me on base for the next few days so that I could participate in the final stages of special warfare training for several of his K-9 teams that were scheduled to deploy. At the crack of dawn the next day, Jeff and I would be on our way to the military base, leaving Heidi and Zachary to spend the day on the beach with Jeff's kids, Rebecca and Adam.

In a large visitor parking lot just off base, Jeff and I waited to rendezvous with two of his commando handlers. I had a visitor's pass to get through the main gate of the base, however, Jeff and I were headed inside the Compound. The Compound was a highly secured area inside the military base that was designated exclusively for the task force operators and their support. After an extensive background check and multilevel clearances, Colonel Edward had issued Jeff a command badge which afforded him the privilege to enter the Compound. This special operations area was so tightly secured that even with his command badge Jeff didn't have the authority to bring me in as a consultant. The only way that I would be allowed into this seldom visited sanctum was under the constant supervision of one of the commandos.

While we sipped coffee and waited on my chaperone, Jeff briefed me on the busy few days that lay ahead. He had four K-9 teams in the final stages of training that had to be ready for deployment within two weeks. Of the four teams, two men were novice handlers and two dogs had yet to be battle tested. Jeff usually paired the seasoned men with the new canines and the experienced war-dogs with the "green" handlers. He felt that this way the bugs in the K-9 team dynamic could be more safely worked out in an active war zone. The seasoned dogs would not only require less handler interaction "in country," which afforded the rookie handlers more freedom to concentrate on the enemy; they would also be less reactive to the "shock and awe" of explosive combat.

Although Jeff went to monumental efforts to duplicate battle conditions for his K-9 teams during the months of preparatory training, he discovered early on (after numerous post-deployment debriefings) that the extreme mortal intensity experienced during actual combat could not be duplicated during instruction. Therefore, the performance of a canine warrior (not unlike his human counterpart) in an active theater of operation could not be predicted, or guaranteed, until the dog had been repeatedly exposed to that uniquely horrifying environment. In Jeff's K-9 Commando program, veteran handlers (whenever possible) guided the new canines through the uncertainties of actual combat, minimizing the distraction risk that an over-reactive dog may place on a first-time handler or squad of men. A seasoned dog-man would possess more skill and composure to calm or direct an excited canine warrior with less risk of losing target-focus.

The rookie handler typically favored the idea of having a proven canine commando at his side during their first engagements as a dog-man. The experienced handlers understood the importance of Jeff's policy, but given the choice would have much preferred to keep their familiar canine partner (idiosyncrasies and all) than to forge a new relationship with another unique animal. The bond between a man and dog grows understandably strong during a tour of duty. Much like human dancing partners, the combat tested handler and canine team learn to interact with one another almost intuitively.

The schedule Jeff had laid out for his K-9 teams over the next several days was exhaustive: fast- roping practice from a helicopter, distance running followed by route clearing, outdoor area searches for the enemy, gunfire practice in the Simulation Bunker, enemy engagement and bomb detection indoors, and a Force-On-Force exercise in "Little Afghanistan." Jeff warned me that the days might be long, but he would like me along for the full ride if I were game. Besides, getting in and out of the Compound was complicated, so once we entered it would be best to stay until we accomplished as much as possible. When Jeff asked me if I was up for the adventure, knowing I could never turn down such an opportunity, I answered with his favorite response to a challenge, "Damn skippy!"

The sun had not fully risen when a blacked-out SUV pulled alongside Jeff's truck. I took that as my cue to switch vehicles; however, one of the four task-force operators from inside the vehicle had to pat me down and check my personal bag for contraband before I could transition. Jeff laughed as he apologized for the inconvenience saying, "Mr. Duffy, I tried to tell them you weren't a spy, but they wouldn't believe me." Once inside the SUV we sped toward the main gate of the base. When the entrance of the installation came into view there was no questioning the seriousness of its security. Tall chain-link fencing topped with razor wire ran from each side of the formidable gate to as far as the eye could see. Attending the gate were four guards, all dressed in battle uniforms and carrying M-4s.

Waiting in line, I watched as two guards approached each vehicle as it slowly encroached upon the entrance. One guard targeted the driver to conduct an interview while the other checked for occupants and contents from the passenger's side. The two remaining guards observed from protective quarters that resembled ominous bastions projecting from a castle wall at either end of the gate. If any one of the four guards experienced the slightest uneasiness over a vehicle, the occupants, or its contents, which was often the case, they would promptly direct the vehicle to a supervised side-lot for further inspection.

As our SUV crawled toward the gate, each commando displayed a special ID tag out his respective window. For us, the high-clearance identification tags meant there would be no delay at the gate. The guards waved us on without hesitation and I was never in question as their guest. I thought as we easily passed through security headed for a top clearance area deeper on base, how difficult it would be for elite commandos like these not to adopt the privileged attitudes that they're known for. The men and women of the regular military often refer to the special operators as "Million Dollar Men," due to the countless hours of training and unlimited resources the U.S. Government devotes to them.

Being an outsider, it appeared to me that much of the accustomed military regulation didn't apply to these upper tier warriors that Jeff instructed. They wore their hair how it suited them, freely used government vehicles, and seldom donned uniforms. However, most in their group did dress in stylish high-tech clothing from manufacturers like Under Armor, Mountain Hardware, and Salomon. Given what they do, it was understandable that the special operators I had a chance to work with, all had a penchant for the latest, quality gear. Their talk and comparisons of raingear, knives, boots, or electronic gadgets was incessant.

I did think it was curious after being with these men for a few days in various venues, that I seldom, if ever, saw them salute a superior officer. This customary show of respect could simply have gone unnoticed by me. However, there was one encounter with a superior officer out in the field during area search drills that made me think the upper tier commandos didn't often concern themselves with such formalities.

Jeff and I, plus a handful of operators with dogs were organizing a canine search for a human decoy that was hiding somewhere in the

The author standing at the base of the "Fast-Roping" tower with the next canine candidate.

coastal scrub that defined our training area. While we were gathered as a group discussing the searching order for the K-9 teams, one of the handlers removed his shirt in order to cool off and soak up sun. Just about that time a superior officer drove up to our location to observe the training exercise. As he stepped out of his vehicle one of the operators standing next to me exclaimed, "The fun vacuum has arrived." I took that to mean regulation and protocol would be expected from that point forward.

The ranking officer confirmed the change to formality by immediately suggesting the handler put his shirt back on. Without discussion the remaining clothed operators promptly removed their shirts and began comparing tattoos that they all seemed to be fond of.

With a more forceful voice, the superior officer said, "I'm serious, put your shirts on. We have an observer with us."

The first handler to have taken off his shirt quips back, "Get off our backs, Tom. It's hot out here."

And then another operator jumped in, "You're just showing off in front of Mr. Duffy and you know it."

Jeff didn't react at all to the young commandos' behavior, instead he began briefing the approaching officer on the area search scenario. I seemed to be the only one in our group who felt retribution must be at hand. But then, much to my surprise the superior officer quietly listened to Jeff as he watched the shirtless handlers go about their busy work. After observing two dogs successfully find the hidden decoy, Officer Tom bestowed his "carry on" approval and stepped back into his very clean truck. As he turned around on the narrow dirt road, Officer Tom and a couple of the commandos jabbed at each other about who would have the cleanest vehicle coming out of the scrub.

I didn't know at the time, that Tom and all of the commandos' immediate superiors were at one time or another active, special operators, and they considered one another brothers regardless of rank. All of the commandos accepted the other as a member of a unique, tightly-knit community. Jeff had become accustomed to this elite task-force culture, so he barely noticed the blatant insubordination. When I asked him if Officer Tom was truly an authority, Jeff confirmed, "Absolutely. He won't be the last ranking officer that you see these guys blow off. Elite operators are well aware of how 'special' they are. I've only seen these commandos impressed by two superiors, Colonel Paul Edward and Gunnery Sergeant William Hawk ('Gunny'). Colonel Edward is the quintessential, 'no bullshit,' high-ranking officer that gets stuff done when no one else can, and Gunny is one of the oldest active operators who has 'been there and done that.' You'll probably get to meet Gunny tomorrow."

We had to drive across a considerable section of the military base in order to reach the operation zone known as the "Compound." The parking-lot adjacent to our destination was exclusively designated for task-force personnel, and access required a key card to open a heavy gate that obstructed the only access to the lot. After parking the SUV in a row of undercover, military vehicles, the five of us grabbed our personal bags and exited toward the secret area. A double row of eight-foot-high fencing enclosed the entire facility. There were security cameras mounted at every vantage point, and armed guards waiting to greet us at the initial check point into the complex. Verifications of identity, clearance-badge examinations, and visitor pass inspections were taken very seriously at this gate. If any questions had arisen over the authenticity of an ID or the purpose of my visit, we all would have been ordered to "stand fast" as potentially unwelcome guests until more information was gathered.

Having satisfied the guard's scrutiny, an electronic gate was activated which allowed us onto the grounds. Walking through the gate I could see several large, utilitarian buildings with an aircraft landing pad not far off to the right of the structures. To the left of the buildings was an elaborate, physical training (P.T.) course for the commandos that utilized all of the open ground that I could see. It wasn't until we had walked between the two closest buildings that I spotted the newly constructed kennel with its connected outdoor obstacle course standing alone at the rear of the compound.

Each of the buildings within the complex was secured with alarms, cameras, heavily armored doors, entry-proofed windows, and electronic key-coded locks so that accidental access to the interior was almost impossible. Once inside any of the structures, the appropriate badge or pass had to be presented to an Officer-In-Charge (O.I.C.) before admittance would be allowed to enter certain areas, such as the war rooms, the armory, the computer bank with its own staff, the team quarters, or any number of classified cells. Also enclosed in these secure structures were medical suites, a swimming pool, gymnasium, dormitory, locker rooms, cafeteria, and fighting rooms. There was enough office space inside the complex to house ranking officers, medical staff, trainers, coaches, nutritionists, logistics personnel, and intelligence agents. Without exaggeration, one could say that the complex was filled with the best technical, mechanical and human support that money could buy. Colonel Edward's elite warriors had every imaginable means of assistance within the doubly fenced perimeter. Nearly two hundred people overall, including the commandos themselves, called the "Compound" their home.

By the time my escorts and I had checked in with the O.I.C. at the kennel facility, Jeff was eagerly waiting in the hallway to show me the dogs that were currently in service for the program. Having my "all clear," I followed Jeff into the canine holding area with the kennel master walking close behind. Inside the holding area were eight immaculately cleaned indoor/outdoor runs that were constructed side by side. Each dog had its own elaborate quarters with an extensive information chart hanging on the gate. The charts contained every conceivable detail about the canine occupant: name, physical statistics, diet requirements, appetite condition, elimination comments, handling cautions, and training status. Although the kennel was designed and built to meet strict military specifications, Jeff had full control over its operation. Over the years he had instituted modifications to the standard military cleaning protocol, diet, and exercise regimen to better suit his elite canine program.

At the time of my visit there were five dogs in the kennel and two that were about to return from active deployment in Iraq. Jeff's task at hand was to complete the training of four K-9 teams on base so that they could relieve the men and dogs in the Middle East. Out of the five dogs there were three Belgian Manlinois, one Dutch shepherd, and one Malinois/shepherd cross. Even at a glance, one could see that all of the animals were athletes. Rigorous daily exercise, along with a custom mix of premium wet and dry food, kept the canine warriors lean, full bodied and firm with muscle. The kennel master had just unlocked each run's outside access door when we arrived. The energized working dogs were racing in and out of their canine-sized portals, torn between the excitement of barking at a stranger (me) inside, or gulping fresh morning air and barking at each other outside. Jeff stopped at the third run and said, "This is Arrow. He's not the largest dog in the program, but he's my favorite. You'll love watching this Malinois transition from obliterating a human target to searching for explosives. He can make a complete mental shift from a bloody, life and death struggle to a composed, meticulous search in less than fifteen minutes."

After the kennel tour, our day officially began as all workdays begin inside the "Compound," with P.T. I was excited about the prospect of exercising with Jeff and the handlers, however, I hadn't worn the appropriate clothing for the planned "Cross training" routine. When I mentioned my conundrum to Jeff he smiled and turned to Adam McAllister (Mac), his most experienced handler, and asked if he thought it might be possible to roundup some proper clothing for Mr. Duffy. Mac, along with the other operators standing by, laughed out loud and said, "Follow me."

Our entire group headed for the locker rooms, or "cages" as they were called. Each commando had his own cage that was the size of a small room. Some of the senior guys, like Mac, actually had two cages, which were chock-full of new P.T. clothing, scuba gear, skydiving equipment, shooting paraphernalia, cold and hot weather battle uniforms, helmets, every imaginable head cover, goggles, glasses of all kinds, rappelling ropes with rigging, and redundant pairs of boots and shoes for every conceivable environment or purpose. As a group we walked from the kennel to the nearest building in the complex that housed the locker rooms. Entering the building Mac asked me what size shoe I wore. When I told him ten and a half he said, "Good that's my size, and I have a pair of Salomons that were designed for cross training. In fact, that's what I'm wearing now." When I exclaimed that I didn't want to take the shoes off his feet, Mac unlocked one of his cages and said he had that particular shoe in three different colors because it was his favorite for P.T. Matching my physique to one of the other handlers, named Mike, I had a choice of brand new sweats from his locker.

Decked out in the latest exercise clothing, I "double timed it" along with Jeff and the commandos to the outside training course for some grueling instruction by an intense female trainer. Elite operators are accustomed to having Olympic grade coaches lead them through Spartan exercises at the top of each day. The professional one-on-one encouragement really felt extravagant to someone like me, who had never hired a personal trainer before. However, to these specialized warriors the best instruction money could buy was what they came to expect in all facets of their lives.

After an hour or so of dragging tires, climbing ropes and snatching kettlebells, we were all physiologically humming and ready to focus on dog-work. Jeff had arranged for the first stage of canine training that day to be at the fast-roping tower. The tower is a ninety-foot-tall structure erected for the purpose of preparing commandos for speedy deployments from helicopters by way of sliding down a long, thick rope. Before the K-9 teams could practice any descents, we had to lug all of their assault gear, including the seventy-six-pound bag of rope, up a narrow staircase with four dogs in tow. At the tower's top platform was a large opening resembling the fuselage doorway of a helicopter. The platform was framed with steel rigging to accommodate rope and safety line attachments, much like a real aircraft. The opening itself was approximately seventy feet above the ground, which meant we needed ninety feet of 1.75-inch-thick rope for a safe descent (that's why the bag was so heavy). All of the commandos had received fast-rope instruction during their basic training where they were taught how to use their two gloved hands and both feet to firmly grip a rope for a controlled downward slide. However, they never had to descend with only one hand devoted to the rope while the other steadied a dog fastened to their safety harness as the new K-9 handlers were about to do. So, this training stage was going to be stressful for the two "green" handlers and the two fresh canine recruits.

To facilitate a one handed descent, the handlers would use a prototype of a mechanical, friction descender that was developed to allow fast-roping with heavy loads. The thick descent rope is weaved through this relatively simple device, which is about the size of a toaster. When a load (handler with a dog attached) is clipped into the upper end of the descender, it causes the device to cant and bind the rope around weaving posts inside the mechanism. The binding of the rope (friction) reduces the sliding action of the load, which in turn allows the handler to brake or regulate the descending speed with only one hand. Provided the descender is affixed properly to the rope, the K-9 team is securely attached to the mechanism, and the handler has a secure one-hand grip; the only thing left to go wrong would be the adverse effects of the helicopter's rotor-wash.

The wash is essentially a miniature tornado within the immediate vicinity of the helicopter caused by the action of the rotor. Consequently, larger tornados are created by larger rotors. At times, a sizable rotor-wash can blow the hefty descent rope out at a nearly horizontal angle to the ground. If the rope were blown out at this severe angle the very moment a K-9 team steps out of the helicopter for a descent, the descender mechanism may fail to engage and bind the rope (due to lack of load and cant caused by the outward rather than downward angle of the rope). Failure of the friction mechanism would shift the full braking responsibility of the heavy load to just one of the handler's hands and the squeeze of his feet. A weighty, seventy-foot, onehanded descent without the aid of a mechanical brake would certainly be disastrous. We had no rotor-wash worries that morning because Jeff insisted on his new handlers and dogs being introduced to team fast-roping from a tower, which allowed them to concentrate (as calmly as possible) on technique. Deployments from a hovering helicopter would come later.

The first K-9 team in line for a descent was Mac and Arrow. My responsibility at this training stage was assisting the handler in securing the dog to the descending device.

Jeff advised all of the teams to approach the tower opening just like they would the fuselage door in a pitching helicopter that was trying to hover in turbulent conditions. Having fast-roped from a helicopter a number of times with his previous dog, Jaeger, Mac had his approach maneuver down pat, so Jeff encouraged him to think out loud for the educational benefit of the rookie handlers. Being a natural lead-man, Mac continuously talked to his fellow commandos as he and Arrow made their way to the rope, out the doorway and down to the ground.

Mac began his monologue with a precept, "Always short-tether the dog's safety harness to yours when you step onto any craft. This prevents accidental separation when you're being tossed around like we always are. The obvious plan as I approach the doorway is to keep my team's center of gravity as low to the deck as possible. So, I choose to scoot on my butt and direct Arrow to low-crawl beside me until the last possible moment when we have to clip into the descender. With a high-energy dog like Arrow, I'm really concerned about him trying to leap through the opening before we're fastened and ready, so I'm going to keep my left hand locked in a death grip around the handle of his harness the entire time. I'm also countin' on Mr. Duffy's assistance with Arrow when I get to the opening. Standing at the threshold of a seventy foot drop struggling to hook into a carabiner with your right hand, while your left is holding back a 'game' dog trying to jump into space, is a special pain in the ass. And I wanted to take this opportunity to thank Franklin for giving me another 'green' dog to break in for the next new class of handlers so that they will have an easy time fast-roping. Isn't that right Mike with my battle-tested "Dutchy?"

When Mac scooted up to the doorway, I immediately secured Arrow by grabbing his collar and harness. Arrow was hyped with nervous energy. He reminded me of an athlete standing on the field just seconds before the start of the game. Almost according to Mac's premonition, a moment after clipping into the descender as he was perched on the outer edge of the deck adjusting his grip on the rope, impatient Arrow attempted to leap from our grasp into open air. Mac never missed a beat. He regained control of Arrow, clipped him into the device, then he stepped away from the tower with a farewell of "Later boys" and down the rope they went. Mac and Arrow's effortless seven story slide completely disguised the imminent dangers of the maneuver, while simultaneously setting a high bar of achievement for the three remaining K-9 teams.

When Mac returned to the platform with the descender, Mike began his scoot across the deck with Jaeger (Mac's experienced Dutch shepherd) in a low-crawl by his side. Mike definitely reaped the benefits of Jaeger's roping experience. Like the professional that he was, Jaeger stuck to Mike's side with no real need of a grip restraint. Even standing on the threshold of the doorway, Jaeger was cool and alert. He exuded the attitude of "Just another day at the shop." On the other hand, this was Mike's first attempt at fast-roping with a dog. He was tense and acutely focused on the details: the descender's locked position, foot placement on the edge of a seventy-foot drop, and a secure one-hand grip on the rope just above the mechanism.

I was standing with Mike on the edge of the high platform when I handed him Jaeger. I could feel that his mind was reeling with the additional burden of the dog on top of the other fast-roping considerations. To offer Mike some comfort I reminded him that he had the "Cadillac" of military working dogs in his hand, and Jaeger should ride down smoothly, if he kept him tight against his body. I had my hand steadying Mike's shoulder while he waited for Jeff's command to go. I could feel him anxiously vibrating under my grip while his eyes were locked on the descender. When Jeff asked, "Are you ready?" Mike responded with a mechanical "Yes sir!" Jeff immediately followed with "Go!" Without hesitation Mike and Jaeger stepped off into space.

The descender once again worked like a charm, landing Mike and Jaeger safely on the ground. With both feet and his dog secure once more, Mike looked up to us on the platform with a huge smile and shouted, "I wasn't sure I could make that slide with one hand like Mac did." Therein lies the essence of a commando. Mike later confessed that he believed he was standing on the precipice of a freefall to death. Yet, when given the directive to "go," he jumped without hesitation into whatever awaited him. I've never forgotten that glimpse of a warrior's courage.

Each of the four K-9 teams had a few successful runs on the rope before we broke for an early lunch. Jeff gave the handlers extra time to pack up all of their combat essentials, including their weapons, for the next training stage. The plan was to spend the rest of the day at a training venue specifically arranged for Jeff's K-9 teams. There, the operators would be challenged to commandeer a hostile, enemy environment under nighttime conditions using their dogs and simulation ammunition. This training station known as the "Bunker," would expose the rookies Trevor, Mike, Bullet, and Arrow to the feel of a legitimate mission.

Eleven

Six-Man-Element

The Simulation Bunker was a partially exposed, but mostly underground structure that resembled a modern, mine shaft. It appeared small and insignificant from the outside when we drove up. However, another world lay underground. While Jeff briefed me on the Bunker's function and the day's training scenario, the K-9 teams donned their entire array of assault gear which included a tactical body armor vest capable of stopping an AK-47 round, a shrapnel stopping helmet, night vision goggles (NVGs), poly-carbonate protective glasses, a full hydration system (bladder), a bungie leash, a wrist mounted camera monitor, a training collar transmitter, a fixed-blade fighting knife, a modified Heckler/Koch M4 long gun, a customized Sig Sauer P226 hand gun, and as many magazines of simulation ammunition that they could fit on their body. Fully dressed, the commandos looked more like cyborgs than men.

Their dogs were also dressed in complete battle attire, giving them the appearance of alien automations. All four canines were equipped with a 4lb ballistic vest/modular harness that provided defense against piercing as well as lifting and loading functions, a remote-control collar to receive handler reinforcements, rubber soled nylon boots for foot protection and tactile control, poly-carbonate lensed goggles as a safeguard against shrapnel or sand, and an enhanced low-light/infrared/camera mounted to the harness above the withers.

When Jeff described the Bunker, it sounded very much like a ride at an amusement park. It was designed and built for the purpose of recreating targeted sites. The Simulation Bunker is one of the last training stages for the elite forces before deployment. Within the structure, the commandos could train in virtually the same theater conditions that they would encounter on any closed-environment mission. Configurations of hallways, room dimensions, staircases, balconies, and latches could all be reproduced to the millimeter to match a designated site. Lighting conditions, colors, textures, noises, even odors could be fabricated to reproduce a proposed theater of operation. When the combat specialists and their dogs train inside the Bunker they are able to plan step by step how a particular mission will be executed. Every detail of an assault can be worked out in advance with "dry runs" through the Bunker, which in turn minimizes the inevitable glitches that are inherent with every mission. The plan on that summer day at the Virginia military base was to have the K-9 teams walk through the portal of the Simulation Bunker and enter the virtual world of a hostile, disabled frigate in the Strait of Hormuz.

The simulation rounds that the commandos would be firing inside the Bunker were known as SESAMS (Special Effect Small Arms Marking System). This type of ammunition works much like a paintball (except at twice the velocity) to mark the accuracy of the shooter, and at the same time possess minimal lethal capabilities. The SESAMS are manufactured for duty weapons. This affords Jeff's handlers the opportunity to fire their personal M4s and P226s under realistic conditions, while managing their dogs.

To prepare his men and their canine counterparts for this day in the Bunker, Jeff spent weeks drilling them through basic obedience skills (Heel, Sit, Down, Stay, Come, and Finish) in a distraction free environment with no combat gear. More weeks of advanced instruction (Jump, Crawl, Send-Away, and Search) follow on the K-9 obstacle course. Finally, Jeff has the handlers dress in full battle array and run through the gamut of obedience exercises in naturally obstructed and distracting environments such as the "hot" firing range, active aircraft hangers, and busy office buildings. During these many weeks of tactical obedience development, the dogs spend equal time learning how to use their bite and their bodies to subdue the human enemy. The Simulation Bunker will not only subject the K-9 units to a tactical obedience test, the handlers will also be challenged to move through a dark environment while shooting marker rounds at pop-up silhouettes and sending their dogs to engage the enemy.

Inside the Bunker Jeff's tactical K-9 handlers will face the arduous task of containing their dogs at "Heel" (the dog positioned on the handler's immediate left) during combat. The colossal challenge of controlling an animal under the stresses of armed conflict isn't hard to imagine. However, it may be a surprise to many that the true difficulty for the handler lies in the task of restraining a dog from prematurely engaging, not from fleeing to quiet safety. All of the dogs that Jeff selects for Colonel Edward's elite group come from a long line of brawling ancestors. After several months of instructional cultivation, the canine's fighting traits are heightened to the point that he is drawn to conflict like a bee is drawn to nectar. With these warfare inclined animals, flight is never really a consideration. The tough assignment for the handlers is holding the canine's motor to an idle until the Team Leader requires their full "horsepower."

A strike force deployed for a small or precision Capture/Kill operation, will often comprise a group of six commandos known as a Six-Man-Element. When a K-9 team is recruited as a member of a Six-Man-Element they are usually referred to as "Dog" for simplicity. The handler's job within the Element is complex. He is responsible for visually clearing or holding a given area just like every other operator on the team. Using his personal weapons, the handler must work in synchronized unison with other members of the Element in order to supply sufficient cover or attack-force to secure a targeted environment. It's critical for a mission's success that the handler and dog operate as a cohesive unit even when receiving or returning gunfire. This means that the dog must be able to heel alongside his handler at a run or a crawl in total darkness and move stealthily from cover to cover with his team. The canine commando must remain close enough to his handler's left leg that his presence is felt, thereby, freeing the handler to devote his eyes and hands to weapons operation. A fully trained dog is expected to preserve his close proximity to the handler as countless 5.56 mm cartridges are discharged over his head, all the while never losing his hunger for the cue to engage.

The handler alone is responsible for containing, deploying, and retrieving his canine under these conditions. An errant canine within the Element could lead to mortal disaster by prematurely announcing the presence or location of the cloaked, tactical team. Mission success can hinge on the K-9 team's ability to fully function with the dog at "heel." A deep connection between the handler and dog blossoms from the many hours of practicing the elaborate "heeling" dance. The genuine trust that develops out of this connection is a magic key the handler employs to shift his dog's mindset from furious combat to methodical searching, when the team is called upon to look for explosives immediately after a battle.

Colonel Edward's canine units are required to operate at levels that far exceed the normal protocol of the trained police dog that K-9 Officer Franklin was accustomed to. Jeff had to create an all new, more demanding training regimen for these highly skilled operators, and he doesn't mince words with his new students on their first day of instruction. After a "good morning" greeting, he welcomes the men with a daunting declaration; "As a member of a Six-Man-Element, the K-9 handler has the fullest plate. Like it or not, that's what you've signed up for. Your special task force, Colonel Edward, and the United States Military expect more from you than anyone else within the Element. So I've set a very high bar for the handlers and dogs in this program, and it's my responsibility to make sure you reach it."

As an integral part of the Bunker's training stage, Jeff arranged to have five other commandos on site to operate as "shooters" and flesh-out a full Six-Man-Element for "Dog" to synchronize with. Strategic coordination and marksmanship was the focus of the exercise. This was the first opportunity for the two new handlers and rookie dogs to function as a unit on a virtual mission. Jeff closely monitors each K-9 team during simulation experiences, noting the details of performance strengths and weaknesses on a clipboard. His notes then determine training protocols for the following weeks when the deficiencies would be worked out.

Mac and Arrow were the first K-9 team selected to enter the Bunker as "Dog." They would be positioned as the third man in a six-man line-up, known as a "Stack." After a quick equipment check, Mac followed the first two "shooters" down to the dark entrance of the Bunker. The "Stack" lined up in the ready position (a point man followed by the rest of the team, one directly behind the other within touching distance and weapons deployed) on one side of the open doorway. Outside the entrance, the men could smell the odor of rusty steel, enamel paint, and diesel fuel belching from the belly of the dark structure. Mac could only speculate on the olfactory nuances Arrow was picking up. Listening carefully, the "Entry Team" heard creaking metal, ocean waves slapping a hull, even the laughter of sea gulls. For all intents and purposes, the Six-Man-Element was about to board a Middle Eastern frigate.

Mac pulled the NVGs over his eyes and stroked Arrow a few times, slowly and heavily to help settle him. Arrow had already encountered decoys (pseudo enemy dressed in protective bite suits) in dark, cluttered quarters during his bite development training in the preceding months. He was trembling with the excitement of a potential engagement, and he began emitting detectable sounds (nasal whining and pre-bark huffing). The Bunker scenario was an exercise in stealth, so Arrow had to comply with the rule of absolute quiet. Being an innately dog-savvy handler, Mac understood in order to extinguish Arrow's noisy behavior, a swift collar-deterrent needed to be applied in the earliest moments of the unwanted conduct. Rattles, clanks, and barks would surely give away the Element's advantage of surprise. On certain Capture/Kill missions, surprise is the only difference between life or death.

Slithering into the blackness of the Bunker, the "Stack" of commandos moved as one silent, deadly organism. Mac used the short bungie leash to assist in compelling Arrow to "heel" tightly at his left side. Climbing a flight of stairs, the men paused on the front of a broad steel platform that led to a passageway running some distance into the Bunker. The passageway had several cubicles with open hatches along either side. Approaching the first two cubicles, the "Stack" divided, and three men lined up along either wall. "Dog" was on the right side just behind the point man who assumed the role of the "Hall Boss." The "Hall Boss" would direct the team's searching movements as they systematically cleared each cubicle and slowly moved deeper into the underground structure.

At the end of the hall was a hatch to a large open area. "Dog" was called forward as the "Hall Boss" slowly opened the hatch. Searching this large area would be Arrow's task. Mac quietly disconnected the bungie leash from Arrow's harness and turned on his wrist-mounted, camera monitor. After checking the signal from the IR camera, Mac vigorously rubbed Arrow's body preparing him for a physical encounter. Football players essentially do the same thing when they bang on each other's helmets and pads before a game. Mac wanted his teammate stimulated and prepared for the worst. Without so much as a whisper, Mac sent his canine warrior into the abyss with a hand signal. From his wrist monitor, Mac and the "Hall Boss" intently studied Arrow's movements. With the speed of a shark searching among the rocks in a murky ocean, Arrow fluidly made his way in and out of every nook and cranny of the largearea. Witnessing the expeditious search from the dog's perspective (via the harness mounted camera) actually made the two men dizzy.

Passing through a hatch to a connecting room, Arrow's camera picked up movement behind a set of cabinets. Mac and the "Hall Boss" watched as their camera perspective took flight over a five-foot-tall cabinet and descended on a hiding assailant. The thrashing, tumbling images coming across the monitor confirmed a target engagement before the sounds of any struggle reached the men in the passageway. Without delay, the "Hall Boss" signaled the strike force to storm the large dark rooms and finish what the canine warrior had begun. Pop-up, enemy silhouettes sprang to life as the commandos charged toward Arrow. Marker rounds sprayed from the M4s annihilating the "kill zone" on every two- dimensional adversary. Not unlike a machine, the lethal Six-Man-Element swiftly and adroitly cleared the Bunker's holding rooms of all the enemy, but one.

The assault on the large holding areas lasted no more than a minute, but it was the longest minute imaginable for the combatant in a protective bite suite. Arrow had savaged the man for nearly ninety seconds before Mac received the signal to "call off the dog." It took some effort from Mack to get Arrow to release his bite and completely disengage. However, once he complied, Arrow fell back into an alert, heeling position while two of the "shooters" zip tied the prisoner's hands and took him into custody. "Dog" fell in behind the prisoner as the strike force escorted the battle worn man out of the dark structure.

For his first pass through the Bunker, Arrow did remarkably well. His nerves were steady and his focus was intense during the entire search.

His responsiveness to Mac's "Heel" command kept him composed and at the ready as the "Stack" moved through the Bunker. Arrow's courageous nature propelled him, solo, through a successful "Seek and Destroy" mission. Jeff was most impressed, however, with Arrow's superior fight drive. The canine warrior never left his charge. He rendered his target incapacitated with the painful clench of his jaws and kept him pinned to the floor with a straddling body position, just like he'd been encouraged to do over the past months.

Although a new dog to the program, Arrow, along with his superior handler, received the highest marks of the day at the Simulation Bunker. There were only two behavioral issues that Mac needed to refine before Arrow would be battlefield ready. Arrow's audible expressions of pre-search excitement had to be quashed before Jeff would risk putting him into a real theater of war. Also, Arrow's reluctance to release the enemy had to be addressed over the short time that remained before deployment.

The overly zealous canine commando was understandably disinclined to give up his hard won prey, which forced Mac into utilizing the remote control to gain compliance.

However, in a real life or death conflict Mac would not have the luxury of extra time to work on delayed response issues.

At the close of the day's training, Jeff expressed that he had no worries over any of the four K-9 units' readiness, least of all Mac and Arrow. Jeff went on to say, "Those two are shaping into the very best I have to offer the United States Military, and that means no specialized K-9 unit in the world will outperform them. And you can take that to the bank." Jeff flashed a half-smile and said, "Wait until you see tomorrow's all-day training venue. I promise, it's going to put these gentlemen and their dogs to the test as well as impress you to see the amount of resources devoted to Colonel Edward's elite group."

In the predawn of the next morning, Jeff and I were driving toward the scrubby coast along the outer reaches of the expansive military base. We were part of a long caravan of commandos and equipment heading for a secret area. Our destination, Jeff told me, was the furthest training venue from the heart of the base for a reason. With that statement alone I was completely intrigued, not to mention that Jeff wouldn't divulge any other facts about the venue until we arrived. He did say that similar to the day before, the K-9 teams would be dressed in full combat clothing and accoutrements. They would also be firing many more SESAMS at this stage and integrating with multiple Six-Man-Elements rather than just one.

Daylight had just begun to break as the motorcade turned off of the main, paved road and onto a sandy Jeep trail. We rumbled over the primitive road and through the brush leaving all signs of civilization. After a good haul we came upon a large, rare, open area within the stunted, coastal vegetation. At the accessible ground the lead driver left the trail and led the caravan to park in the unobstructed sand. When all the vehicles came to a halt we had nearly formed a circle. Our parking pattern made me think of the pioneers who circled the wagons as a defensive maneuver in the American West.

Jeff could see the question on my face as I stepped into the sand looking at the untamed landscape. He exclaimed with some laughter, "Well Mr. Duffy, we are here!" To which I replied, "Where is here, pray tell? Besides the middle of nowhere, of course." With that, Kyle walked up to hand me a pair of binoculars and pointed southeast toward a narrow ravine.

It took a bit for me to bring the binoculars into clear enough focus to see anything but endless sand and scrub. As I stared into the small topographical opening at the end of the ravine, a man-made stone wall came into view. Just behind the wall I could make out a primitive dwelling that looked to be made out of mud bricks. I carefully steadied the binoculars and more details popped into focus. A second sand-colored structure came into view behind the wall. I saw smoke from a cooking fire, a trash barrel brimmed with garbage, and a line full of drying clothes blowing in the breeze. As I studied the distant scene, I watched a man come out from the closest structure and walk toward the trash barrel. Even though he was far away, I could clearly see that the man was dressed in a traditional peraham, tunban and waskat (the long top, baggy pants, and outer vest often worn by men in the Middle East). When he turned to leave the garbage container, the early morning light illumined an AK-47 assault rifle strapped to his back. In the dwelling farthest from view, I could make out the image of two women standing in the doorway. Both women were wearing a classic firaq partug (the upper dress-like garment and loose-fitting pants commonly worn by women from the Afghanistan/Pakistan region) with their chadors (head scarf) blowing about their faces.

Before I had a chance to lower the binoculars and comment, Jeff walked up close behind me and whispered, "Welcome to 'Little Afghanistan,' the next theater of operation for my K-9 teams." The obvious question that came to mind was who are those Afghani looking people? Jeff informed me that they were Middle Eastern role-players from various backgrounds that were hired by the United States Government to be themselves. Jeff went on to say, "During long stretches of weeks into months, these full-time role-players eat, sleep and fight in this reproduction village. Every minute aspect of this rural, Afghani, farm village is to spec. The height of the fortification, the dimensions of their interior rooms, the mud and straw roofs, the clothes that they wear, even the garbage spilling out of the trash barrel is identical to what our men will encounter when they deploy overseas. Within the village they have cached food, water, firearms, ammunition and explosive components just like our teams are likely to find 'in-country.' These role- players fight in Force-on-Force (gunfire against gunfire) training exercises routinely and they are exceptional combatants as a result. Of course, they are using simulation ammunition like we are, however, nobody likes getting tagged by those little devils, so these dudes fight for real. Gunny has known for a while that our commandos would be headed to Afghanistan, so he arranged to have us participate in this particular Force-on-Force exercise that Colonel Edward organized."

Jeff also told me that the role-players never know when a strike will be made against them so they keep "lookouts" posted twenty-four hours a day, no differently than they would in a real theater of war. Our wilderness camp, which was actually being set up as a F.O.B. (Forward Operating

Base), all made sense after Jeff enlightened me about the training stage. The plan for the day was to develop an overall invasion strategy for the multi-team task force, assign a K-9 team to each Six-Man-Element, have the teams gear up, and "hump in" to the target area from the F.O.B.

The Force-On-Force training exercise was intended to replicate a real combat situation as closely as is possible. Therefore, all four of Jeff's dogs would operate in a muzzle during the mission because there would be no bite-suit-wearing decoys planted within the multi-dwelling village. This meant that the K-9 handlers would deploy their muzzled canines like battering-rams to engage the enemy, knocking them to the ground and keeping them out of play with repeated, violent strikes. Once the village of five primitive structures was secured and all of the combatants had either been neutralized or taken prisoner, the dogs would have their muzzles removed and be used to search the dwellings and communal grounds for hidden explosives. While the commandos were gearing up, Jeff went over the muzzle protocol with his handlers. He stressed that although their "fighting" muzzles were well ventilated, they should not be put on the dogs until all of the teams were in position along the fortification and ready to penetrate. Jeff's concern over when to muzzle the dogs centered on adequate respiration and temperature control.Panting is an active dog's primary means of regulating body temperature on a hot, sunny day. However, a panting dog doesn't exchange heat nearly as efficiently as a perspiring human being does, especially if air-flow is somewhat restricted by a muzzle.
Jeff's general rule of thumb was,if the handlers felt uncomfortable in the summer sun, the dogs were already stressed under those same conditions and needed to be tended to. Add a muzzle to that equation and devastating heat exhaustion or deadly stroke would be just around the corner.

Jeff made it clear that morning to all involved, if the risk of over-heating became a problem, he wouldn't hesitate to disrupt the practice mission to pull his dogs. Days before the operation, Jeff conveyed to Gunny (the staunchest supporter of the K-9 program, and the man who set up the "Force- On-Force" opportunity) that he didn't like the idea of his dogs working in muzzles on hot sunny days. However, his K-9 teams desperately needed a real-life training scenario before they deployed overseas, so he was cautiously onboard. Although the K-9 commandos would not be muzzled during a midday raid in the Middle East, overheating, dehydration, and scorched feet were serious problems in that part of the world. Jeff intentionally used the day's venue to drive home heat awareness to his handlers. That day's training exercise had been designated a "daylight" mission for the purpose of evaluating tactical execution and to afford the commandos an opportunity to hone their stalking skills. Minutes before the teams were ready to hike toward the target, Gunny radioed for distracting helicopter activity to occur roughly a mile southeast of the village. Given that their F.O.B. was northwest of "Little Afghanistan," Gunny's plan was to create an area of interest (not threat) that would attract the attention of the enemy lookouts. This in turn would give the four separate Six-Man-Elements a better chance of strategically positioning themselves along the outer wall of the village without being detected.

The K-9 Team is purposefully positioned in the middle of the "Stack."

Jeff and I concealed ourselves at a high point near the end of the ravine (still a good distance from "Little Afghanistan") and we watched the raid unfold with binoculars. Gunny was advising onsite and evaluating the tactics of the four separate Elements. He was also maintaining radio contact with Jeff apprising him of the K-9 teams' performance. For me, observing the operation from afar was much like watching a football game. There were no lives on the line, but an element of stress accompanied the excitement of watching the home team aggress against the opposition. It was a much more serious experience for Jeff, however, because he knew that one day in the very near future lives would depend on how his K-9 teams implemented the skills that he had taught them.

As the multi-team strike force divided and covertly positioned themselves within a "stone's throw" of the stone wall, the helicopters came into sight on cue, a mile southeast of the village. Like clockwork, the Six-Man-Elements moved into their strategic positions along the wall. On Gunny's command, the first Element with Kyle and Bullet (a new Malinois to the program) formed into a "Stack" and entered a small breach on the north side of the wall. Mac and Arrow immediately followed through the same opening with their Element. Gunfire instantly broke out signaling the remaining two Elements to storm the village through a gate on the western portion of the fortification. In only minutes, the strike force had neutralized the enemy "lookouts" and trapped the remainder of the opposing force inside their dwellings.

Elements two and three locked down the communal grounds between the five structures by positioning men on the roof tops and strategic points on the ground. Element four formed a "Stack" outside of the largest mud-brick dwelling and called "Dog" (Mike and Jaeger) forward to the secured side of the small, main entrance. There were no cameras mounted on the dogs for this operation. That meant once Mike sent Jaeger in to search the dwelling, the "Hall Boss" would wait for sounds of engagement before storming in with his team.

True to the construction of habitations in rural Afghanistan, the dwellings within the village were relatively diminutive with numerous rooms, narrow halls, and occasionally false walls for ambush and caching.

After a quick check of Jaeger's protective vest and muzzle fit, Mike rubbed his warrior's shoulder as he disconnected the bungee leash. On the signal from the "Hall Boss," Mike whispered into Jaeger's ear, "Take 'em!" The K-9 commando shot into the dwelling like a missile, alone and fearless. Even though Jaeger had legitimate combat experience, he didn't treat the training exercise as a game. Mike reported to Jeff at the end of the day that the hair on Jaeger's neck was bristling when he bolted into the little doorway. Mike said, "Without question, he was out for blood! It seemed like only nanoseconds passed before we heard the undeniable sounds of a man and dog fight. Hysterical screams from a Middle Eastern man crashing into a table mixed with the guttural growls and barks of a muzzled animal sent chills up our spine as we charged in to finish what Jaeger began."

When gunshots rang out from the structure under siege, two armed adversaries jumped through a couple of rear windows and crouched along either side of a storage bin that was attached to the back of the dwelling. Operators from the second and third Elements, who were holding the communal courtyard, were unable to fire at the enemy lying in wait (due to the risk of striking commandos from Element Four who were on the other side of the frangible, mud-brick wall conducting their search). With little time available to protect Element Four from walking into a potential ambush at the rear windows, Gunny radioed the team leaders from Elements Two and Three and directed them to simultaneously deploy their dogs from lateral vantage points on the closest, designated combatant. To afford their canine teammates a tactical edge, the roof-top commandos held the attention of the hiding adversaries with random fire at benign targets within their proximity.

Gunny didn't realize to what degree he was putting Jeff's K-9 program to the test. Jeff and I watched as Mac launched the rookie, Arrow, from across a small courtyard at the partially concealed enemy. At exactly the same time, Trevor, the other handler, launched his experienced Malinois, Griff, from the opposite side of the yard. Jeff's visceral response, "Oh my," summed up what we were both thinking. If either dog was not precisely "zeroed in" on their designated human target, the two agitated, canine warriors could likely focus on each other resulting in a delayed attack (or in a worse case, engage each other out of misdirected hostility) and expose themselves to enemy fire. Although Jeff ran his K-9 teams through tandem deployment scenarios, seldom would two commando teams use their canines in such a challenging juxtaposition. Since Gunny and the team leaders were not educated in the nuances of dog behavior, they had no idea of the potential debacle that could have been the result of such a tactic.

Gunny, in particular, had enough faith in Jeff and the K-9 program that he seldom entertained any doubts about the ability of the four-legged commandos to fill their specialized niche. After all, from Colonel Edward on down, everyone connected to the task force program fully expected Jeff to produce the most elite K-9 teams the United States had ever seen. It was on Jeff's shoulders to figure out how to get the dogs to do what the commando teams required of them. According to the centuries old maxim, "The proof of the pudding is in the tasting," the Special Tactics Group recognized the Force-On-Force training exercise as an excellent, non-lethal opportunity to taste Jeff's pudding.

If there was any hesitation on the part of Arrow or Griff to slam into their assigned targets, it could not be seen from my and Jeff's vantage point. Arrow's opponent did have time to pull his weapon around but was not able to depress the trigger before the canine battering ram struck him shoulder high. When Griff's adversary caught sight of charging Arrow, he frantically tried to position his weapon over the top of the storage bin to fire a protective shot for his comrade. Consequently, Griff struck the unprepared man with full force from the blind side. The hard-hitting, canine missile jammed his muzzle squarely into the combatant's ribcage, causing the man to lose his breath. Most importantly by Jeff's assessment, neither dog let up on their quarry as their scuffle rolled into the courtyard where the four combatants nearly wound up on top of one another.

Each adversary lost control of his weapon as a result of the canine impact. This allowed Mac and Trevor, along with four other "shooters," to safely rush the enemy and take them into custody. Both handlers allowed their muzzled dogs to assist in keeping the enemy pinned to the ground while their hands were zip tied behind their backs. Due to weekly practice, as well as amplifying the muzzle fighting training that Jeff employed in his Police K-9 days, all of his war dogs were proficient at using their entire body to relentlessly knock their opponent off balance. Jeff made it clear to his handlers that there was no hurry in calling off the canine assistance. He advised, "Let your fighting machine keep the bad guy busy until they are no longer a threat."

Compared to the previous day's training stage, calling the muzzled Griff and Arrow off their quarry was made a little easier from the fact that they possessed no satisfying grip to give up like they had in the Bunker. Even so, it was no surprise for Mac that he had to supply some moderate training collar corrections to compel Arrow to walk away from the downed enemy. Being the more experienced dog, Griff disengaged with a strong verbal command and promptly returned to Trevor's left side, although still bristling from the brawl. As the four men and two dogs quickly evacuated the prisoners from the open communal ground, Mike, Jaeger and his team were exiting from their dwelling by way of the rear door and moving as a "stack" to clear an adjacent shelter.

Jeff and I were absorbed in the action around the largest structure when his radio keyed up. Kyle, with Element One, wanted to send Bullet through a high window by way of a human ramp. Kyle's team leader made the call to "stack up" and clear the dwelling closest to the front gate. This was the only structure with the tactical advantage of an upper level. It was actually Kyle's suggestion to deploy Bullet through the upper window at the same time the rest of the team stormed the front entrance. Before the team leader would run with the plan he wanted Gunny's approval. Gunny in turn radioed Jeff: "Franklin, 'Dog One' wants to deploy through the upper window of the forward most dwelling. What do you think?" With no thought, Jeff sent his confidence back across the radio, "Easy day, Gunny." Kyle required one of his teammates to act as a ramp by placing his forehead and forearms against the wall directly below the window, then backing his feet out to about a forty-degree angle. With a "go" signal from the "Hall boss," Kyle sent Bullet scrambling up the human ladder and into the window. The plan of creating havoc from above and havoc from below, thereby trapping the inhabitants in between, worked like a charm for Element One. No team members went down and no prisoners were taken from that search. All of the inhabitants that the "stack" encountered were hostile and resistant which resulted in their termination. Also, during the execution of the dwelling search, Bullet located an armed assassin hidden in a false-wall. Were it not for Bullet's strong alert, an ambush would have occurred in a rear hallway on the first floor, after the strike team felt the structure was already clear. A frightening thought for all of those in Element One. Training exercises like "Little Afghanistan" brought into clear perspective the true value of a well-trained canine commando.

When the last structure was cleared, and Gunny confirmed that all of the hostile inhabitants were either captured or terminated, the muzzles were removed from the four war dogs in order to prepare for explosives search. According to Jeff's recommendation, the team leaders allowed their K-9 handler the requisite time to transition their dog into a methodical mindset. Each dog required the necessary minutes to properly eliminate, rehydrate, and relax their mind with a little shade time. It's not uncommon for some working dogs that are exposed to a period of heat and stress to develop diarrhea. Those individuals would require a few extra moments for their system to cool down and return to normal. Griff happened to be one of those dogs. Unfortunately, the team leader for Element Four was known for his impatience. Less than ten minutes from clearing the last shelter, he called his K-9 team forward to begin a bomb sweep. When Trevor responded with "Not ready," the team leader confronted him with intensity and ordered the search to begin. With no hint of a backing down, Trevor stood nose to nose with the team leader and calmly responded, "When it comes to Griff, I take orders from Franklin! Franklin takes orders from Gunny, and Gunny answers directly to Colonel Edward. Make of that what you will, but Griff doesn't search until I say so."

Again, Jeff's radio keyed up: "Franklin, this is Gunny. Dog Four is bucking the team leader saying his canine isn't ready to sweep yet." Jeff hated to give Gunny grief of any kind, given his support of the K-9 program, however, he felt obligated to stand by his men. Jeff radioed back exactly what he tells his handlers throughout their instruction: "Gunny, I teach it this way, the handler is the canine expert for his Element, and he is solely responsible for the dog's well-being. Therefore, it's the handler who says the K-9 team is ready, and no one else." Gunny's respect for Jeff came through loud and clear in his concise response, "Roger that."

Jeff was aware that Trevor and Griff were not pushing the limits on a transition period. The friction was a result of a restive leader and not an unwilling handler. Over the years Jeff had averaged the time for transitioning out of excited combat and into meticulous, bomb searching. He calculated the time could vary from fifteen to thirty minutes, depending on the dog's personality and the handler's management skill. The first two handlers to give their team leaders a "thumbs up" was Mac and Mike. As Jeff had already mentioned, Arrow was one of the fastest transitioning dogs that he had ever worked with. The dogs had not quite taken a fifteen-minute break, yet Mac was already warming up Arrow with ball-reward games (catching, chasing and speaking for his round treasure). The moment each handler felt that their canine partner was more interested in the ball than anything else in the environment, it was "go time."

At their handlers' direction, Jaeger and Arrow began the careful search of the open communal grounds from opposite sides of the courtyard. Mike guided Jaeger around the exterior of the largest structure while Mac and Arrow worked around the outer wall. Moving toward the central courtyard, Jaeger stretched his nose high into the air and cast his head back and forth. Mike instantly recognized Jaeger working into odor, so he better positioned his companion on the downside of a prevailing breeze and gave Jaeger a full leash to cast into the wind. The scent detection dog used the breeze to his full advantage, bouncing from left to right as he made his way up the invisible scent cone. At first Jaeger's casting was a few body lengths to the left, followed by two to the right. As he hurriedly made his way into the wind, his movements reduced to a couple of steps to the right, then one to the left. By the time he had narrowed his casting to a single head sweep to the left and one to the right, all onlookers could see where the source of the odor must be. Jaeger approached a small inconspicuous water-well where he dropped heavily into a sit. Mike walked up to his companion, who was staring at a primitive pumping mechanism and tossed him the bouncing "paycheck." Mike told Jeff afterward that Jaeger's search and subsequent indication was so "textbook" that he could almost see the imperceptible odor, and he didn't need verification to justify the reward.

After marking the water-well, Mike and Jaeger continued their search of the courtyard only later to find out that the EOD (Explosive Ordinance Disposal) Technicians retrieved a bag of bomb components (charges, detonators, and fuses) from the narrow hole in the ground. The bag was suspended many feet down into the hole by fishing line that was anchored to the base of the pump which was thoroughly buried in soil. The EOD Technicians commented in their report that the bomb components were undetectable by human investigation.

While Mike and Mac were sweeping the outside area of the little village, Trevor and Kyle were directing their dogs through each dwelling one at a time. Searching one of the smaller structures inside the fortification, Griff hit pay dirt despite unintentional interference from his inexperienced handler.

Trevor stepped into the main room of the dwelling from the front entrance and directed Griff into a clockwise search pattern as Jeff had taught him to do. Jeff has always stressed the importance of a systematic search in order to minimize the possibility of overlooking a nook or cubby. Halfway around the room Griff broke from the pattern and followed his nose to the fireplace where a couple of dirty cooking pans were stacked. Trevor, stopping short of a correction, sternly called Griff back to pick up the search pattern where he'd left off. In short order the K-9 team reached the fire place where once again Griff demonstrated a change in behavior (which often precedes a target-odor indication) by slowing the search to a near halt. Being a new handler, Trevor quickly insisted that Griff pick up his pace and move on past the cooking pans, assuming the food remnants were the attraction rather than a distraction that the experienced dog was trying to work around. The team finished sweeping the shelter with no finds.

Standing at the front door ready to exit, Trevor was haunted by some words of wisdom from his mentor, Franklin. Trevor heard Jeff's advice as clearly as if they were standing next to each other, "If you're in doubt about a change in behavior, trust the dog who has been proven trustworthy." Griff had clearly earned his stripes with multiple finds over a couple of tours "in country," so Trevor felt that he ought to make one more pass around the main room before walking out. Coming up on the fireplace, Griff put on the brakes once more, but this time Trevor demonstrated patience and said nothing to his companion. With unbroken focus on the fireplace, Griff eased into a sit position as if he were mesmerized by a siren singing from the ash. Trevor called out for EOD, "We have a hit," then he tossed Griff his ball for what he hoped was a job well done.

Trevor was anxious as he watched the technicians examine the fireplace. He didn't want to be known as the handler who ruined a good bomb-dog by rewarding false indications. It only took moments for Trevor's fears to be alleviated. The technicians discovered a large cache of IED (Improvised Explosive Device) elements, including artillery shells and bags of potassium chlorate, buried under a hollow hearth in front of the fire pit. When the EOD tech complimented Trevor for the nice find, the rookie handler quipped back as he rubbed Griff's ears, "I appreciate the compliment dude, but all I did was get in the way of this 'scenting machine.' He insisted there was something special about the fireplace besides the food pans that I was hung up on."

The balance of the day was spent reenacting specific, engagement scenarios that Gunny and Jeff deemed necessary practice for combat orchestration. The operators were also able to trade positions and responsibilities, which gave each Six-Man-Element (including the K-9 teams) an opportunity to experience multiple facets of realistic conflict, "Afghanistan style." The role players proved to be enthusiastic, hard-working people who made the replica of the Middle Eastern village come to life. They brought a realistic fight to the theater of engagement and never complained about the stray marker round that connected with an unprotected body part. Jeff was very pleased with the role players selected as decoys for his dogs. At every encounter, they scrapped with the canine warriors until the handlers called them off. And no one knows better than Jeff and his handlers, who routinely decoy for each other's dog, how exhausting a muzzle fight can be (not to mention the discomfort from the bruises and scratches).

"Four wheeling" down the sandy, makeshift road away from the little village, I felt like a foreign correspondent leaving the Afghani war zone after a long day with the troops. The sun was setting when Jeff and I reached the paved road. We were both too tired for much idle talk, but after thanking him for the opportunity to hang out in his world for a while, he said, "I have one more surprise, if you can stay until tomorrow.

Jonas Bushman, one of our operators, is coming to the 'compound' to pick up a dog. Jonas was my first K-9 Commando handler to be deployed. He did two tours in Iraq with a dog, and I wanted Jonas to tell you his story in person. I promise it'll be worth your time."

Twelve

Dog Down

It was the first part of 2005 when Jonas Bushman joined Jeff's one-of-a-kind, K-9 program for commandos. He wasn't sure what to expect from the newly formed program except that it would involve special operations with dogs, and that's all he needed to know. A classic image of a Midwestern farm boy in both looks and background, Jonas was first exposed to the idea of police dogs back in his small hometown in Illinois. On one occasion at his rural high school, Jonas gave up his lunch period to watch a K-9 officer and his narcotics dog search endless rows of students' lockers for a reported drug stash. He has always been mesmerized by news videos of police dogs assisting with riot control and apprehensions. Jonas also holds on to the memory of good fortune and the feeling of invincibility that dogs brought him on his first tour of Iraq the previous year. On that deployment, he, along with his strike-force, moved "in country" on foot behind several Marine K-9 units that swept for bombs and ambush along the way. Jonas doesn't remember a time when he didn't feel a strong affinity for Canis familiaris. However, up until Jeff's program, Jonas had only really handled one dog, the family hound- mix that he loved and grew up with.

The very day that chatter around the Compound became serious about developing K-9 commandos, the twenty-four-year-old Jonas jumped into action. He tenaciously campaigned to everyone associated with the program about being one of the first handlers. Although he didn't have the resume for the task, Jonas possessed enough passion for dogs and the bold, new project that he convinced Jeff Franklin to take him on as his first student. In the opening class, Jonas made mention of his large stature and announced his preference for a substantial dog. Jeff conveyed to Jonas that successful handler/canine pairing was not a matter of looks or preference, but a matching of personalities. Much to Jeff's chagrin, Jonas responded with a relieved, "Good deal! Then I'm bound to get a large, robust dog to match my personality." Jeff simply shook his head at the insistence and said, "We'll have to wait and see what comes down the pike, I guess." Jeff realized in that inaugural handler's class, that the single-minded determination he admired in Jonas could also be his undoing as a dog-man if it weren't channeled correctly. Jeff had coached many professional handlers by the time he met Jonas. He knew that stubbornness wasn't always an asset when it came to working with dogs.

After days of traveling and testing dogs at police-canine breeding kennels, Jeff wound up with four that he thought were the right caliber for Colonel Edward's program. On the evening of Jeff's return, he saw a sizable silhouette standing in front of his covert, kennel headquarters as he parked the dog trailer under a security light. Before Jeff had a chance to step out of his truck, Jonas came walking out of the shadows to greet him; "Good to have you back Franklin. Gunny said that you'd probably roll in sometime tonight, so I decided to camp out over here and see if you needed any help unloading the dogs." Road-weary, Jeff didn't argue. Instead, he directed the enthusiastic Jonas to the right side of the trailer; "Your dog is in the middle box, by the way."

Peering into the trailer compartment, Jonas saw a broad, confident countenance looking back. The dog's dark eyes were so relaxed, it was hard to imagine him as a warrior. Jeff could almost read the new handler's mind: "Don't let his calm demeanor fool you; he's a bona fide 'man-stopper.' In fact, I can't believe he's not carrying on right now. Until this moment, his menacing growl has challenged every new face that's crossed his path, including mine!" Jonas felt like he knew this dog already. Later that night, he told his wife that Jeff had found his sidekick from a previous life.

Each of the dog compartments had a strip of tape above the gate which served as a nameplate. When Jonas noticed that his dog's tape was blank, he asked why. Jeff said that he bought him with an ill fitted name, and he hasn't thought of a new one yet. Without hesitation, Jonas offered: "I'd like to call him Cooper, if that's all right with you." Jeff had no objection, saying, "He kind of looks like a Cooper. Alright, let's unload Cooper and see if he meets your standards."

Cooper was a two-year-old half Belgian Malinois and half Czech shepherd. He had a football size head and was heavy boned for his breed cross. After several months on Franklin and company's Olympic regimen, Cooper's body weight topped out about eighty pounds. When the

Maliherd (Malinois/shepherd) poured out of the trailer, his feet hit the ground with a substantial thud. Cooper lowered his shoulders, raised his rump as high in the air as he could, and reached way out with his front feet at the same time. When Jonas laughed at his dog's cat-like antics, Cooper immediately turned the stretch onto his new handler by placing his front feet high on Jonas's chest and pressing in his nails. Quite content in that vertical position, Cooper surveyed his new surroundings while Jonas quietly stroked his companion's head. As far as Jonas was concerned, Cooper was tailor made for him. The next morning when Gunny asked what he thought of his new canine recruit, Jonas summed it up in one word, "Perfect."

The bond between Jonas and Cooper strengthened with each day of training. Even on his off days, Jonas would pick Cooper up from the kennel, just so they could spend leisure time together. Reflecting back on that early period of the program, Jeff said from the moment they were introduced, you rarely saw Jonas without Cooper. They were an exemplary K-9 team when they were working and best friends when they weren't.

Cooper couldn't have taken to commando training more readily. He was as comfortable in the heat of armed conflict as was Jonas. True to Jeff's early assessment, "man stopping" was Cooper's forte. He excelled at disabling hostile combatants. Nothing satisfied the warrior in that Maliherd more than a physical struggle with a human being. Cooper was ferocious with or without a muzzle. He gleaned as much pleasure from battering the enemy into submission as he did in mangling them. Cooper was also head and shoulders above the average dog when it came to scent work. Unlike a large percentage of working canines who must be conditioned to think through their nostrils, Cooper naturally defaulted to his olfactory system to solve problems. It wasn't possible for a decoy to hide high enough or deep enough to escape his nose. And when Cooper's mind was put on explosives he was relentless. A single blasting cap was sufficient to send him into a searching frenzy. The only weakness in Cooper's war-dog performance was his slow mental transition from bite work to explosives detection. Regardless of the redirection techniques that Jeff and Jonas applied, Cooper required a full forty-five minutes to disengage from an embattled mindset to a methodical search mode. Even after months of conditioning, Cooper needed twice the time required by the average dual-purpose canine (a police or military dog trained to both aggressively apprehend human subjects and locate specific target odors) to effectively shift his cognitive gears. Both Jeff and Jonas eventually resigned to accept Cooper as a slow transitioning operator, and they made it a policy to allow him the preparation time to balance his intense drives.

Being Jeff's lead handler and one of the initial K-9 commando teams deployed to the Iraq war- zone, Jonas had to haul a massive quantity of dog supplies with him on his first flight over. He had to oversee the loading and unloading of a small mountain of dog food (enough to last four dogs for six months plus an emergency supply). Jonas was responsible for two first aid trunks, which included I.V. saline bags for hydration; four complete sets of extra K-9 battle gear; two protective bite suits and explosives training aids; extra batteries and chargers for the remote collars and cameras; duplicates of pans, buckets and grooming equipment; additional leashes, longlines, training collars and tennis balls (for play and reward). With each successive trip over, the K-9 teams added or replaced necessary components to their remote Middle Eastern kennel. When it came to sheer volume, no subsequent supply trip compared to Jonas' maiden voyage.

"In country," Cooper wasn't housed in any kind of kennel. He bunked with Jonas inside an air conditioned, storage pod that had been converted into private quarters. After exhausting training or a stressful capture and kill mission in the intense heat, Jonas and Cooper would crawl into their dark, cold pod to crash. Cooper claimed his choice sleeping spot right up against the door. Even though Jonas encouraged Cooper to climb onto a spare cot that he had set up, he would only stay on the elevated bed as long as Jonas insisted. At first opportunity, Cooper would slip off of the cot and sprawl out against the door. Although frustrating at first, Jonas quickly grew accustomed to his guard dog blocking the door. When anything living approached Jonas' pod, a diabolical rumble would roll out from under the door, announcing to all, "Enter at your own risk." Within the first weeks of combat action in Iraq, Cooper developed a ferocious reputation. Subsequently, Jonas was afforded more privacy than the other commandos at base camp, and he was seldom bothered after retiring to quarters.

Daytime operations in Iraq were hell during the many hot months of the war. Jonas felt powerless trying to keep Cooper protected from the heat. At first, he followed protocol when preparing to launch a day-time mission. Jonas was adamant about Cooper wearing his heavy pro-tective vest, boots, and goggles. He also had Cooper carry a ration of water and a first aid kit in the two side pockets of his vest. But as the hot weeks raged on, Jonas began trimming Cooper's load. The first items eliminated were the water bottles and first aid kit. Then the goggles and boots came off. Jonas couldn't forget scenes from a previous tour in the Middle East where soldiers carried their dogs who were unable to walk because of blistered feet, so he kept Cooper's boots handy just to wear over the scorching surfaces they had to traverse in the hottest part of the day. Lastly, Jonas removed the cumbersome and stifling protective vest. He hated to take off Cooper's lifesaving, ballistic garment, but he felt that the heat was killing him anyway. Prior to particularly long, hot mis-sions when it wasn't possible to consume enough water, Jonas resorted to giving Cooper saline saddlebags (pouches of fluid formed by subcutane-ous injections just behind each shoulder) to help prevent dehydration.

On Jonas and Cooper's first nighttime mission in Iraq, they ran into an unexpected plague that would haunt them through nearly every Capture/Kill mission in the Middle East. Shortly after dark, Jonas' assault team set out from base camp in an IAV (Interim Armored Vehicle) Stryker. After two hours of "lights-out" driving, the assault team parked the Stryker approximately a mile from the target destination (a complex of dwellings). Setting out on foot, the Six-Man-Element, including Jonas and Cooper, planned to quietly hike the remaining distance under the cover of darkness. Unsure of the amount of armed resistance they would encounter at the complex, the Element was counting on stealth to give them the edge. During a covert operation of this nature, the commandos went to great lengths to ensure they would generate no noise or light as they crept into assault position. During mission preparation, "no rattle, clank or shine" was the team leader's cue for his men to tape over or take off any part of their gear that could possibly emit noise, light or reflection. Even their weapons were fit with noise suppressors in the event an early kill shot was necessary.

Whispering through their helmet "Coms" (Voice Activated Radios) and viewing hand signals through their "NVGs" (Night Vision Goggles), the Six-Man-Element carefully made their way to within a quarter mile of the target. Just about that time Jonas noticed Cooper becoming agitated as he sniffed the breeze wafting over his left shoulder. He passed along the observation to the team captain, telling him that Cooper seemed uneasy about something he was smelling in the air. After another cautious one hundred meters, Cooper began to bristle and vigorously cast his head from left to right deciphering all the information the tail wind was delivering. That's when Jonas gave his group a heads-up, "Gentlemen, Coop is definitely alerting on a threat approaching from behind." The team captain followed with, "Eyes and ears commandos, eyes and ears." As the complex came within sight, the fourth "Shooter" called out over the "Coms," "Movement at three-o-clock!" When the Element collapsed to the ground, the fifth "Shooter" echoed, "Movement at seven-o-clock!" More movement at ten-o-clock sent a gut-wrenching sense of "surrounded" over the men. As the commandos instinctively scrambled into a defensive formation the team leader blurted, "I see dogs!" They were everywhere, moving in from all directions. The assault team had inadvertently crossed paths with a pack of feral dogs. A ubiquitous nuisance in Iraq (numbering in the hundreds of thousands), the animals were being drawn in by Cooper's presence. The realization of being surrounded by a pack of mid-sized canines, rather than armed combatants, was somewhat relieving to the Element, except for the fact that the four-legged nuisances were becoming noisier as they closed in on their intruding cousin. The yips and barks were rapidly increasing as the seconds ticked by, posing real danger in exposing the commandos' position.

Initially, the men tried to shoo away the feral pack by charging towards them and throwing rocks, but the tenacious animals were not deterred from confronting the canine competition. As the ruckus escalated, Jonas spoke up, "We're not going to run off these indurate dogs like this. They're determined to get to Cooper!" With that comment, the team leader quickly ordered, "Shoot 'em!" When one of the commandos asked, "Are you serious?" The lead man demanded, "Now!" Under the circumstances, the men felt there were few other options. Even a successful retreat would have been challenging given the growing disturbance. With heavy hearts, the team carried out the order. In less than a minute the desert was once again deathly quiet.

Unfortunately for Jonas and company, that wasn't the last time they ran into feral dog trouble. In fact, pack interference proved to be so common that the commandos carried extra ammunition to deal with the problem on their covert missions. Neutralizing the canine pests never became easy for Jonas, because he was a dog-man at heart. If the truth be known, Jonas actually admired the wiliness and adaptability of the autonomous, Iraqi residents.

When Jonas and his Element reached the periphery of the complex, they surmised that only one, large dwelling inside the fortification was inhabited. Based on that information and the fact that the mission was targeting two specific al-Qaeda terrorists that may not be there, the strike team decided to quietly surround the two-story structure to offer the inhabitants an opportunity to surrender. After hearing the announcement, the occupants stirred into a noisy frenzy which triggered the team leader to offer a final chance to peacefully evacuate. During the few minutes the team waited for a surrender, "Dog" was directed to the rear entrance of the habitation to prepare for an assault. In the final moments before storming the structure, Jonas began to perspire profusely; his respiration cycled up, and his heart began to pound rapidly as it always did. This wasn't Jonas' first real raid so his pre-entry ritual was etched in stone: regulate breathing, check his M4 breach to make sure it was charged, jam the magazine to fully seat it, click the safety on and off, grip his P226 to check its placement, adjust his NVG straps, tighten his gloves, and regulate breathing again. Taking on the role of K-9 handler, Jonas expanded his preparation ritual to include his dog: tighten Coop's vest, adjust his goggles, tighten his boots, remove the leash, hold the harness and rub him down, then start the whole process over. Much like Jeff, Jonas was a "detail man," and he firmly believed that attention to the particulars kept him, and now his dog, alive.

Waiting for the "go" signal outside the doorway, Jonas noticed that Cooper was behaving strangely compared to the numerous Live Fire and Force-On-Force training exercises they had been through together. With his head dramatically canted to one side, Cooper's full vibrating attention was locked on the back door, and he refused to look back at his handler when Jonas spoke to him. Also, Cooper's stance was unusually rigid as he lurched toward the portal. Jonas noted that the most striking difference in his companion between that real-life situation and a training scenario was the absence of bristling. Cooper always bristled as Jonas prepped him to assault a structure, but not this time. As Jonas stroked his eighty-pound warrior while they waited, Cooper's mind remained calm even though his body hummed with anticipation. Jonas recounted, "If Coop could talk, he would've said, 'No bristling because I was born for tonight. I know the realness, and I'm obsessed with the hunt. I'm going to taste the enemy when I hear the screams this time.'"

Outside the Iraqi structure, Jonas considered Franklin's understanding that war-dogs intuitively know the difference between sparring and war. Even in their inaugural battle, they cannot be fooled into thinking that it is some kind of training exercise. By the same token, regardless of training scenarios, props and acting, Canis familiaris is far too savvy to be convinced that he is in the throes of genuine conflict when in actuality he is only practicing. Jonas also rationalized that Cooper's unusual behavior could have been the remnant effect of the feral dog incident and their mortality. Or, Cooper could have simply been responding to a psychological undercurrent of group tension experienced by the strike team over their precarious situation. Maybe, since Jonas and his companion were so closely bonded, Cooper was naturally reacting to his handler's physiological reactions to the combat environment. After much thought, Jonas concluded that Cooper's physical, mental, and emotional state at that threshold of his first, authentic fray was probably a product of all those palpable influences as well as his own potent canine instincts. Without knowing how his dog garnered the information, Jonas picked up on a sobering thought in Cooper's eyes that night, "This ain't no game."

Still holding onto Cooper's vest, Jonas saw a line of hysterical people file out of the entrance to the dwelling. Men, women, and children, holding their hands in the air and talking a "mile-a-minute" marched out into the courtyard like it was a practiced drill. One of the "shooters" in the Element acted as a translator/negotiator attempting to gather information about any other inhabitants or contraband. After passing around photos of the wanted terrorists and receiving no cooperation, the team leader directed "Dog" to "go." With one last pat on the ribs, Jonas carefully opened the back door then gave his companion a protective blessing and a command, "Take 'em!" Jonas immediately communicated, "'Dog' in!" The team leader responded over the "coms," "Lock and load, we're moving." With one of the team members left outside to guard those that surrendered, the remaining five members of the Element "stacked up" and cautiously entered the structure.

Entering the lower level, the team watched Cooper finish his first-level search and race to the upper floor. The "Stack" systematically cleared the ground floor while listening for engagement from Cooper above. Before the team had a chance to completely cover the lower level, Cooper flew down the steps to join them. He was drooling and looked almost frantic that he had possibly missed some concealed quarry. Satisfied that the first floor was safe, the team leader directed Jonas to send Cooper once again to the second level as the "Stack" followed. Finding no threat, after sweeping all the way to the flat roof, the lead man ordered the team to evacuate the structure.

While the negotiator interrogated the captives, Jonas and Cooper were assigned to search the habitation for explosives. So, Jonas led Cooper to the far side of the courtyard in hopes of quickly calming his companion's mind and generating interest in the ball reward. Right away, Jonas could tell that Cooper was more than just frustrated over missing the opportunity to brawl; he was beside himself for not receiving some kind of bite satisfaction for his effort, especially given his psychological buildup over the authentic circumstances. Jonas struggled for nearly thirty minutes to disengage his companion from a "Seek and Destroy" mindset. Still, Cooper persisted in keying on one of the boisterous captives, who was resisting the interrogator. Noticing his team leader's impatience, Jonas decided that he and Cooper had to make a run at sweeping the dwelling whether they were ready or not.

Being the first K-9 commando team to work with Colonel Edward's Special Tactics Group, Jonas attracted some skeptical looks from his teammates as he wrestled with Cooper's strong will to continue the human hunt. Jonas was humiliated over his inability to properly channel Cooper's energy. He felt the explosives search was quickly turning into a disaster, and he nearly apologized to his fellow operators for letting them down. However, Jonas kept his thoughts to himself and imagined Franklin was there to consult. Thinking of Jeff watching the "clown dance" between him and Cooper, Jonas laughed out loud as he imagined his instructor's comments, "What in the hell is all of this 'jackassery about?' Jerk a knot in that dog's tail and grab his attention!" With the image of Jeff still on his mind, Jonas belted out "heel" in an imposing tone that Cooper was definitely not accustomed to. The terse command coupled with a stiff collar correction as they passed by the yet distracting interrogation, effectively shocked Cooper into handler focus. By the time they had "heeled" to the front entrance, Jonas and Cooper resembled a synchronized K-9 unit once more.

Although attracting the feral dog pack and coming up empty in the terrorist search was not Cooper's fault, Jonas was secretly anxious over proving his companion's worth when he set up for the explosives sweep. Jonas was confident in Cooper's abilities because he had worked through many successful scenarios with his canine counterpart, but most of the Special Tactics Group had never seen Cooper in action. They were supporting the K-9 commando on faith, and so far on his inaugural mission, the four-legged operator hadn't contributed much.

All of Jonas' comrades watched as he gave Cooper a final pat before commanding him to "Find." With his first foot through the door, Cooper's nose was on fire, sniffing at high speed for what Jonas hoped were bombs or components. Working at the end of a six-foot leash, Cooper led Jonas in and out of two small, lower level rooms without a hint of an indication. Entering the main, living area on the ground floor Cooper seemed to be rushed as he sniffed in an undulating pattern along the walls. Jonas wasn't completely convinced that his dog was in a hurry for explosives. It was possible that Coop was still rushing after the elusive human target that he was supposed to have dismissed. Inwardly, Jonas was trying to convince himself that Cooper had made the appropriate mental shift. However, outwardly Jonas portrayed the highest confidence to his teammates as he encouraged his companion from behind.

Sniffing at a rate of one hundred and seventy breath cycles per minute, Cooper was scurrying past a substantial, open-faced wall-cabinet when his tail end dropped like a lead weight. Sitting at the front edge of the cabinet with his hocks pressed to the ground, Cooper's nose continued to move from side to side in an undulating pattern. The lead man and another team member, who was a bomb specialist, stared for a moment at the mostly empty cupboard then looked at Jonas. Praising his dog for the strong indication, Jonas glanced back at the two operators and said, "I know they look like empty shelves, but I'm callin' it a hit and movin' on because Coop is an honest detection dog."

Carefully investigating the cupboard, the bomb specialist found it to be built into the mud-brick wall and asked the lead man what he wanted to do. The team leader called out to Jonas as he and Cooper were making their way outside to finish the search, "'Dog!' How confident are you about the indication?" Jonas stopped and replied, "Either there was a wheelbarrow full of explosives stacked on those shelves not long ago, or there is something in that wall, because Cooper's change in behavior was unmistakable."

Jonas and Cooper swept the outer premises while the two men left on the inside worked to break the cabinet away from the wall. Once the exterior search was completed, Jonas rejoined his teammates inside in the desperate hope of finding at least some miniscule evidence of explosives. Thinking back on that day, Jonas remembered wanting validation for Cooper as much as anything in his life up to that point. However, he was not encouraged by the stoic postures of the team leader and bomb specialist peering into the wall cavity that was left from the cupboard removal. Looking over the shoulders of teammates, Jonas' face lit up when he spied a small, Russian-made arsenal that was tightly packed from floor to ceiling (three AK-47 assault rifles with stacks of 30 round magazines, two RPG-7 launchers with a box of HEAT [high explosive anti-tank) warheads, a belt-fed PKM sniper rifle with numerous 250 round box-magazines, and IED initiators/switches/fuel). The bomb specialist voiced what Jonas was thinking, "Dude, we owe Coop a steak or something.' I had no idea he could smell like that. We would've never found this stuff without Cooper. And now we have concrete evidence that this location and our two 'High Value' targets may be connected." The team leader added, "Congratulations 'Dog.' You not only proved that this place is a hideout for Sunni extremists, you also demonstrated that our Special Tactics Group has a new secret weapon, the K-9 Commando."

Feeling fully vindicated from skepticism after the colossal find, Jonas never again worried over Cooper's standing among his fellow commandos. In fact, as the weeks turned into months Cooper repeatedly demonstrated his abilities to perform like an operator. Mission upon mission, Coop located bombs and ferreted out assassins with precision. His ferocity in battle earned him a wide-spread reputation among the coalition troops. It was rare for Jonas to travel anywhere with his companion that someone wouldn't holler out, "Go get 'em Coop!" Jonas still laughs about his own anonymity while accompanying the canine celebrity. Cooper's ruthless manner in battle also earned him a high-dollar bounty offered by the dominating Islamic insurgency group of the area. From time to time, flyers with Cooper's telephoto would circulate among the local villagers offering a handsome amount for anyone who terminated the four-legged terror.

The commandos, who lived and fought beside Jonas and Cooper, became so dependent on them that they rarely considered an operation without the support of "Dog." For certain, everyone at base camp expected the K-9 Commando to always be in the mix of his human brothers. It didn't matter if it were a mission briefing, a cookout, or an Evac of a wounded comrade, Coop was there. By the conclusion of Jonas and Cooper's initial six-month tour, there was little doubt left in the minds of the Special Operations community that Jeff's K-9 warriors had become a permanent fixture in Colonel Edward's Elite Task Force.

After a brief respite back in the States, Jonas and Cooper shipped out for their second deployment to the Middle East. It was the height of the Iraq War when Jonas and Cooper, along with a second K-9 team, settled into base camp along the Turkey/Iraq border. Only a few weeks into this tour of duty, the two K-9 teams and the four Special Tactics Units that they supported (one K-9 unit per two Six-Man-Elements) were recruited for a multi-team strike-force. The commander of the operation had his sights set on a high-profile target that had been known for some time to be an al-Qaeda stronghold and a training camp for Mujahidin guerillas. Reliable intelligence described the mission's objective as a substantial complex of fortified structures that were heavily occupied by fully armed combatants and their families. At the operation's briefing, the commander expressed the goal of the mission as the dismantling of a terrorist production facility. He also psychologically prepared the multi-team, combat unit for a small-scale war and said, "Gentlemen, although we are relatively few in number, our job will be to pierce the virtual 'hornet's nest' and neutralize the enemy while sparing the civilians. Two Six- Man-Elements and one K-9 team (Alpha Force) will spearhead the assault from the north by way of separate breaching points and pass through the small village exiting by way of an existing southern gate. The remaining two Elements, along with their K-9 team, (Bravo Force) will hold at a rendezvous point established approximately two hundred yards north of the stronghold. When Alpha Force radios from the southern gate, Bravo Force will infiltrate through the northern breach points and join the assault as support."

The al-Qaeda stronghold was located far enough "in country" from the Coalition's Turkish base camp that a Forward Operating Base

(F.O.B.) was needed as a staging area for the assault. Twenty-four hours prior to the operation that was dubbed "Hornet," the F.O.B. sprang into life somewhere east of Dohuk in Northern Iraq. The raid on the guerilla complex was planned as a covert, nighttime mission, which meant that expeditious execution would be a priority in order to complete the strike under the protective cloak of darkness.

Efficiency was a priority, so two waves of attack were deemed necessary. Jonas and Cooper were assigned to Element One of the Alpha Force and labeled "Dog One." The plan was for Element One to enter the fortified village via a northwestern breach and clear the peripheral western structures as they pushed through the compound. Simultaneously, Element Two would breach the security wall in the northeast corner and sweep the eastern most dwellings as they fought their way through the village. Ultimately, each Element would reach the southern gate at which time Bravo Force would be signaled to begin their drive through the center of the complex.

The goal of the first attack was to soften the target by scattering and dividing the enemy while minimizing the chances of a multi-team, commando bottleneck. A meticulous "seek and destroy" action would begin with Bravo's follow up assault. Given the two-wave strategy, half of the commandos would have to painfully wait at the rendezvous point while their brothers-in-arms initially pierced the "hornet's nest" without them. One of the more stressful situations in a warrior's life is holding "on deck" while someone else confronts the enemy. Jonas called that the unlucky draw. So, he felt fortunate that he and Cooper would be some of the first to encounter the adversary that night.

As the sun dropped below the horizon on the designated evening of operation "Hornet," Jonas and Cooper made their routine pre-battle visits to all the commandos involved in the mission. Jonas liked the idea of re-familiarizing Cooper with the men that he would be fighting alongside. He thought at the time that it may not be necessary, but it certainly didn't hurt to reacquaint the scrappy canine warrior with some of the operators he hadn't seen in a while. Besides, Jonas knew that his commando brothers would be deeply disappointed if they didn't have a chance to pat their courageous mascot before engaging in such a high-risk assault.

Jonas was a favorite among Colonel Edward's men, partly because he was an exceptional caretaker for the most popular commando of the Special Tactics Group. Mostly Jonas was favored because he had demonstrated many times that he would go to great lengths to care for any one of his fellow commandos. Jonas had been known to drive all the way across town just to get a fish sandwich for the one teammate who didn't eat red meat like everyone else who wanted ribs. He was also adamant about never leaving one of his brothers alone to struggle on the obstacle course, even when it meant that his own allotted time would expire forcing a second run of the course. Although a big man himself, Jonas had little tolerance for bullying and more than once had stepped in to defend a smaller man. Within the Special Operations community, Jonas was known as one of the few who were good to the bone.

Darkness settled in fast as the commandos ran through their final equipment checks. After Jonas offered Cooper one last chance to eliminate and drink some water, they loaded into the Stryker with the other teammates of their Element. Despite the mortal challenge that lie ahead, spirits were high throughout the strike force as the armored caravan drove to the hike-in point. As usual, Cooper was humming with energy, especially since he was well rested and in peak condition from his recent leave back home in Virginia. The canine warrior had yet to see any real action since arriving in the Middle East for his second deployment. He was so excited to be on a nighttime mission that he virtually squirmed inside his skin and popped his jaws waiting to disembark the vehicle. Always amused by Cooper's aroused antics, Jonas couldn't keep from laughing as he massaged his companion's ears in an attempt to calm him. One of the commandos inside the Stryker commented on the K-9 team's apparent worry-free demeanor and said, "You guys are a great morale boost. Every time I go on a mission with the two of you I feel like everything is going to go as planned."

A relatively short drive from the F.O.B., the motorcade slowed to a stop. The men had reached their "hike in" point, and it was time to unload for the dark, silent, one-mile trek to the target. Marching side by side in two lines, each of the two columns was led by their designated Force leader. Scarcely three hundred yards from the vehicles, the ominous barks and howls of feral dogs could be heard closing in. Before an opportunity for discussion arose, Jonas passed along a suggestion over the "coms" to shoot any approaching dog within range. Unaware of Cooper's allure in regard to the orphaned canines, a percentage of the commandos (who had never fought alongside a K-9 team before) thought that Jonas' advice was harsh and disregarded his suggestion thinking the Iraqi pests would wander away on their own. As the men closed in on the guerilla complex and reached the designated rendezvous area, the feral pack not only failed to lose interest in the intruders, it increased in number. By the time the Force leaders acknowledged that the canine clamor was a problem, the disturbance had grown into a potential alarm for those inside the small fortified village. Although possibly too late, Alpha Leader issued an order to dispatch the dogs with their suppressed M4s. At this juncture, the commandos felt uneasy about their noisy entrance onto the scene, but the consensus among the men was that the assault should be executed as planned. So, without ceremony, Alpha Force marched for the al-Qaeda stronghold, leaving Bravo Force behind.

Upon reaching the outer wall of the complex, Jonas and his teammates assessed that the village was far busier than it should have been for that time of night. The hustle and bustle inside the dwellings virtually confirmed their concern over the feral dog announcement. Still, the unanimous vote was to strike as planned.

Preparing to breach the mud-brick wall, Alpha Force split into Element One, who would make entry at the northwest corner, and Element Two, who would enter from the northeast. Jonas and Cooper were the third and fourth commandos to pass through the small, self-made opening in the wall. Looming immediately in front of them were two substantial structures with an alley between them that led to more dwellings down the western perimeter of the village. Element Two entered the compound to find a similar arrangement along the eastern border. After both Elements completed their ritualistic equipment checks, they stalked to the rear entrance of their respective, first structure and braced for a synchronized assault. Arranged in "stacks" along the rear walls of the dwellings, twelve commandos waited for Team Leader One to say "go."

There would be no announcement to the inhabitants on this strike. This was a confirmed terrorist hideout and a known launching point for insurgents.

The goal for the task force was straight forward: neutralize all armed combatants and practice due diligence in sparing the innocent throughout the process. Jonas would not be instructed to send Coop into such a "hornet's nest" alone. He and his eager canine commando were securely tethered together until the enemy had been engaged. At that time, Jonas would decide when and how to best deploy his four-legged terror. Cooper wasn't seen by Jonas or any member of the Elite Task Force as simply a weapon. He had aspired to the moral status of personnel. Coop was one of the warriors and his wellbeing mattered. This meant that Jonas would give him the opportunity to fight when the odds for Cooper's success were at least level. Being armed with only his bite and speed, timing and darkness would be the great equalizer. Quickly destroying all illuminating devices inside the dwelling would be a top priority for the stealthy commandos, who were geared to fight in the dark.

When "go" rang through the waiting helmets, twelve men and one dog stormed into an AK-47 firestorm in two separate structures. Bullets rained down on their position from above, grazing vests and disintegrating the walls. The enemy had indeed been alerted by the discordant feral pack and had established an emplacement on the second level. With no time or place to take cover, the commandos unleashed their own M4 furry, taking down lights and guerillas. Once the guerillas had been backed off and the darkness returned, the commandos secured themselves only an instant to assess their situation. The team suffered no debilitating wounds, Cooper was sound, and the enemy no doubt had retreated to the flat rooftop to make a stand. Divide and conquer was the Team Leader's strategy, so he asked Jonas, "Can you, Coop and

Tony as an extra 'shooter' make an assault on the roof from inside, after four of us divide and attack from two points outside?" Jonas responded with confidence, "Cooper will rock their world, and we'll be right on his tail to see to it. When you guys engage from the outside we'll storm the roof."

The plan was set into action immediately, before guerilla reinforcements moved to their location. Events transpired in such rapid succession that night, Jonas recalls the entire conflict as a long, dark, blurred moment. Carefully creeping to the base of the crude steps that led to the second level and the roof, Jonas unleashed Cooper directing him to low-crawl at heel. Kneeling at the base of the steps, a flash of Jeff came across Jonas' mind, "I'm so glad Franklin pushes us so hard in training." Before the thought fully left his mind, Jonas and Tony heard gunfire erupt from the rooftop. It was time. Jonas gave Cooper a strong hug and said, "God will protect us, Coop. Take 'em!" Like a hound from hell, Cooper charged up the short flight of steps with Jonas and Tony firing over his back.

There were too many guerillas to easily count, and they were scattered in the darkness firing in all directions. Cooper leapt onto the roof and grabbed the closest combatant by the buttocks. While those two writhed on the deck, Jonas and Tony sprayed bullets from a low position in the stairway opening. A few of the guerillas fled the roof by way of a ladder to join the fight on the ground. Jonas called Cooper off of the downed adversary, and in the seconds it took for Jonas to fire two lethal rounds into the combatant, the canine commando had engaged another guerilla that was shooting from his knees at the commandos on the ground. Cooper clutched this man by the base of his neck in a death grip. Jonas and his teammates found themselves in the middle of a barrage when they began receiving gunfire from the structure across the alley. Their situation quickly deteriorated from bad to worse as the commandos fought in all directions. There was no time for worry or thought. There was only fighting, dumping empty magazines and more fighting. Jonas had to leave Cooper to battle on his own and hope that his animal-speed and the darkness would protect him.

Shooting at combatants on the adjacent roof, Jonas witnessed Cooper out of the corner of his eye slam into guerilla attempting to climb onto their rooftop. Calling out for his fearless companion to retreat from the edge of the roof, Jonas and Tony watched in slow horror as Cooper tumbled off the deck with the guerilla in his grip. Cooper was propelled into space by his own momentum, and Jonas was helpless to do anything about it.

Finally clearing their roof of the last combatant, the two men crawled under gunfire to the roof's edge and saw the lifeless Coop lying in the alley next to the dead enemy. Tony immediately called out over the radio, "Dog down! Dog down!" Jonas couldn't believe it. He wouldn't accept it. He hollered down to Cooper, "Don't move Coop! I'm comin'!" Racing to the aid of their comrades, who were battling for their very lives further down the alley, Jonas and Tony had to run past the inanimate canine warrior to engage the overwhelming enemy. Jonas remembers purposefully not looking down at his companion as he passed by. He said, "There wasn't a spare second to hesitate. My living brothers needed me and my M4 to survive the next minute. As I left Coop there in the alley, I whispered 'Don't move my friend. I'll be back to get you.'"

Listening to the raging battle back at the rendezvous point, Bravo Force had barely been able to contain themselves. When Tony's "Dog down" distress call came across their "coms," the commandos all thought it was Jonas who had been mortally wounded, and they had no intention to stand by while the best of them bled out on the battlefield. Instantly, Bravo Leader radioed back to base camp to get permission for an immediate attack. Transmission problems plagued Bravo Leader's communication attempts, which painfully delayed a supportive assault. Kevin, who was one of Jonas' close friends, stepped forward and declared, "No more waitin' for me. I'm going in." With Kevin's announcement, every commando, including Bravo Leader, charged his M4 and ran toward the stronghold.

Inside the village Elements One and Two gained enough control over the ground conflict to retreat safely to the first structures that they seized. Jonas led the way for his Element hoping to see his Cooper up hobbling around, but as he approached the first dwelling, his heart sank. Jonas could see through his goggles the lifeless body of his canine warrior still lying in the alley where he had left him. Slinging his M4 over his back, Jonas knelt down next to Cooper to check his respiration and pulse. Still intensely vibrating from the blazing conflict and unable to sense subtleties, Jonas wasn't certain, but he may have detected shallow breathing in his companion. When Jonas stood up with Cooper cradled in his arms, Tony patted his teammate on the shoulder and said, "I'm sorry, dude." Jonas wasn't of the mind to accept a gloomy fate for Cooper in that moment, so he told Tony, "I've got to get him to a medic. Can you do without me?" Tony responded just as he knew Jonas would for him, "Sure. Take off, we've got this covered."

It was only because of adrenaline that Jonas could run at all with the big dog in his arms. After Jonas passed through the wall headed for the rendezvous point, he could barely lift his legs, but he intended to get Cooper to the medic even if he had to crawl all the way to base camp. All but out of gas and barely able to hold onto his companion, Jonas saw his friend Kevin running towards him out of the dark. When the two men met, Jonas wanted to tell Kevin that he didn't think Cooper was dead, but Jonas was far too exhausted to speak. Kevin didn't need his friend to tell him anything; he slung his M4 over his back, grabbed Cooper out of Jonas' arms and took off running toward the rendezvous point where the Strykers were headed in high gear. Like the rest of the commandos in theater, when the armored vehicle drivers heard "Dog down" they also thought Jonas had been wounded. After listening to Bravo's radio attempts for an early assault, they decided to act on their own and drive toward the combat zone.

Before the first driver on the scene had a chance to park, he saw Kevin, who by this time was struggling with his armload, hobbling towards him. Racing out to pick up his fellow commandos, the driver was somewhat relieved to find out that Jonas was in one piece and headed that way, but seeing Cooper down was gut wrenching. Kevin laid Cooper in one of the backseats and the men sped toward Jonas and the village. Reaching Jonas, Kevin hopped out of the vehicle and encouraged his friend to jump in and get Cooper to the F.O.B. As Kevin charged toward the conflict, Jonas climbed into the back of the Stryker so he could hold onto Cooper during the rough ride to the medic. Jonas didn't have to encourage his teammate to hurry, the driver pushed the armored vehicle to its maximum over the undulating terrain.

The short drive to the F.O.B. seemed like a trip across the whole of Iraq to Jonas, who was clinging to his yet lifeless Coop. Radioing ahead, the medics met the Stryker with a stretcher as it pulled into camp. Helping to lift Cooper out of the vehicle, Jonas swore he heard his companion moan, he wanted desperately for one of the helpers to verify the claim, but no one could. Refusing to leave Cooper's side as the doctor began the examination, Jonas told him what had happened and kept assuring him that he felt Coop breathing on the ride, and he definitely heard a moan getting him out of the vehicle. The doctor was morbidly quiet as he closely examined the canine commando. Although not a veterinarian, he was more than capable of evaluating the vital signs and reaching a diagnosis. The doctor looked up at Jonas after his second meticulous pass over Cooper and said, "Your companion is tenuously clinging to life. There are no outward signs of extreme trauma, but he is definitely fighting off the effects of shock and possible internal injuries. So I suggest getting him to a veterinarian back at the Coalition base camp as quickly as possible." Jonas didn't have to be told twice. With no more than a "thanks," he snatched Cooper from the table and ran toward the Stryker. As Jonas was climbing into the vehicle with Cooper secured in his arms, the doctor hollered out at them, "Your dog is tough, he does appear to be stabilizing." With that tiny bit of good news, Jonas' eyes began to water as he smiled back at the doctor and nodded.

Having been advised of Cooper's situation, the veterinarian hospital was operational and fully staffed when Jonas arrived in the wee hours of morning. The medical team swarmed the Stryker as it rolled to a stop in front of the clinic. Taking Cooper from Jonas before he could step out of the vehicle, the veterinarian and his technicians launched into "around-the-clock" shock/concussion treatment for the canine warrior. The doctor briefed Jonas the next day, and summed up Cooper's condition as nothing short of miraculous. He told Jonas that he found no evidence of internal bleeding or organ damage, and X-rays turned up no broken bones. He went on to say that given Cooper's strong rebound from the shock and concussion in the first twenty-four hours, a full recovery should be expected with enough time allowed to heal from bruising. Not only did the four-legged commando completely regain his health after weeks of rehabilitation, he was able to finish his tour in Iraq with Jonas. Eventually, Cooper went on to work with another handler during his impressive war career.

I met Jonas at the "compound" on that last day of my summer visit with Jeff in 2007. The one-time K-9 handler had traveled a long way to pick up a dog from Jeff. Jonas had eagerly awaited weeks for that trip because he was picking up much more than a dog; he was reuniting with his loyal companion, Cooper.

Colonel Edward's Elite Task Force had a unique policy put in place when they formulated their Canine Commando Program. Unlike the majority of U. S. Military war-dogs who suffer from an unknown and often gloomy future beyond retirement, the very day one of Colonel Edward's dogs receive retirement status they are immediately adoptable by one of their commando handlers. Lucky for Jonas, given he and Cooper's strong bond, the initial handler to deploy with a dog has the first right of refusal before that right is passed along to the next commando in line.

Jeff called Jonas the very day Cooper received official retirement status, which was barely twenty-four hours before Jonas arrived at the "compound." He told Jeff that he knew that Coop's retirement had to be getting close, so he had a travel bag packed and ready to go. When Jonas walked into the kennel he grabbed Jeff by the shoulders and said, "What a good day Franklin. I've missed that animal as much as I've ever missed a human being." After a good bit of wrestling and ball-play, Jonas loaded Cooper into the cab of his truck, and both of them were looking out the window as he pulled away. Jonas didn't get three truck lengths across the parking lot before he hollered back, "Thanks for everything, Franklin! I mean that. I love this dog."

Thirteen

GLITCH AND THE GOAT PEN

A t 2300 on a mid-winter's night in 2007, Jeff was jarred from sleep by his vibrating pager. With the exception of a shower, he was never without the troublesome, digital companion next to his body. The pager and Jeff's immediate accessibility were part of his agreement with Colonel Edward. Jeff officially worked for and with the top-tier fighting force in the world. That meant when any member of the elite group had questions or concerns about one of Franklin's dogs or handlers, they wanted it addressed immediately. Jeff's location, the time of day, or any activity that he may be involved in were of no consideration when the group needed Franklin. His obligation to be available was laid out in no uncertain terms when he signed on with the task force. Jeff never outwardly complained about the pager, but he did grow to dread its signal.

It seemed to Jeff that the pager never alarmed him for uplifting reasons, like an accolade from the Colonel, or a group celebration over a K-9 commando mission well executed. When the dog program was running smoothly and the K-9 teams were performing flawlessly, Jeff's pager was quiet, which was the way he liked it. If and when the pager signaled, there was probably an issue relating to one of the K-9 teams, and Jeff was afforded only two acceptable responses to the digital alert according to Colonel Edward. He could either make his way to a secure room at the "compound" for an in-person meeting, which may include a "red phone" (designated for "high clearance" conversations only) conference, or he could call into the "compound" on a secured line and transfer to a "red phone" if necessary. With either option, Colonel Edward made one condition very clear, "now" was the common denominator.

On this particular winter's night, Jeff happened to be on a mountainous training excursion with four of his K-9 units in northern California when he was awakened by the ominous signal. As he sat up in his sleeping bag, clearing the fog from his head, Jeff nearly panicked over his situation. He was roughly twenty-eight hundred miles from the "compound," and there were obviously no secured lines near their mountain campsite. The only thing Jeff could think to do was call his "go to man," Gunnery Sgt. William Hawk ("Gunny"). Having only poor cell phone signal where they were camped, Jeff alerted his handlers to the "stat" situation and his need to find higher ground in order to reach Gunny. Without so much as taking a drink of water, Jeff cinched up his winter clothes, turned on his headlamp, and hiked out to the vehicle that was parked a thousand yards away at the trailhead.

Embedded with his teams on the western side of the Sierra Nevada, Jeff disconnected the dog trailer from his truck and drove to the nearest mountain pass heading east toward Nevada. Watching the rising values of the elevation signs along the highway, he kept checking the strength of his cell phone signal. Finally, as he crested the highest mountain range in the contiguous United States, Jeff determined that he had acquired enough signal to contact Gunny, who was probably at home somewhere in Virginia. Too impatient to look for a pull-off or legitimate parking area, Jeff eased his truck as far as he could onto the gravel shoulder and dialed up his friend. Much to Jeff's relief he made it through to Gunny on the first attempt. It was 2100 back in Virginia when Gunny answered:

"Franklin! I thought you were up in the Sierra Nevada Mountains somewhere training with your guys. What's going on?"

"You are correct, sir. I am in the mountains with my K-9 units, and unfortunately, I was just paged. Gunny, I have no clue what to do now. This was an urgent message and I am obviously nowhere near the "compound" or a secure line. Do you have any suggestions?"

"Hang on and let me think for a minute. Can you give me your location, a mile marker, or trailhead and GPS coordinates?"

After Jeff gave Gunny the necessary information, Gunny instructed him to go back to the trailhead and wait. Gunny said that he would contact the "compound" in regard to Jeff's situation and he would send a solution to meet Jeff. Having no idea what his friend had in mind, Jeff followed his instructions and headed back to the trailhead to wait. He fully trusted Gunny's influence, and spent a couple of cold hours hunkered down in the cab of his truck. True to his word, Gunny's assistance arrived as two headlights rolled up to Jeff's truck. A man dressed in plain clothes stepped out of the typical SUV and walked up to Jeff's truck and asked, "Franklin?" Jeff responded with an affirmative and presented his security-clearance identification. The man handed Jeff a satellite phone and said, "Here's a gift from Gunny."

Although Jeff had been immersed in the Special Forces community for years by that time, he was still astounded by the far-reaching network of the elite group and their capabilities. Colonel Edward's resources seemed to have no limits; in less than a few hours from his urgent page, Jeff was presented with a secured phone line on the fringe of a legitimate wilderness.

When Jeff called into the logistics office at the "compound," he was immediately transferred to the commander in charge of covert operations in Iraq. Flushed with anxiety, Jeff felt his heart-rate rise by the second as he waited for the connection. Speaking with the O.I.C. (Officer-In-Charge) of all the elite forces in the Middle East was very serious business. Usually Jeff was paged to council a handler, or evaluate a dog's performance after a mission. On occasion, he had to appease a team leader over K-9-unit protocols, but never had he been summoned to conference with the overall operations commander. For Jeff there was no getting around the feeling of dread. Something very grave must have gone down on the other side of the world, and he feared his dogs had something to do with it.

The commander was abrupt and to-the-point when he came on line: "Franklin, this is Lieutenant Colonel Westcott. You and I have a problem. One of my operators took a 7.62 round to the head because one of your dogs did not manage his designated adversary. This is the second glitch of this nature that my men have experienced in the past two months, possibly due to a modification in the enemies' behavioral response to the K-9 commando units. Regardless of the reasons why, it was the last mistake of this kind, I assure you! This morning I pulled all four of your canines from active duty. They are waiting for you at our Turkish Base of Operations. I want you to immediately terminate your training exercises in California, return to Virginia and arrange transportation to the Middle East. I want you here yesterday to deal with this complication. Am I clear, Franklin?" Jeff was quick to respond: "Absolutely, sir."

The Lt. Colonel went on with his instructions: "After you arrive at the Turkish base, you will meet with Gunnery Sergeant William Hawk and a squad of commandos under his command. Sergeant Hawk and his men will escort you 'in country' where you will observe the performance of the scrutinized K-9 units in person under real battle conditions. Also, upon returning from this Middle Eastern theater of war, I will expect you to brief me on any identifiable adjustments in the enemies' response to the canine teams. Our Task Force requires that you remedy the deficiency in canine functionality with one hundred percent assurance, or the K-9 Commando program will be terminated. I won't allow for any ambiguity here, Franklin. You have one opportunity to correct this glitch. Make the best of it." Again, Jeff was swift with his response: "Yes sir."

The Lt. Colonel curtly ended the conversation with a final comment: "Franklin, once across the border of Iraq you will be in hostile territory, and as an unarmed, civilian observer, Sergeant Hawk will be responsible for your safety. Report directly to me when you arrive at the base." With the commander's last word, Jeff's satellite transmission from the side of the mountain ended, and he was left sitting alone in the dark cab of his truck to mull over the heavy news.

Jeff was so disturbed by the troubling situation that he had no intention of waiting until morning to begin the long trip back to Virginia. Hiking into camp, Jeff immediately roused his handlers and told them that there had been a drastic change in plans handed to him directly from the "high brass." He informed his groggy headed men that they were getting an extra early start on the day and they needed to immediately exercise the dogs and pack up their gear. Jeff didn't tell his handlers exactly why they were hiking out to the trailhead in the dark. He simply said that a Lieutenant Colonel Westcott ordered them back to the "compound" and they were only given three days to get there. Jeff added, "That means we're going to drive in shifts while we eat and sleep on the road."

Forty-four hours after leaving the Sierra Nevada trail head, Jeff and his K-9 teams pulled into the fortified confines of the "compound." Although drained from the taxing, cross-country trip, the handlers dragged themselves out to the obstacle course and gave their dogs, who'd been cramped inside a trailer far too long, a vigorous and satisfying workout. As soon as the young men fed the dogs and secured them in the kennel, they were free for a little Rest and Relaxation because their temporary ordeal was over. Jeff Franklin, however, came home to an entirely different set of circumstances. As soon as he had unloaded the truck and trailer, he was on the phone making arrangements to fly to Turkey. Using a headset for his cell phone, Jeff planned his itinerary while he packed enough clothes and gear for a two week visit to the Middle East. It was evident to Jeff back on the mountainside that he wasn't going to experience any kind of relief from his intense schedule for some time to come.

The next afternoon Jeff was on a military transport plane headed to Frankfurt, Germany. In Frankfurt he connected with a Task Force flight crew who flew him into Turkey where he was picked up by another unit of commandos responsible for carrying him overland to the Base of Operations. By the time Jeff reached the base to meet with the commander that afternoon, he was physically and mentally numb from the exhausting seventeen-hour leg of his long journey. He had essentially been on the move since he left California four and a half days earlier and nine thousand miles ago. The only positive aspect of the trip that stands out in Jeff's memory was Gunny, who had already settled into the expansive camp and met with Lt. Colonel Westcott even before Jeff's arrival. During that brief period of stressed relations with the Special Tactics Group, Gunny never deserted Jeff, nor did he hesitate to intercede as an advocate on his friend's behalf. Jeff was never sure whether it was he or the dogs that attracted such loyalty from Gunny. But one thing is certain, were it not for the influence of this trusted insider, Jeff may not have been afforded the opportunities which ultimately led to the development of the indispensable, Canine Commando Program that the U. S. Military employs today.

After a hurried debriefing with the handler of the dog in question and Gunny, Jeff made his way across camp to the Lt. Colonel's quarters for the dreaded meeting. Stepping into the commander's virtual office, Jeff was confronted by the teammates of the operator who went down and the Lt. Colonel. Not surprisingly, all six men displayed depressed countenances and the only greeting Jeff received was "Franklin, take a seat," from the commander. The discussion opened with good news. The wounded commando was saved from the AK-47 death blow by his helmet and would return to duty. Jeff was relieved to hear that his comrade was alive and well and he was fully prepared to accept any admonishments that followed.

Once Lt. Colonel Westcott wholly expressed his disappointment over the canine commando's performance, he turned the meeting over to the team leader to describe the mission's details and the particulars surrounding the dog's engagement of the enemy.

The strike team was executing a daylight "Seek and Destroy" procedure in a multi-room structure that was occupied by a small band of armed terrorists. The combatants had been fiercely fighting allied troops from the sizable stronghold for days and were well ensconced. Upon entering the dwelling, the team was faced with a hallway having rooms staggered on either side. Ulysses, the dog in question for the Six-Man-Element, was deployed from the third position in the "stack" as was customary. On the team leader's signal, the handler directed Ulysses to search the nearest room on the right. Quickly in and out of that space, Ulysses was sent to the next compartment on the left where he engaged in what was determined by the waiting "stack" as a light scuffle. Hearing Ulysses' engagement the team launched into sweeping action; the leader and the second operator stalked toward the first room on the right which allowed the handler and the fourth operator to follow Ulysses into his space. The last two commandos were left to search the next cubicle in line, up the hall.

Heavy gunfire erupted from the far end of the hall before the men had a chance to clear any of the rooms. Returning fire, the team was forced to duck into their prospective rooms for cover. As the handler and his teammate jumped into Ulysses' room they witnessed the canine commando release his bite on the motionless adversary (who was lying prone on the floor) and eagerly trot towards the door in hopes of a livelier engagement.

Consumed with the battle in the hallway, and the barrage of bullets exploding through the walls, the handler and his comrade counted on Ulysses like they counted on each other. All three commandos were trained and expected to carry out their duty to fruition. That meant never walking away from an enabled combatant which greatly increases the risk of mortal danger.

With a glance toward Ulysses to command him to "down," the handler saw the not so immobile guerilla sit upright and point an AK-47 at his teammate's head. Turning his M4 on the enemy, the handler shouted a warning to his partner when both his and the combatant's weapons discharged simultaneously. The fourth operator's head bounced off the wall as the guerilla slumped into a lifeless form on the floor.

Simply recounting the incident raised the team leader's ire, so he went on to say that a very similar premature disengagement occurred with another K-9 unit on a different team about four weeks prior. He directed his stare at Jeff and said, "That's two too many mistakes, Franklin. Our group doesn't allow for any. So, if you can fix this issue, you're going to have to prove to us that we can trust your dogs again. Because right now we don't." The Lt. Colonel added, "Until the K-9 program gets a 'green light' from me, the dogs are restricted from any 'man' work outside of your assessment. Understood?"

Always a Marine at heart, Jeff looked each speaker in the eyes as he intently listened to every critical word directed at him. He offered no excuses when he gave the commander the only acceptable response, "Yes sir." The Lt. Colonel concluded the meeting with two questions; "Franklin, can you get on top of this glitch? If so, how long?" By this time Jeff was standing, and purposely facing the inculpating team leader when he answered the questions; "You will have new dogs by the next round of deployments which is in four months. Count on it." After the commander nodded with approval, he reminded Jeff that he had a predawn commitment on the parade ground the next morning. Gunnery Sgt. Hawks and a squad of commandos, along with two K-9 units, would assemble with Jeff there, then escort him to an actual target site to observe canine functionality and enemy comportment during the execution of a real mission.

Jeff began addressing the problem no sooner than he walked out of the commander's provisional office. His first piece of business was to grill all four handlers at the Operations Base Camp about their dogs' mindsets. Then the K-9 units would be subjected to bite-scenario training where the prospect of an enemies' "opossum maneuver" could be explored more deeply. One thing Jeff was sure of, Ulysses didn't lack courage or prey drive, and he fully expected him to be the decoy's strongest opponent of the day. Ulysses was actually credited in an After Action Report (A.A.R.) with one of the few solo kills of the K-9 Commando program at that time. The report outlined in considerable detail the eye witness account of Ulysses being sent by his handler to neutralize a shooting, al-Qaeda terrorist positioned beneath an armored truck.

Ulysses, along with his handler, and two other operators were pinned down by steady enemy gunfire coming from two separate locations. A well concealed guerilla sniper fired at the team from a rooftop which forced the commandos to crawl through the rubble of a recently leveled structure toward an open courtyard that was controlled by the combatant firing from underneath a truck. At the handler's suggestion, the commando team agreed to send Ulysses to attack the guerilla under the truck as the operators opened fire on both sniper positions simultaneously. Clearly, Ulysses would be at high risk of mortality running across the open courtyard under heavy gunfire to engage a mostly concealed adversary. Unfortunately, the commandos were in a desperate situation, and they were not only counting on Ulysses to visually identify the well-hidden assassin and make the exposed dash across the courtyard, but they needed their canine counterpart to disable the enemy without their backup.

From a prone position, Ulysses' handler carefully directed the canine warrior to focus on the only visible part of the assassin, the slight barrel movements of his AK-47. When the handler felt confident that Ulysses was zeroed in on the appropriate target, he revved up his animal-missile with strokes of praise and alerted the teammates that all was ready. On "go" from the lead shooter, the commandos attempted to knock the snipers back on their heels with streams of 5.56mm rounds from their modified M4s as the handler sent Ulysses to "Take 'em" amid the rain of bullets. In an attempt to protect his dog, the handler furiously fired over Ulysses' back, doing his best to keep the concealed enemy's AK-47 quiet during the charge. Ulysses crossed the open courtyard with Olympic speed and dove under the truck like a torpedo to seize the guerilla by his neck in a death-grip.

Confirming that Ulysses had made contact, the commandos coordinated cover fire as they ran across the courtyard to a structure beyond the armored truck. Passing by Ulysses, the handler called for his companion to release the neck-bite of the blood-soaked adversary who had been partially dragged out from under the vehicle. As the commandos hunkered down inside the structure, the handler inspected his dog from head to tail, looking for an injury. The entire front half of Ulysses was covered with a muddy mix of blood and dirt, but there was no wound to be found on the panting warrior. Looking at the amount of blood smeared on Ulysses and the spreading, red stain underneath the lifeless guerilla, the commandos surmised that Ulysses' neck grip must have severed either the assassin's carotid artery or jugular vein. As a direct result of Ulysses' superior effort, the commandos were liberated from a potential death-trap.

Could this be the same dog that let his teammates down so terribly? If so, why? And is there some truth to an enemy strategy of "playing opossum" during a dog attack? Those questions Jeff intended to answer before he left the Middle East.

Jeff spent much of the day talking with his four handlers at the camp, especially the two that were traveling "in country" with him the next morning. Each handler took his turn to describe the execution and result of their last mission in great detail. Jeff followed each description with pointed questions about any noticeable hesitations in their dog's initial contact with a combatant, or any measureable differences in their dog's response due to environmental conditions. Jeff also explored the possibility of the dogs developing premature bite-releases due to some type of battle fatigue or a rush to engage multiple targets. After a few hours of discussions and working through bite scenarios with decoys in full Middle Eastern costume, Jeff noticed an ugly behavior-pattern immerge.

Throughout the afternoon, all four of his K-9 teams were expeditious in locating the enemy, regardless of how high, low, buried, or quiet the hiding place.

During the bite tests, every dog ferociously encountered both hostile and passive adversaries. As the men expected, all of the canine commandos demonstrated tenacity during extended physical battles, and released their hold on the prey with acceptable variances of reluctance when commanded by the handler. The dogs also scored high under close-quarter, weapon discharges and strikes to their body with no inclination to retreat. In fact, the more violent the foe became, the stronger the dogs responded. Jeff did pick up on one troubling tendency during the canine fighting exercises though. When engaging a lifeless appearing opponent, Jeff detected a measureable loss of target-interest in his dogs after only a brief period of contact.

To further explore the problem, Jeff had his handlers repeatedly send their canine counterparts to attack a lifeless combatant under multifarious conditions. Initially the dogs worked frantically to arouse the sleeping foe with fierce bites and scratches. However, if the decoy (following Jeff's direction) endured the probing teeth and claws for a few agonizing moments without responding, the four-legged warriors would invariably seek out more satisfying action elsewhere. He wanted to attribute their letup in concentration to the effects of the extended training sessions that afternoon, or possibly being somewhat out of condition. But deep in his dog trainer's psyche, Jeff knew that the propensity for his canine commandos to prematurely release their debilitating grip of a non-reactive enemy had to come from either a lack of instruction or a shortfall in the dogs' fighting character. Either way, the glitch was real, and it was his to fix.

In order to execute an "opossum" tactic with Jeff's highly driven and easily stimulated combat dogs, a victim needed to withstand a flesh-tearing thrashing for a few long, gruesome moments without reacting. To achieve total non-responsiveness to the attacking dogs during the training exercises, Jeff's mute decoy (dressed in a bite-protection suit) had to maintain physical rigidity and steely mental focus while ignoring the canine's bruising bites. To Jeff and his men, the possibility of an al-Qaeda guerilla summonsing the fortitude to accomplish that same task in a true conflict without the aid of a body-preserving protection suit seemed inhuman and highly unlikely. Yet, after a full day of experimentation and evaluation, it was looking more and more like the enemy was adopting this lurid, self-sacrificing tactic in order to nullify the effectiveness of the canine commando as a fighting machine.

Conditioning canines to vigorously attack a passive decoy is common practice within the disciplines of war and police dog training. Almost without exception, a strategy of "playing dead" for the purpose of ambush is unsuccessful due to an assailant's inability to resist the shocking, initial impact of a trained combat dog. Jeff made sure that Colonel Edward'selite canines, including Ulysses, excelled in this area. He even went as far as to have non-reactive decoys explosively attack any dog who attempted to walk away from a boring encounter. This ploy fostered a desirable distrust in the commando dogs for all sleeping prey. Jeff felt certain that the glitch that nearly caused the death of one of the operators was not a product of a weak attack or poor focus on his dog's part. It was possible that the combatant in this situation sustained unresponsiveness longer than any of Jeff's dogs had ever experienced, especially given the After-Action Report (A.A.R.) presented by the Strike Force. Considering the recent assessment of his four K-9 teams, along with the fact that not one of his dogs had failed to aggressively engage a targeted enemy in two and a half years of battle testing, Jeff came to the conclusion that Ulysses prematurely released his bite on an adversary that he had tenaciously probed and determined to be dead or "out of play," rather than just lying still.

Regardless of whether the "opossum" tactic was a new strategy employed by the enemy or not, Jeff knew that in order to keep the elite K-9 program alive, one way or another he would have to extinguish the commando dogs' habit of prematurely releasing an unresponsive combatant. There would be nothing easy about that task. Jeff would have to push his dogs to the limit of their instinctive fight-drive, and compel them to maul an opponent who gives nothing back in the way of brawling satisfaction. Since trained war/police dogs do not reap the reward of a freshly killed meal after a ferocious battle like their wild cousins do, their incentive to fight comes from the inherent satisfaction of dominating a foe and the natural titillation of physical combat itself (assuming a dog is strongly predisposed to hunting, fighting, and killing from generations of selective breeding to that end). If the thrill of domination and physicality is removed from a struggle, there is no incentive left to keep a combat dog engaged with an adversary for any extended period of time. This conundrum, however, would have to wait until Jeff returned from traveling "in country." There he intended to observe his K-9 units functioning in an active war-zone and hopefully gain additional insight into the problem.

Despite being bone tired, Jeff didn't sleep well that night. Anxious thoughts of his dogs' performance during the upcoming mission made relaxing impossible. He roused early the next morning, dressed, and packed his gear bag well before dawn and the rendezvous time with Gunny.

That mission was the first opportunity for Jeff to see his friend in action. Although the two had spent quite a bit of time together, Gunny traditionally acted as a facilitator or supporter for the K-9 program, and he tended to take a back seat to Jeff. For this operation, however, Gunny would be the senior enlisted man and therefore the team leader, as he usually was out in the field.

In his forties, Gunny was old for an operator. In fact, he was the oldest active commando within Colonel Edward's elite group. That being said, Gunny was the polar opposite of washed-up or worn-out. He considered himself, like those around him did, as being in his "special operations" prime. Tall and powerful, he seldom encountered his physical match. Even so, Gunny never rested on his laurels. He spent more time in the gym and on the P.T. course than any man he worked with. From two decades of covert operations, Gunny had accumulated more combat experience than most of his superiors combined. He was proficient with all the small arms and special weapons that the commandos employed, including land and sea craft. Gunny was cool, confident, and savvy like an authentic hero. He was a quintessential warrior, and everyone respected him for that.

Jeff was well aware of Gunny's reputation, so he felt little trepidation following his friend into a hot combat-zone, unarmed. Besides, Jeff had enough to worry about with his troubled K-9 program. He was more than willing to allow Gunny the responsibility of group safety while they were "in country."

Gunny assembled a "strike force" that consisted of five shooters other than himself, the two K-9 units, and Jeff. The group traveled south out of the Turkish Base of Operations in two Strykers with enough provisions for a few days. Their designated target site was a cluster of dwellings north of Mosul, Iraq that were identified as a staging area for local insurgents. Considered a low-profile mission, Gunny and his men were expecting armed, but light resistance from a small band of guerillas. This operation represented a classic situation where the K-9 units would assist in clearing the structures of combatants and explosives, precisely the activity that the Lt. Colonel wanted Jeff to witness.

Daylight found Jeff and the commando team rolling through the parched countryside of northern Iraq. Since landing in Turkey, Jeff had waves of emotions washing over him as he remembered his tour in Desert Storm as a Marine Tanker. He had not been to that part of the world since he left the war zone seventeen years ago. Back then he was an armed warrior on the front line of battle. On this trip, however, he was assigned an inferior position as a civilian and observer. The current mission was a distinctly different role for Jeff.

En route and not quite halfway to their destination, Gunny received a radio transmission from Base Camp warning of extensive enemy movement due south at an upcoming crossroads. The Strike Force was advised to take cover at an abandoned compound that was situated off the road a short distance from the busy intersection. There they would wait for the "all clear" before proceeding to their target location.

Jeff remembers driving up to the central portion of the compound and thinking it resembled the ruins of an old monastery that had been converted into bucolic living quarters. There were even a couple of live-stock pens containing a number of goats precariously built into the partially walled structure. A few hundred yards southwest of the central ruins was a tall multistory building that was curiously standing alone at what would be considered the periphery of the complex that also contained a few mudbrick outbuildings. The expansive, open acreage surrounding the structures terminated in a scrub zone that formed a distant perimeter in all directions except the broad corridor that led back to the main road. Scattered among the sparse brush and trees at the purview were a dozen or more dilapidated dwellings that appeared to be uninhabited.

Unanimously, the team decided to conceal the two Strykers by parking them inside the courtyard of the central structure next to the goat pens. Gunny assigned guard duty immediately for the three corners of the deteriorated dwelling. Jeff also suggested having the K-9 teams posted along the westerly edge of the ruins where they would be away from the agitated livestock and facing the breeze that may carry an early warning of intruders. The men settled in around the quieting goats, and they prepared to wait out the afternoon thinking that it would be close to evening before the enemy movement at the crossroads would sufficiently subside to allow them to proceed with their mission.

Outside of an undercurrent of anxiety over the return of the resident herders and the pungent animal odor that filled the air, the first couple hours at the impromptu shelter passed pleasantly. Peace didn't last long, however; the lazy afternoon changed abruptly when Gunny's radio keyed up again. An urgent message from Base warned of a shift in enemy movement towards the team's encampment. By the time of the radio transmission, the main road had already become busy with mobilizing guerillas. Gunny and the group were advised to hold fast within their cover and evacuate the area at their first opportunity, which was likely to be nightfall. Very shortly after the communication from Base Camp, Ulysses' handler called out: "Franklin!" Jeff made his way over to his two handlers and saw both dogs standing erect with their front feet on the short wall. Their ears were prick straight, and their noses were pointing rigidly into the prevailing westerly breeze. The message transmitted by the dogs' alert postures was easy for Jeff to read. As he and Gunny approached the two canine sentries their whining confirmed what Jeff was thinking out loud: "Crap! We have 'incoming,' and the dogs are screaming that they're on foot." Gunny gave an overt sniff after Jeff's comment, then calmly announced; "Well, it looks like we need to prepare for a gunfight, huh, gentlemen?"

Minutes after the canine alert, one of the commandos positioned as a guard on the south corner confirmed a visual of numerous insurgents slowly occupying the tall building at the southwestern edge of the compound. With that sighting the stress level instantly spiked for the Strike Force even though they were still undetected for the moment. They all knew it was only a short matter of time before they would be exposed and chaos would ensue.

Gunny was on the radio informing Base Camp of their situation when another commando spotted more guerillas carefully investigating the dwellings among the outlying scrub. Jeff noticed no negative reactions from the operators with that announcement even though each man was well aware that the main road behind them was alive with mobilized guerilla units, the brushy perimeter was crawling with insurgents, and the compound's tower was filling with the enemy. In less than an hour the Strike Forces' circumstances escalated from serious to critical. Surrounded, is the way Gunny described their condition over the radio.

Outfitted with only small arms, the commando team dispensed their stores of ammunition, tightened the straps on their ballistic gear, and took up defensive positions as they prepared for the fight of their lives. Jeff was also issued a helmet with goggles and a protective vest for this mission. Once he secured his equipment, he took it upon himself to care for the dogs so that the two handlers would be unfettered with that worry. Jeff fitted the dogs with their vests, boots, and goggles, then heeled them in tandem over to the Strykers. Until the adversary overran the crumbling ramparts, Ulysses and his counterpart would have no role to fill in this battle. Being unarmed except for his tactical fighting-knife, neither would Jeff, for that matter. This conflict was sizing up to be a medium-range gunfight, and unless it reduced to close quarters, all Jeff and his dogs could do was lay low.

Jeff directed the two canines to crawl under the Strykers and "down-stay." That was as close as he could get them to protective cover. Gunny called the group to huddle-up against the goat pens near the center of their fortification. For Jeff this was a poignant repeat of Sarge's rally just before the opening "charge" of Desert Storm that he has never forgotten. Gunny cautioned his men to steady their nerves when the first hair-raising screams sounded from the enemy. He went on to say, "Their hysterical execrating will be as wild and ineffective as their aim, but they will be coming at us from all directions so it will seem much worse than it is." Jeff was secretly thinking it couldn't get worse than it was, and being unarmed made the situation all the more unnerving for him. He repeatedly told himself that although the similarities were very frightening, he and his comrades were not the Texans at the Alamo and they would create a different outcome.

Gunny assured the commandos that even though they had limited personnel, limited ammunition, and limited mobility, they would certainly win the day if they'd adhere to only three requirements: steady nerves, low center of gravity, and accuracy. Gunny's prep talk was acridly truncated by frenetic shouts from the tall structure. Their position had been compromised. It was on! Yelling and AK-47 gunfire spread like wildfire around the complex periphery. The operators crawled to their designated positions and began doing what they say they do best: "Taking it to the enemy." Jeff snaked his way over to the Strykers to soothe the canine warriors, who like him, chomped at the bit to engage the "bad guys." But, for the moment there was nothing the three of them could do except keep low while the 7.62 rounds rained down on them like hail from a copious storm.

From his cover position Jeff admired Gunny as the seasoned combat veteran cared for his team. He made a continual, circuitous route to pat each man on the shoulder and check on his status while he simultaneously talked on the radio. Jeff witnessed the truth in one of the first acclaims he'd ever heard about the team leader: "When you fight on Gunny's team, you never fight alone."

Before Gunny came to Jeff in his circuit, a PKM (Russian 50 caliber machinegun) opened up from the rooftop of the tall building. The heavy sniper-fire wreaked havoc on the commandos' ancient fortress, allowing insurgents to spill out from the tall building like termites and take up offensive positions. The 50 caliber rounds easily burst through the double and triple layers of the mudbrick walls, blowing goats to smithereens and punching holes in the Strykers.

By the time Gunny made it over to the Strykers, the Ak-47 fire had doubled, adding more misery to the existing barrage and sniper fire. Every commando was shooting to full capacity and the Strike Force was barely able to stave off their own massacre. When Gunny reached Jeff, he leaned against one of the vehicles and coolly asked: "How are our dogs doing?" Jeff remembers what a calming effect Gunny's presence had on him and the dogs alike. Jeff recalled: "I couldn't tell by Gunny's demeanor that bullets were ripping through our structure from every possible direction and we were only moments away from annihilation."

Gunny dropped a duffle in front of Jeff and said: "Franklin, I brought this bag along for a moment just like this. You are no longer a civilian. You are a Marine, and I never met a Marine who wasn't a sharp-shooter. I need you to buy me some time. Use the M4 in that duffle and keep that 'son- of-a-bitchin' PKM pinned down. Can you do that for your ole friend?" As Jeff crawled out from under the Stryker with a half-smile across his face, he answered Gunny: "Damn skippy! That sniper is going to have to work for it now." Gunny slapped Jeff on the shoulder as he quipped: "That's what I'm talkin' about!" Jeff reached in for the M4 and charged it before he pulled it out of the bag. He was trembling with energy to get in the fight. Slinging the duffle bag full of rifle magazines over his shoulder, Jeff called for his two dogs to join him at "heel" as they positioned themselves along the southern wall. He told Gunny that if this was his day to "check out," he was going with his dogs.

Jeff's suppressing fire quieted the sniper instantly. Having a man devoted to stifling the machinegun lightened the mood of the entire Strike Force. Jeff remembers his own gloomy feelings of dread that he'd been carrying since the gun battle began vanishing the very moment he joined the other men in the fight. Taking a successful attack to the sniper even caused Jeff to think that maybe they wouldn't die that day after all. However, the air of confidence was short lived for the commandos. Over the span of an hour the gun battle intensified dramatically due to truckloads of insurgents flooding the area with increased armaments. With the buildup of enemy vehicles surrounding the fortification and a rapidly thinning ammunition supply, feelings of desperation once again took hold of the Strike Force.

The following hour brought no change in the relentless guerilla attack that appeared to have no end in sight. Were it not for adrenaline, Jeff and the commandos would have collapsed from the extended and concentrated effort of discharging thousands of rifle rounds at countless moving targets. Even though he was severely stressed from the extreme conditions like every other man in his group, Jeff couldn't put his two canine charges out of his mind. Each time he changed an empty magazine, he took a moment to examine both dogs and reassure their "down" position with a couple of pats.

Being true to his nature, Gunny displayed no outward signs of worry or despair as he made his support rounds from man to man. Most of the time he walked upright around their degenerated fortress talking a mile-a-minute over the radio and occasionally wiping shattered mudbrick or goat blood off his face. Gunny wasn't pretending for the sake of his men's confidence that this was simply a rough day at the office. Close quarter combat was Gunny's livelihood of choice, and he was genuinely comfortable at work doing what he did best, leading men in battle. Jeff will never forget Gunny's final check-in of the conflict. Squatting down to pat the dogs, Gunny asked if Jeff were holding up alright. After an answer of "affirmative," Gunny commented on how impressed he was with the dogs' stability under such heavy gunfire conditions. He said, "They're true warriors just like you, and I know you three are good for the day, but we're dangerously low on ammunition and I've had about all of this party I can stand. So I'm about to open up hell on these boys. When the "devil" arrives, huddle down over your dogs and don't lift your head until all is quiet. Comprende?"

By the time Gunny reached the last commando to deliver his message, the ground beneath the compound roiled with shock waves as brain-jarring thunder engulfed the air above them. Everyone knew that the "devil" had arrived. As Jeff retreated from his shooting post to cover the dogs, he witnessed out of the corner of his eye the tall building at the edge of the complex actually liquefy. The substantial structure that was filled with combatants didn't explode, it melted in a single instant. There wasn't even a rubble pile left. From Jeff's perspective, he couldn't say whether a single missile flattened the enemy stronghold or a barrage of rockets turned it into a shallow depression in the desert landscape. The explosions throughout the compound were so numerous and continuous it felt to Jeff as though he were encamped at the top of an erupting volcano. In every direction around the fortification vehicles burst into fireballs while human bodies vaporized in mere flashes. Jeff recalled that the noise and concussions pounding his body as he shielded the dogs were indescribable.

Huddled over his companions as the world came apart, it occurred to Jeff what Gunny had done. He had called in the help of an AC130 Spectre (long-endurance, heavily-armed gunship). Jeff had only heard about its capabilities but had never seen anything like that in action. He later found out that is exactly the "hell" Gunny had ordered.

The Spectre is a converted C130 cargo plane that is filled with long-range ammunition and has been fitted with various configurations of armaments on one side of the craft. With this modification, the monstrous Spectre can fly in a continuous circle high above the target zone while it accurately unleashes devastation from multiple 40 mm Bofer's cannons at a rate of hundreds of rounds per minute. The gunship is well prepared to disintegrate any structure with its 105mm howitzer cannon which delivers more than 100 rounds per minute. The Spectre completes its destruction with multiple, six- barreled, 20mm, Vulcan Gatling guns which fire at a rate of thousands per minute. Accurate, deadly and out of reach, an AC130 is one of the more devastating US Military weapons that is capable of bringing the most pugnacious enemy to its knees. Long minutes went by as the Spectre decimated the guerilla's offensive positions in a 360-degree radius around the commando's meager fortification. When the gunship departed the area, the insurgents along with their motorcade of vehicles had been shattered, yet Jeff and his group were left unscathed.

Before the enemy forces had a chance to regroup, the second half of Gunny's hell arrived. Two DAP (Direct Action Penetrator) helicopters flew "in theater" from the north. Although nearly deaf from the long, unprotected exposure to gunfire, Jeff remembers standing up with his dogs during the brief respite to survey the damage and hearing the distinct sound of the powerful Black Hawk helicopter. Seeing the two stub wing DAPs racing toward the compound over the top of the scrub, Jeff immediately commanded his dogs to "down" and fell on top of them once more. These modified Black Hawks were known as the "special operations" cleanup crew, and they flew in with an attitude of "Take no prisoners." No sooner than Jeff and the dogs hit the ground the DAPs made their first passes over the adversary, launching their Hydra 70 rockets and Hellfire missiles at the remaining intact perimeter dwellings and moving vehicles. On their third and fourth passes both Black Hawks opened up with their large, GAU-19 machine guns. They literally cut down anything left standing with a firing rate of 2000 rounds per minute. Before the DAPs signed off and left the "theater," they scoured the compound and all its surrounding area for any living or moving object. Like sharks in the sky, they hovered quickly and closely over the contour of the ground emitting bursts from their M134 mini-guns at any viable target. On the last crisscrossing flight pattern, their mini-guns were quiet. The helicopter's muted weapons were a clear, audible sign to their comrades that it was done, the exhausting struggle was over. Tightly circling the commandos' fortification, the men from the Black Hawks saluted Gunny and his men then shot away to the north.

Absolute was the word that came to Jeff's mind after the helicopters departed: absolutely no noise, no movement, nothing taller than a bump off the ground as far as the eye could see, no living thing existed outside of their fortification, not even scrub. Gunny's "hell" amounted to total annihilation of the enemy and a free pass back to the Base of Operations for Jeff and the commandos. With only a small cache of ammunition left, Gunny's group wasted no time loading into the bullet riddled, yet functioning Strykers and motoring towards home. At camp they would be debriefed and spend a couple of days recuperating before launching on a new mission to test Jeff's K-9 units.

Weeks of "in country" observation gave Jeff all the information he needed to draw a conclusion about the functionality of his K-9 units. In his report to Lt. Colonel Westcott, Jeff cited multiple incidents where the dogs were deployed to engage both dynamic and static combatants. Under varied circumstances the canines performed in stellar fashion. Only in one encounter did either dog demonstrate any sign of waning hostility during an attack. On that one occasion, an al-Qaeda assassin was observed by multiple members of the Strike Force curling into a ball on a bed then tolerating a long and intense savaging from Ulysses without a response. The canine commando eventually gave up on the non-reactive combatant and had to be resent on the assassin when he jumped from the bed in an attempt to escape through a window. Jeff reported that the enemies' counteractive "opossum" strategy appeared to be real and at least moderately effective.

The solution to the conundrum that Jeff presented to the Lt. Colonel centered on his own new concept of "corpse attack." Jeff intended to push all of the canines within the elite program through intensive training that directed them to focus on relentless and ferocious physical contact without the reward of adversary reciprocity. Jeff also made it clear to the Lt. Colonel that any dog incapable of sustaining such a degree of aggression under those conditions would be washed out of the program and replaced by one with genetically-superior, fighting drive. Jeff also assured all those involved with the Canine Commando program that regardless of whether the existing dogs adjust to the new training protocol, or they are replaced by new candidates, their bomb and explosives detection ability would not diminish. Reiterating his promise to develop and maintain the most elite multipurpose canines any military has ever seen, Jeff excused himself from the Middle East and headed for Virginia to refine the details of his "corpse attack" stratagem.

Fourteen

Dog Brokers

B ack in Virginia, Jeff went straight to the drawing board to create a retraining strategy that would correct the "opossum" glitch plaguing his K-9 program. Determined to keep the good dogs that he had and salvage the considerable investment they represented, Jeff worked for weeks with his prize canines to heighten their combat traits during engagements with unresponsive adversaries. Throughout the extensive retraining exercises, the four-legged commandos consistently demonstrated superior hunting and fighting drive. However, in the end Jeff was forced to concede that although his prize canines had more possessive/ guarding instinct than the average war-dog, they still fell shy of engaging "sleeping prey" long enough to satisfy the new demands on the K-9 units.

That tough realization pointed Jeff to one solution for his conundrum. He had to find working dogs with extraordinary genetic material that could meet the demands of his adjusted training procedures. Not only would it be necessary for his new, war-dog prototypes to indefinitely engage a nonreactive opponent, they also must be socially balanced in order to intimately work with a multi- member Six-Man-Element. And like his previous class of dogs, the new canine commandos must also be olfactory experts in locating explosives and searching for the enemy.

Jeff was somewhat intimidated by the task at hand. He was well aware that the tractable yet adamantine canine warrior that the Task Force required would be very rare (genetically speaking) and difficult to select from the masses of working dogs available. Also, Jeff's skill in assessing canine potential would be put to the test trying to ferret out the one percent of inherently remarkable dogs from the pack of capable animals. Ultimately, he would have to refine his testing protocol in order to detect the exaggerated possessive/guarding instinct that the new canine commandos required.

There was no debate in Jeff's mind where the quest for choice wardogs should begin. His plan was to fly to Europe's working-dog hotspot and hook up with a few contacts that he had formed while employed at Neue Welt Kennels. Germany, the Czech Republic, and Holland were home to three of the world's most prolific dog brokers. Among those,

Eduart Haghen of Holland was the quintessence, and Jeff's first choice as a supplier.

When Jim Buckley introduced Eduart, a stylish and sharply dressed businessman, to Jeff four years earlier, the two men instantly meshed. Jim even commented at that introductory meeting how he felt like the outsider despite the fact that he'd purchased dogs from Mr. Haghen for some time. Eduart in later years confessed that when he first met Jeff, he saw in him many of the business and dog-savvy traits that he possessed. Like Eduart, Jeff was athletic and insisted on decoying for all the dogs that he tested. Laughing at Jim's impatience over Jeff's meticulous evaluation process, Eduart said that he felt exactly the same about testing each dog's abilities under multifarious conditions, regardless of how long it took. Sitting at the bargaining table on Jeff's inaugural buying trip, Jim remembered after all the testing was done, Eduart and Jeff respectfully haggled over the potential of certain dogs like a father and son debate over whose favorite sports team is better prepared for the playoffs.

A self-made millionaire exclusively from buying and selling dogs, Eduart was a "type A" businessman who happened to be passionate about working dogs. His knowledge of canine behavior and training techniques were on par with his proficiency in marketing and economics. Mr. Haghen's influence and connections within the dog-world were far reaching. There was scarcely a breeding kennel, a K-9 trial judge, or a sporting-dog club in all of Europe that didn't recognize his name.

From young manhood Eduart committed to building a career around dogs, even though his overbearing father was vehemently opposed to the plan. Haghen Senior, a successful Amsterdam businessman and politician, was deeply involved in the Show-Horse world. He firmly believed that people of money and status invested their disposable resources in fine horses rather than common dogs of the working class. The rift between father and son only grew as Eduart matured into adulthood clinging to his canine passion. Haghen Senior could not understand nor would he accept a son who willingly snubbed the upper-echelon equestrian circles in order to frequent neighborhood dog clubs. When Eduart announced his plan to enlist in the military to become a K-9 handler,

Haghen Senior wasted no time in virtually disowning his son. Young Haghen walked away from a privileged lifestyle in pursuit of his dream. To Eduart, the intuitive relationship between man and dog surpassed in value anything that his father's world had to offer.

During his military service, Eduart excelled as a canine handler and was quickly promoted to a higher rank of Kennel Master. He successfully served in that position until his honorable discharge back into the civilian world where he put his canine skills to work as a trial decoy in the Royal Dutch Police Dog Sport (KNPV) as well as in civilian dog training circles. In the world of police-dog competitions, Eduart excelled just as he did in the military-dog realm and ultimately ascended to the coveted status of a championship decoy. Although reaching that pinnacle in canine sports and establishing a local name for his training/breeding kennel, young Mr. Haghen wasn't able to support a family on the humble proceeds from his canine talent alone, so he established a hauling service to bolster family revenues until his dog business took off.

After a few lucrative years of hauling all conceivable forms of inanimate objects, Eduart expanded his company to include a canine transportation service. Modifying one of his two moving vans to accommodate dog crates, Eduart advertised at dog shows, sporting events and K-9 trials that he could expeditiously transport any type or number of dogs from one destination to another for a nominal fee. He slowly became busy picking up dogs from sellers and delivering them to buyers, hauling dogs to and from the airport for breeding kennels, and rounding up canine candidates for police programs. While Eduart was crisscrossing Europe transporting dogs, he was also generating a colossal network of breeders, trainers, competitors, and handlers along the way. Every spare dime the young businessman could get his hands on went to purchase KNPV and police quality dogs for himself to resell. By the late 1990s, Eduart Haghen had evolved into "The Contact" for working canines in Central Europe, and he was generating enough income from his animal endeavors to allow his hauling company to fade away. By the start of the new millennium it was known in Europe's working dog world that if Eduart didn't have the animal to fit the situation, he knew where to get it.

Over the following years, Eduart's reputation spread outside of Europe and his kennel grew to house over one hundred dogs for sale. In the spring of 2004, when Jeff visited Mr. Haghen's facility with Jim Buckley, he recalled walking through Eduart's kennel to view the available dogs and counting two hundred and twenty healthy and welled cared for animals with more new-arrivals out in the parking lot. Jeff remembered being awestruck by the sheer size of Mr. Haghen's operation. His facility nearly doubled that of Jim Buckley's in square footage and dog numbers. Eduart had just as many employees as Jim, and they were frantically busy simply selling dogs. Unlike Neue Welt, Haghen's kennel did no breeding and little training. All man hours were devoted to the care and presentation of their canine commodities to an endless stream of police, military and civilian buyers from around the world.

By that time in his life Haghen's lucrative kennel business was generating multiple millions in dog sales annually. Although having reached the status of a tycoon, Eduart was still quick to help his staff when they were in danger of becoming overwhelmed. Even as a mature man, he wouldn't hesitate to put on a bite suit and decoy for a dozen dogs being demonstrated to a police department. It also wasn't uncommon to find Eduart at his Kennel in the wee hours of the morning loading purchased dogs into trailers for their trip to the airport.

At the age of forty-five, Eduart Haghen had far surpassed his father in wealth and had accumulated an impressive stable of show horses that were the envy of his father's social circle. As Jeff came to know Eduart in later years, he asked him why he never rode any of his expensive horses. Eduart confided that he didn't buy the horses to ride. He sincerely told Jeff: "I buy the horses and pay people to show them, simply because I can. It's a statement to my father, who disowned me, and all of his upper-class associates. I want them to witness what a working-class dog-man has accomplished each time one of my horses beats one of theirs in the competition ring."

Before Jeff scheduled his European itinerary, he called Eduart and confided in him about his situation. During their lengthy conversation, Eduart responded to Jeff more as a friend than a supplier. The millionaire dog broker was compassionate and vowed to find suitable animals even if he had to send Jeff to his competitors. Eduart reassured his American friend that the dogs he needed did exist, they just had to be located, and it was going to be his personal mission to secure them. Before the phone call had ended, Eduart asked Jeff to give him two weeks, and he would have multiple canine candidates at his kennel to assess. Having a large measure of faith in his friend, Jeff planned a very streamline, buying trip to Europe. As soon as he disconnected the call with Mr. Haghen, he arranged a flight to the Amsterdam Airport Schipol and booked a week's stay at the closest hotel he could find to Mr. Haghen's kennel. Jeff didn't schedule any evaluations at other kennels. He was counting on the legendary Holland broker to come through with the canine specimens his Special Tactics Group required.

Unaware at the time of Mr. Haghen's "searching soldiers" and their far-reaching connections, Jeff had no idea how Eduart intended to secure eight dogs of the caliber he needed in just a couple of weeks. In truth, Jeff didn't worry about how he did it, he knew that Mr. Haghen didn't become a world's top supplier of working dogs by chance, and he was instantly comforted to have a broker like Eduart on his side.

Part of Eduart's successful business equation was his employment of full-time dog-buyers that scoured Europe's local training clubs and breeding kennels 365 days a year. Eduart's soldiers attended every significant dog-sport competition and K-9 trial inside a four-country fertile zone looking to purchase young canine prospects even if harassment was necessary to seal the deal. Over the years Eduart groomed two of his senior kennel employees into

Franklin with Marcell and tough Czech shepherd for his program.

shrewd dog-buyers. Both of these men he found as teenagers, subsisting on the urban streets of Central Europe, and he took them in as family.

Dusan was born to an impoverished family in the Czech Republic and spent much of his boyhood roaming the old-world streets of Prague. He was a familiar face at many of the merchant's shops around his neighborhood. Dusan was poor, but proud, and he would stop in routinely at the local businesses with friendly proprietors to ask about work, but never about handouts. He became somewhat of a spectacle in his quarter of the picturesque hometown because of his well-behaved canine accompaniment. Dusan was seldom seen without a dog or two at his side, weaving as a synchronized team in and out of frantic traffic and dense crowds. Any time he would enter a marketplace or a business that was unwelcoming to his companions, Dusan would direct his tail- wagging entourage to sit and stay out on the sidewalk alongside the building while he went in. It was a scene much like this that initially attracted Eduart's attention.

During this time in Eduart's career, his brokering business was growing at an alarming rate, and he was having a difficult time keeping enough dogs in-house to cover demands. To complicate matters, Mr. Haghen's trusted kennel manager had just been lured away by an arch competitor, taking with him the "green book" with all of Eduart's contacts' information. Those harried conditions forced Eduart into double-duty. He had to manage the day-to-day operations during the week and travel the dog-buying routes over long weekends in order to keep his business running smoothly. Eduart was in desperate need of some trustworthy, skilled dog-men to fill in his ranks, and he needed them yesterday.

On an excursion through the Czech Republic, Eduart stopped at a roadside café for a midday break one Saturday afternoon. Eduart watched Dusan amble up with a small Czech shepherd heeling in perfect competition form at his left leg. Sending his dog under an outdoor side-table to "down" and "stay," Dusan went in to inquire about employment. Although on his own for quite a while, the little shepherd didn't budge from his duty as a regular stream of patrons strolled by, wholly unaware of his presence. Swallowing the last bite of his sandwich, Eduart was startled by a sharp whistle that sent the shepherd tearing out from under the table to the far side of the café where Dusan was standing. As the eager little herder slid onto his hocks in a beautiful sit-in-front position, Eduart witnessed Dusan feeding his companion a small crumb from his pocket before he had his four-legged friend jump up into his arms.

Noting the young man's outerwear and gaunt appearance, Eduart surmised that the youthful dog-man may be unemployed, so he asked Dusan in English, as he passed by with his heeling shepherd, if he were looking for work. Halting in mid-stride Dusan and his lean sidekick turned to face Eduart. Slowly nodding his head, Dusan answered in broken English, "Yes, we hungry."

Eduart responded, "Have you ever worked with sporting dogs or been a decoy?" Dusan lowered his gaze and shook his head "no." Immediately after shaking his head, Dusan seized the moment with a magical surge of confidence,"But, I do anything with dogs. I know them, they know me. I have no fear and learn fast." Eduart couldn't help but smile at the certainty in Dusan's every word when he said, "Good. I need some help testing and buying working dogs around your part of the world. When could you be ready to ride with me?"

Dusan didn't hesitate, "Now, we ready." With that, Mr. Haghen stood up to shake hands with his new handler and asked where his shepherd could be kept while they visited some clubs and kennels in the area. Dusan's gaze fell once again as he looked at his devoted companion and answered, "No place. We have no home. He my friend and I not lose him. Thank you for work. Larben and me must keep lookin'." As Dusan and Larben turned for the street, Eduart blurted out, "Nonsense! We have plenty of room in the van for your friend. What kind of dog-man would I be if I split up a team like you and Larben? Your attachment to Larben is what landed you the job-offer in the first place. Let's start your employment by getting the two of you a decent meal." Dusan couldn't find any words to say in gratitude, but his watering eyes and a seldom seen smile already repaid the million-dollar dog broker for his generous offer. On that Czech dog-buying trip, Dusan proved to be the quick study that he claimed, and he adeptly took on the role of decoy and handler for Eduart.

The second most prolific buyer for Mr. Haghen's kennel was Marcell. A Belgian by birth, Marcell had no real parents to claim. He lived much like a gypsy with some extended family bouncing through parts of Germany, Holland and his own country picking up odd jobs here and there. On his own and unemployed when he encountered Mr. Haghen one day in a parking lot, Marcell observed Eduart exercising a trailer full of dogs on their way to the airport. An extravert and multilingual by necessity, Marcell was a dog-lover by nature, so he called out to Eduart first in German, then in Dutch and offered his assistance in handling some of the animals. True to his type-A nature, Eduart had taken on too many of his overwhelmed, kennel techs' duties that day and was running behind on his trip to the airport, so he accepted this young stranger's offer.

Marcell had no idea that each dog he handled was worth more Euros than he'd ever seen. He was simply elated by the opportunity to touch and talk to such handsome animals. Marcell's rapport with the energized police dogs was immediate and effortless. He needed no coaching in his manner of communication or leash handling. Eduart was so impressed, as well as relieved, by his competent, vagrant helper that he asked Marcell if he could be hired to accompany him to the airport and help unload the live cargo. Marcell affirmed that he was for hire and said, "Food and drink is good pay. I not eat in a while." After an evening of jostling dogs through the airport, Eduart took Marcell out for a hardy dinner. He also gave his helper enough money to buy new boots and a jacket to replace the worn-out versions that he was wearing.

Driving back toward the parking lot where they first met, Eduart asked Marcell where he was staying and offered to drop him off there. Marcell casually replied that the parking lot would be fine because he wasn't sure where he'd be sleeping that night. Pulling into the parking area Marcell attempted to exit the van just as soon as the vehicle came to a stop, but before he had a chance to step out, Eduart presented a proposition. Being a direct communicator, Eduart said, "Marcell, you're gifted when it comes to managing animals. You're a natural dog-man and you proved that tonight with the ease in which you handled those challenging police canines inside the chaotic airport. I own a large kennel with more than a hundred dogs like that. If you don't mind long, noisy days of cleaning dirty runs and exercising aggressive animals, then I could use a man like you as a kennel tech. I have small, but comfortable living quarters for you and a couple of other techs right there on the property. If you stay with me, I'll teach you how to evaluate, train and sell dogs better than any of the competition. Working for me you can develop the skills to turn your natural ability into a real money-maker. What do you think?"

Marcell didn't have to think. He shut the van door and buckled up for the ride to his new home. When Eduart asked if he had any family or friends to inform, Marcell replied with a single word that reflected his lonely, brief history, "No."

Eduart cared for Dusan and Marcell as he would his own nephews. He compensated them well enough that they could live like respectable hard-working people. To Dusan and Marcell, hard work came easy, so having all the daily necessities covered with a little left over for some comforts was the same as living a life of royalty. Until their fortuitous meeting with Mr. Haghen, neither of the young men had any inclination to think about life direction or purpose. Day to day considerations of food, shelter and clothing consumed their thoughts most of the time. However, under Eduart's employment, Dusan and Marcell were able to soak up their mentor's weekly tutelage and dream about advancement in a lucrative dog business. And for the first time in their lives, Dusan and Marcell also had a supportive friend in each other.

Several days before his two dog-buyers set out on their epic journeys for Jeff's replacement dogs, Mr. Haghen contacted a few of the larger breeding kennels and used his considerable influence to convince them to release some of their prized animals for testing. Eduart wasn't forthcoming when he contacted the prestigious breeders about the final destination of any purchased dogs. Eduart, like many of the dog-brokers of

Europe, felt the disdain of training clubs and kennels in their respective countries towards the idea of shipping the best dogs to the United States. For a business minded dog broker, national pride takes a backseat to a lucrative contract, and Eduart was fully aware of his potentially profitable relationship with Jeff, given his position within the U.S. Military. So, he gave Marcell and Dusan explicit instructions not to divulge the customer or ultimate destination of the special dogs they were looking to buy.

On the morning of their departure, Dusan and Marcell had the vans fueled up and had neatly placed six empty crates on the inside, allowing a mattress to fit squarely on top. The dog trailers attached to their vans had been meticulously cleaned and readied with fresh water and bedding for new occupants. Both men had personal bags packed with two weeks' worth of ready-to-eat food (the two-roving dog-buyers never cooked and rarely dined out while on the road) and a single change of clothes. Marcell and Dusan viewed their canine-purchasing excursions as competitions to see who could secure the highest number of marketable dogs with the money Mr. Haghen had allotted them. So, they traveled in a Spartan style with little interest in comfort or fashion.

This particular trip was going to make an especially challenging competition, however. Not only were the two "dog-soldiers" needing to ferret out only the toughest/hardest canine candidates available throughout Central Europe, they also had a very limited time in which to locate, purchase, and deliver them to the kennel. Under normal circumstances Dusan and Marcell would make several buying runs over a month's period before they would spend all of the money that Mr. Haghen had given them for sourcing animals that month. Nevertheless, neither Marcell nor Dusan were the slightest bit intimidated by the demands placed on them for the Franklin-dog project. Over the years the two men had developed a vast network of club and kennel insiders who kept them abreast of the possible working dogs available within a given circle. Also, Dusan and Marcell had become experts at canine selection and handling, so they rarely missed a viable candidate or committed to one who fell short in the end. Both of Mr. Haghen's "dog-soldiers" intended to come home with a van and trailer full of canines suitable for Jeff, so they each packed enough dog food and supplies to care for twelve dogs for a two-week period.

Mr. Haghen had planned for Marcell to take a southern route through Holland, Belgium and into Germany before circling back at about Austria. Dusan on the other hand would pull his rig through Northern Germany, the Czech Republic, Slovakia, and turn around at Hungary. Mr. Haghen was essentially having his trusted representatives make a quick sweep of Central Europe, stopping at designated kennels and clubs along the way. Eduart's ultimate goal was to have his "dog soldiers" return in about twelve days with at least eight prime canines to fill Jeff's initial order.

Before sending Marcell and Dusan off with handshakes and well-wishes, Eduart handed them each forty thousand euros. That was substantially more money than he normally gave them for a buying trip; however, this expedition was unique. Eduart gave Dusan and Marcell specific instructions to thoroughly test any potential candidate and buy any qualifying canine regardless of price. He made it clear that no Franklin-dog could be left behind. Eduart had his buyers deal only in cash; there were no checks, credit or I.O.U.s considered. Mr. Haghen insisted on simple transactions, the way he had always done. His men exchanged cash for a healthy, suitable dog, along with his registration papers and medical records, then they moved on to the next deal. Fast and efficient was Mr. Haghen's model to be followed.

Based on the detailed conversation with Jeff about his conundrum, Eduart and his two right hand men devised an exhaustive testing strategy that was sure to bring only the most elite working canines to the front. Mr. Haghen was also savvy to Jeff's new evaluation protocols for his commando dogs, so he conveyed to Marcell and Dusan that any dog purchased on this trip had to have met Jeff's testing requirements without a hiccup. Eduart had every intention to satisfy Jeff and the U.S. Military's special demands and position himself as the sole supplier of this high-caliber canine type.

Before Eduart had filled the first order for Jeff, he was scheming about a loose partnership and future plans with his American friend. Mr.

Haghen was confident that Marcell and Dusan could find and evaluate the elite canines that the U.S. Task Force required for their covert operations. He was also quite sure that he could afford to purchase and house as many of the expensive animals as Jeff could venture to train. The more Eduart learned about Jeff and his training abilities, the clearer it became to the dog- broker tycoon that these uniquely tempered and trained, special-forces dogs would fetch a high price from any commando group in the world. Eduart would need to convince Jeff that such an enterprise would be lucrative, because without Franklin's resume and skill the "commando dog" concept would not be tangible enough to sell to other governments. The European magnate envisioned an arrangement where he secured the canine candidates and shipped them to any location or Special Tactics Element where Jeff would carry out the training. However, the first step in the extravagant scheme was to satisfy Franklin's immediate need for eight superior working-animals.

It was early 2008 when Jeff's plane landed in Amsterdam. He had arranged transportation from the airport directly to the kennel with Mr. Haghen's gregarious kennel manager, Carlos. Carlos was a transplant from Spain, and a successful dog trainer in his own right from the Madrid Police Department. He had visited Mr. Haghen over the years buying dogs for his K-9 Officers, and on one trip Eduart offered him the managerial position at a salary Carlos couldn't refuse. Eduart told Jeff at one point that he didn't pay Carlos a handsome salary because of his dog training skills. He said, "Carlos has loads of charisma. He can sell dogs like nobody's business, and he happens to be a pretty good manager to boot." Eduart couldn't keep himself from being Jeff's mentor so he added, "It's simply a plus that Carlos is good with dogs. He makes us a lot of money because of his exceptional personality and communication skills. Now it's much different with Dusan and Marcell. They must be superior dog-men first, because they make us money by purchasing sound dogs. I really don't care how well they get along with people, as long as they can buy quality dogs. Besides, when you're buying something, money does all of the talking and charisma takes a back seat."

Jeff and Carlos arrived at the kennel around 0530, about an hour before the cleanup and feeding routine began. The kennel complex was comprised of two large modified barns which housed nearly 200 dogs, a small apartment, and training grounds that surrounded the structures. Angled across a number of empty vehicle spaces at the rear of the parking lot was a long dog trailer hooked to a utility van. Jeff was ambling around outside in the early morning air waiting for Carlos to open up the office area of the primary building, when he detected some rustling coming from the long trailer. About that time, Marcell stepped out of the apartment and walked over to the van and knocked on the passenger door. He waved at Jeff as he continued on to the secondary structure. When Marcell rapped on the van, he triggered a thundering of barks and growls that roared from the interior of the vehicle as well as the dog trailer. The staccato of barking drew Jeff in like a magnet. As he approached the van, the side door slowly opened exposing a young man precariously perched on a flimsy mattress atop four rumbling crates that were housing very aggressive canines. Jeff peaked into the odiferous van and greeted the groggy passenger, "One hell of an alarm clock you have here. Good morning! Does it take long to get used to sleeping on top of filthy, rowdy dogs?" Without missing a beat and with very little expression, the young man replied, "It matters how tired a man. Twelve hours ago, I almost to Hungary picking up shepherds. I sleep good two hours. My name Dusan. You American, maybe Franklin? Haghen said, come early, Franklin will."

Shaking his head in slight disbelief, Jeff replied, "I am Franklin, and Eduart told me about you and Marcell. He called you guys "dog soldiers" and said you two can smell a good canine candidate in the next country and you never come home with an empty trailer."

Dusan nearly smiled, but didn't, when he confirmed, "I been gone nine days finding Franklin dogs."

Jeff felt excitement rising when he asked, "Did you have any luck?"

Dusan crawled out of the van and put his hand on top of the noisy trailer when he answered, "I always have luck. Marcell too. He come yesterday with Belgium and German dogs. We ready!"

Jeff connected with Dusan and Marcell at the first greeting. He marveled at their high energy and smooth handling skills, but he couldn't help to be struck by their severe countenances. Jeff later learned about their dismal, destitute past, which helped to explain the painful reflection in their eyes. With the exception of admiring a working dog going through the paces, Dusan or Marcell seldom seem to smile. Jeff suspected that both men had been so deprived of humor and pleasure that they had failed to develop any appreciation for such things. He also noticed that even during discussions about their favorite subject, the young dog-men found it difficult to sustain eye contact and would often fall into a subservient downward gaze whenever they were engaged in conversation. Despite their hardness, Jeff liked Dusan and Marcell, and he was delighted to have them on board to help sort through the large number of intense dogs that Eduart had collected. Jeff needed a couple of assistants who could work long days, manage dangerous dogs, and be equally comfortable handling or decoying. Eduart promised Jeff that Dusan and Marcell were more than qualified for the task, and they were at his service for the entire week.

Coming from different cultural backgrounds, Dusan and Marcell had very dissimilar appearances. Dusan was a stocky 5' 7" with a rough complexion and course black hair. Marcell had a slender 6' frame with fair skin and thin light-brown hair. Both men, however, were identical in their severe physiognomy, hollow cheeks and dark, deep eye sockets. When it came to work ethic and perseverance, Jeff's two assistants resembled brothers. They also shared the same penchant for wearing an abundance of oversized clothes and hoarding food in every nook, cranny, and pocket. The better Jeff got to know Dusan and Marcell, the more evident it was that they had grown up in the same street-hard fraternity.

Even after a week of working with his two new friends all day long, Jeff was unable to distinguish who was the better handler or decoy. Much like a tag-team, Marcell would don the bite suit to give his adopted brother some relief before receiving any expressions of fatigue from Dusan. Marcell didn't have to be told that working ten dogs through realistic combat scenarios was exhausting. He kept a visual check on his counterpart, and if he noticed Dusan routinely hitting the ground, or consistently stumbling during a series of violent impacts, Marcell wasted no time in shouting to his friend, "We switch now!" Both men seemed ever aware that the robust combat dogs they handled for Jeff were very capable of taking advantage of a "grounded" decoy and inflicting debilitating injuries to unprotected extremities. So they were diligent about not exposing the other to such a fate.

On several occasions Jeff witnessed Dusan, who was decoying in a bite-suite, jogging toward a struggling Marcell as he wrestled with a belligerent canine student. Although taller, Marcell was not as strong as Dusan in regard to handling the powerful Czech shepherds. When Dusan stepped within arm's reach of his friend, he insisted, "Hand me leash. You rest. I give back." Marcell and Dusan worked well together, and they were capable of training the most challenging dogs, despite the limitation of different language backgrounds. The two-young dog-men watched over each other as one would expect brothers to do.

Eduart's personal interest in Jeff and the U.S. Military's Commando Dog project was evident on that first morning. No sooner than Carlos had invited Jeff into the main facility's reception area for coffee, in walked Mr. Haghen with enough pastries to feed the entire staff and as many guests. In an unusual fashion, Eduart took control of the day's agenda by announcing that he and Carlos would organize the nearly forty canine candidates he had assembled for Jeff into groups of ten. Eduart assigned Dusan and Marcell to alternate as decoy and handler for each dog to be tested.

Before Eduart had the opportunity to blurt out his next directive, Jeff interrupted, "Excuse me, Mr. Haghen, but on this buying trip, I'm the decoy for each candidate's initial test."

Eduart's response reflected what all of the men in the room were thinking, "You don't mean for all forty dogs?"

Breaking into a half smile, Jeff replied, "I do. This week's selection process will either make or break the Commando Dog program. With no disrespect to Dusan or Marcell, my career will necessarily hinge on the decoy's performance during each dog's initial fight, and I don't intend to give that responsibility to anyone but me. Provided that at least a few of the four-legged candidates on your property get through me, there'll be plenty of follow-up decoying opportunities for your two 'dog soldiers'. I do need to borrow a bite-suit, though."

As Dusan headed out to the van for his suit, Eduart called for him to stop and announced, "I have one that will fit my American friend, perfectly." Eduart walked out to the waiting area and took down a suit that was hanging on the wall as a display. When he handed it over to Jeff he said, "This was my personal suit that I wore when I was invited to decoy at the KNPV National Championships. I would like for you to wear it."

Slapping Eduart on the shoulder, Jeff concluded the early, morning meeting with his own dictate, "I'd be honored to wear your suit Mr. Haghen. Now let's go work some dogs."

While Jeff was strapping on Mr. Haghen's bite-suit he gave Marcell and Dusan specific instructions for handling the dogs during their first encounter with the decoy. Jeff first handed Marcell a blank gun and two boxes of blank cartridges, he then gave Dusan fifty meters of rope securely fastened to a heavy, leather buckle-collar. Jeff explained, "Attach this collar with the rope to each dog, then one of you handles and one of you shoots, understand?" Pointing to a dilapidated structure at the back of the property, Jeff continued, "I will be hiding in that old barn and watching the two of you approach from the kennel with the dog and the revolver. When you get within thirty meters, I will step out of the building waving my gun and shouting. Whoever is holding the handgun fires two blanks my way which will trigger me to return fire while I continue to shout and run back inside the barn. As soon as I step out of sight, stimulate the dog and send him toward the structure to find me. Once you send the dog, hold on to the end of the rope, but do not follow or say another word to him. I'll repeat, it's critical that you do not touch or communicate with the dog until I tell you to do so. You got that?"

Jeff went on, "This is all about how the dog engages the 'bad guy' on his own. This is not about teamwork. If you two have found the right dogs with the appropriate backgrounds, they'll recognize me as a hostile target, pursue, locate, and bring the physical battle to me without support from you. And if they're the right dogs for the commando program, they'll chew on me for a long time without me providing any stimulation or reaction over their biting and clawing. Once I determine they've fought long enough with the nonreactive "sleeping" prey, I'll give them the fight of their life. I'll pin them on the ground and bite their ears. I'll punch, kick and scream before I drag them outside to you with their teeth still latched onto my body and fire my revolver over the top of 'em."

Jeff concluded with, "We'll further evaluate any candidate who passes my initial combat test for the other mandatory skills like bomb detection, obstacles, and area searching. But, if any dog disengages from me at any time, even once, they fail and there is no more testing or second chance. What I must have in this new grade of special tactics dog is an extreme fighting instinct with a highly exaggerated possessive drive and calm intelligence. I need a dog that will not consider walking away from the adversary whether it's lifeless or ferocious. There aren't many dogs born like that, so, if I leave here at the end of the week with the eight canine warriors I need, I'll give you each five hundred euros for being the adepts that Eduart said you were. I just spit out a lot of English, did you get most of it?"

Marcell didn't hesitate to respond, "You scream, I shoot, you shoot and run, Dusan send dog, you fight dog, we wait, you bring dog to us. Franklin pay euros to Dusan and Marcell. We find good dogs!"

Nodding his head up and down, Jeff was putting an extra-large tunban, perahan and waskat over his bite-suit to better simulate a Middle Eastern fighter as he reacted to Marcell's boastful statement, "Well we're about to put your confidence to the test, my friend. Find Carlos and Mr. Haghen, then bring around the first dog that they've selected. I'll be waiting in the barn."

Carlos put together the first strings of candidates to be tested from Mr. Haghen's top choices of "in-house" dogs. That would allow Marcell and Dusan's new acquisitions a day or so to settle into the kennel environment before having to perform. Eduart was hanging his reputation on the eighteen new arrivals, and he wanted to give them every chance to be on their game. Some fresh meat with their kibble, a spacious pen to exercise in, and a good night's sleep on a cot in a climate controlled building would go a long way in heightening their execution.

A high-capacity dog trailer for full-time "Finders."

After the first long day of testing, Jeff felt that only one dog soundly met his new requirements, and another dog was marginal. So only these two out of twelve otherwise outstanding, police-dog specimens of Eduart's deserved further testing. When Jeff went out for a lonely dinner that night, he was physically spent, substantially bruised and emotionally down.

He felt that maybe the dogs he was looking for were too rare to be collected in any numbers. He was also in doubt about the test he'd set up. While he picked at his food, Jeff thought that the test might be too hard, except for the fact that he did have one dog that passed, and the challenge in the Middle Eastern theater would require such mettle. That night it really didn't matter whether it was the test or the caliber of canine, Jeff felt there was little hope of finding even half the dogs he needed that week to appease Lt. Colonel Westcott.

Early the next morning, Jeff arrived at the kennel stiff and sore, still emotionally down but ready for another day of decoying. Walking into the facility's reception area for a strong cup of pain medicine, Jeff said "Good morning" to Marcell who was standing by the coffee maker. Marcell nodded while he sipped his coffee and watched Jeff double-brew a potent mug of fuel. Marcell broke the weighty silence in the room with his version of a pep talk, "Franklin, today be better. We work my dogs now. You smile tonight, and you pay me euros Friday." Jeff did feel a little more hopeful after the small infusion of confidence; however, he considered himself a negative realist who approached life from an angle of skepticism, so "We'll see" was the best he could do in response.

Standing inside the run-down barn, Jeff had his two helpers set up for the exact drill they had run candidates through the previous day. Jeff watched through a broken window as Marcell was practically drug out of the kennel by a quiet, sinewy Malinois that he found at a sporting club in Belgium a week before. When Marcell and Dusan reached the thirty-meter starting-marker for the drill, Jeff saw a distinct smile on Marcell's face as he hollered out, "You be ready, Franklin!" Jeff stepped out of the structure waving his gun and shouting like he'd done twelve times the day before. When Dusan fired his revolver the Malinois never hiccupped in his leash-straining stare at the human target in a bite suit. Jeff fired his gun twice and the lean canine remained transfixed on the adversary but didn't make a sound. Just to throw a little twist into the routine, Jeff reentered the building by scrambling through the open window rather than the gaping doorway.

From inside the barn, Jeff watched as Marcell stoically released the Malinois with no words of encouragement or pats of stimulation like they had done with every other canine the previous day. The Malinois covered the thirty meters to the barn so fast that Jeff barely had time to get into his defensive "turtle" position on the cot he had set up. Marcell's first candidate of the day bolted past the open door and shot through the window without touching the frame. Although one of the smaller dogs tested thus far, the Malinois hit Jeff with such energy that it jarred his curled-up body to the floor. The impact to Jeff's back was so forceful that he had to scramble to protect his extremities as he recovered his defensive "turtle" position.

Jeff painfully allowed the canine dynamo to bite and thrash for an extended period while he offered no retaliation. The Belgium dog savaged Jeff until it was clear that there was no equal among the candidates tested so far. Once satisfied, Jeff aggressively engaged his wiry opponent by rolling over and pinning him to the floor. Marcell's warrior freed himself and reattacked in less time than it took Jeff to draw a breath of relief. Jeff used knee and elbow strikes, as well as ear pinches in an effort to run off the Malinois, but none of his tactics were effective. In fact, the harder Jeff fought the more energized the Belgian became.

Struggling as he drug the Malinois outside, Jeff fired two blank rounds alongside the candidate's ribs without as much as a twitch from the dog. Out of breath and whooping with excitement, Jeff waves Marcell and Dusan over to secure their "tiger." After Dusan removed the dog from the shredded perahan, Jeff fell to his knees to catch his breath and looked up to see both his helpers grinning from ear to ear. Trying to talk and breathe at the same time, Jeff conveyed his thoughts in segments: "So you guys can smile. Now that's a dog. I don't care how much 'ball drive' he has, I'll get him to find bombs. He's a keeper. If you two have any more like him, we're in business and I'll be forkin' out some euros on Friday."

Dusan handed the heaving Malinois over to Marcell so that he could help Jeff stand up, and said, "He not best, he no Czech shepherd. We have more for Franklin, maybe ten." Then Dusan slapped Jeff on the shoulder and headed back to the kennel with Marcell to get their next candidate.

Marcell had presented an impressive string of dogs. Out of his eight candidates Jeff tagged four as first-class keepers and one additional was marginal. The day's testing wrapped up with a couple of borderline, bi-colored shepherds from a North German police-dog kennel that Dusan had picked up. As Jeff prepared to leave that evening, both of his helpers agreed that some of their stronger dogs have yet to be seen. Dusan advised him to eat and sleep well that night because he would need all of his energy for the next string of dogs.

Jeff was in the reception area double-brewing his coffee the next morning when Eduart stormed in with more pastries and asked, "Are you sore? I hope my suit is bringing good luck while it protects you." Eduart was transparently wanting to get a tally on the number of dogs Jeff had found acceptable after two days of evaluations.

Jeff responded; "We had a slow first day and only found one suitable and one maybe. Yesterday was great though. Your 'dog soldiers' are the 'bomb' by the way. They demonstrated ten of the dogs they had just picked up and four were outstanding while three were 'maybes'. Dusan tells me that he saved the best Czech and Dutch shepherds for today, so it looks like you and the staff have made good on your promise of finding me eight specimens for the commando program."

With a smile and a nod, Eduart said, "I always make good on my promises, Mr. Franklin, and I have another promise I'll make right now. Before you leave my kennel this week, we're going to have a meeting about an international proposition that I have in the works that is sure to make you a wealthy man."

When Friday morning rolled around, Jeff's entire body was tattooed with all shapes and colors of bruises. Mr. Haghen's bite-suit did its job though. Like Eduart said, it fit like a glove and allowed Jeff to use his athleticism and move freely while he fought with the dogs. Just as importantly, the championship suit kept Jeff free of debilitating punctures and tears.

Sitting in Mr. Haghen's office that morning, Jeff handed Eduart a list of ten dog names and said that he's buying two more than he intended because their quality was too high to pass up. Jeff then handed Eduart a check for fifty thousand dollars which was in accordance with the price per dog they had agreed upon. After the two men shook hands, Jeff said, "It's up to me now. I have to shape all of that canine potential into the toughest commando dogs the world has ever seen. If I can get this done, I will be back in four months for more warriors just like these. Also, in regard to your proposition, I'm all in. In fact, I have a Special Forces Group from Ecuador who contacted me about fixing them up with some dogs. So keep your 'dog soldiers' on the hunt, I may be back sooner than later. And speaking of Dusan and Marcell, I owe them a handshake and some money before I skedaddle."

Jeff's "super dogs" proved to be the solution for his floundering K-9 program. It was early fall of 2008 and nearly six months after purchasing his superior canine specimens before one of the commando teams ran into an "opossum" ambush as earlier deployments had the year before. After reviewing an A.A. Report which highlighted the performance of a commando dog's prolonged engagement of a concealed assassin, Lt.

Colonel Westcott called Jeff to congratulate him on the successful fix of the lethal problem. Westcott also contacted Colonel Edward to request a K-9 team for each of his Special Tactics Groups in the Middle East, especially those Elements that were moving into the Afghanistan Theater. Jeff's colossal effort to address the devastating glitch ultimately resulted in the expansion of the Canine Commando Program.

Fifteen

Two Warriors

At the beginning of 2009, the focus of operations for Jeff Franklin's K-9 teams shifted from Iraq to Afghanistan. Travis Poteet joined the dog program around the time of this transition. Poteet transferred to Franklin's group from a special weapons outfit that was once commanded by Lt. Colonel Westcott. Jeff knew little about Poteet's background except that he was a favorite of the Lt. Colonel, and he had already been involved in a number of covert missions to the Middle East.

As Jeff found to be common practice among the Top Tier Operators, the name Travis Poteet was probably not his newest recruit's real name. His clandestine background was likely by design. Many elite commandos are adamant about hiding their true identities and places of origin in order to protect their families from terrorist retaliation.

Possessing a favorable demeanor that naturally coupled with his handsome appearance, Poteet came across as very approachable. Wavy dark hair topped his five-foot, ten inch frame, and he weighed- in with a well chiseled physique at one hundred and seventy pounds. Jeff guessed that his new recruit was in his late twenties when he first signed onto the K-9 program, but even after working closely together for two years he was never sure of his age.

Poteet was fiercely competitive and that mindset dominated every aspect of his life, especially his exercise regimen. He often declared that few activities satisfied his athletic pursuits like Triathlon Sprints. His lean muscular stature reflected his obsessive pursuit of that goal. Despite his competitive intensity, Travis was amiable and easy to like. However, he seldom allowed anyone a peek into his deep and ominous emotional realm. Jeff felt that Poteet purposely kept people at arm's reach to protect them from his "dark side."

Franklin has never forgotten his first glimpse into Poteet's psychological interior. One afternoon, early in the handler course before canines had been assigned to the men, Jeff took his four new handlers out into the Virginia countryside to discuss the fundamentals of ground tracking. As the sun reached its zenith, the commandos began shedding their shirts. When Travis peeled off his top layer he exposed a richly colored mosaic of tattoos. A striking display of morbid and gruesome depictions formed an inky dark shirt that normally lay hidden from view. From belt to collar to cuff, no pinpoint of Poteet's natural skin color showed through the diabolical scenes. Jeff had never seen such an exhibition of body art in his life. He actually paused the instruction session just to marvel over the lurid messages scribed onto his student's torso.

Some weeks later, Jeff was talking about Travis' artwork at a group gathering when Gunny spoke up and divulged what little background he had on the tattooed handler. Poteet's previous stint as a "small arms specialist" really meant that he operated as a commando assassin, and he wasn't an ideal team-player. Gunny relayed that some of Westcott's most clandestine operators described Poteet as a "natural born killer," saying: "He's definitely the kind of guy that you want with you, not against you. In certain areas of Afghanistan, the guerillas have dubbed him 'the devil.'"

In the early weeks of instruction, Jeff wasn't sure what to think of Travis Poteet, especially after Gunny's insights. He felt sure of one thing; Poteet was the hard and keen commando that he needed to handle Razor, the latest canine recruit from Eduart Haghen. This Dutch shepherd was cut from the same tough cloth as Travis, and Jeff intended to turn them into an unparalleled K-9 Unit.

Razor was a two-year-old brindled dog weighing about seventy pounds. Like Poteet, he was a handsome, athletic specimen that never ran low on energy. Marcell came across Razor at a small Schutzhund club not far from Haghen's kennel. Although too young to enter a working dog program at ten months old, Razor was already much too aggressive for his competitive owners to manage. Recognizing his warrior characteristics, Marcell purchased the young dog for the sole purpose of raising him to be one of Franklin's canine commandos.

Razor lived with Marcell for nearly a year before Jeff had a chance to evaluate him. When the day finally came for Razor's assessment, he was ready. For twelve months, Marcell had prepared Razor for Jeff's full range of Herculean tasks. The young canine recruit had battled decoys in many different styles of engagements. He had also become proficient with area searches and bomb location techniques. Marcell gave Razor every opportunity to develop his innate talents, and that was readily apparent when Jeff ran the Dutchy through a day of challenges. Since the implementation of Franklin's revised evaluation protocols, no canine recruit had scored as high across the board as Razor. At the end of the day, Jeff gave Marcell the ultimate compliment by offering him the highest price that he'd ever paid for a canine recruit and labeling the special Dutch shepherd a "force to be reckoned with."

The morning Franklin handed Razor over to Poteet, he watched as both commandos sized each other up, while waiting for their first drill on the P.T. course. Only moments after transferring leash control to Travis, the cocky Dutch shepherd looked up at his new handler with a wagging tail, then grumbled a threat. Having only childhood dog interaction before joining Jeff's group, Poteet wasn't very dog-savvy and didn't know quite what to think about Razor's "hello." Without much thought, Travis responded viscerally to his new partner's threats by growling back at the Dutchy as the two stared at each other. Remembering Franklin's repeated warnings about Razor's tendency to test a handler's mettle, Travis calmly prepared himself to use defensive leash maneuvers in the event his canine counterpart actually followed through with the challenge of authority.

Jeff watched the situation quickly unfold from a short distance and called out, "Poteet! Be ready, your dog is sending a clear message that he's not in the mindset to take direction from his new handler yet." Poteet couldn't have responded to the warning any better as far as Jeff was concerned. He answered back; "I've got it, Franklin. Razor and I are about to work out our differences."

With that Travis decided to throw down the gauntlet and gave his dog a pleasant, but firm directive to walk. As Travis took his first step, he encouraged Razor to cooperate with a small leash tug which proved to be the minor provocation the canine companion needed to fight.

Razor's fearless brown eyes were locked onto his handler's as he bristled, his growl deepened, and his respirations quickened. When Razor's rapid tail-wagging slowed into a rigid, erect position, the hair on Travis' neck stood on end. He realized the moment of truth had arrived, and his canine partner was eager to test the team leader's constitution.

Poteet was a calculated and deadly operator in the face of mortal combat. On more than one occasion he'd killed an enemy in close quarters, and Poteet was comfortable with those memories. However, the moment Razor launched his animalistic aggression up the leash, Travis was shocked by his own goose-bump reaction and near loss of emotional control. Never had the seasoned commando experienced such explosive, raw hostility. The seventy pounds of relentless fury nearly took Travis to the ground. Razor was almost more force than could be managed on a leash. Poteet felt as if he were in a life and death struggle with a tiger. After a long and exhausting couple of minutes, Travis finally regained control using "release" commands and an extended correction (at Franklin's prompting) to calm his challenger.

Until that confrontation, Travis wasn't entirely sold on the battle effectiveness of a canine commando. He appreciated their searching and location abilities, but he wasn't convinced that a medium sized dog could offer genuine "back-up" in the heat of a lethal struggle. However, Razor changed Poteet's way of thinking. The powerful and brawling Dutchy left a permanent impression on the "operator's" psyche. Although considering himself a loner, Travis confessed to Jeff at the conclusion of handler's school that after being trained as a K-9 team, he would never again feel complete in a warzone without a Razor at his side.

Poteet took to dog training as naturally as a Border collie takes to herding. The very day he was assigned his dog, Travis augmented Franklin's regular training regimen with his own version of "repetition with variation." Applying his obsessive concentration and energy to Razor's training, Travis essentially doubled his and Razor's workload. He hung onto details that most handlers felt were unnecessary. Hearing Jeff tout the importance of "authentic targets" in bite-work, Travis couldn't keep from taking the element of realism to the limit during his off-hours training. When a comrade was commandeered to act as a decoy for the Poteet/Razor team, Travis required them to wear the genuine attire of their enemy like a soiled perahan tunban from a Mujahideen guerilla (brought back from the Middle East). Travis also insisted that his helpers speak only in the limited Pashto/Dari (the two dominant languages of

Afghanistan) that they knew and carry a decommissioned AK-47. Razor would be familiar with every detail of his enemy, well before he encountered them in battle.

Following Jeff's training criteria to the letter, Poteet and Razor could often be found at odd hours on the outskirts of the operations complex sweeping for explosive components (procured from a previous Middle Eastern deployment) that one of the other handlers had planted for them days earlier. Although Poteet and Razor excelled at searching open areas for ambush under Jeff's instruction, Travis would routinely bribe fellow commandos into playing the role of a hidden assassin long after the regular training day was over. Travis Poteet didn't believe in resting on his laurels. From the starting block, he intended to create the superlative K-9 commando team.

It took nearly six months of instruction, relationship building and relentless application before Travis Poteet and Razor were assigned to a Six-Man-Element. The combat specialists that Travis was committed to were being prepared for a covert operation against associated Taliban/al-Qaeda forces in Afghanistan. Even though this mission would represent Travis' inaugural tour as a dog handler and Razor's first exposure to real combat, Jeff possessed enough confidence in his newest K-9 team that he didn't hesitate to recommend them for the high-risk endeavor.

In September of 2009, Poteet's "element" boarded a monstrous C-17 Globemaster at an airbase in Quantico, Virginia. They flew directly to Panzer Kaserne, a Special Forces Headquarters in Boblingen, Germany. There, the men were further briefed on the specifics of their secretive mission, as well as attached to a larger tactical group composed of personnel from various branches of the U.S. Military.

Inside the main building at Special Forces Headquarters, Travis' "element" and Razor, along with eight commandos from the multi-branched tactical group, positioned themselves around a large table in the planning room. The operation commander stepped to the head of the table and laid out the details of a discrete and unsupported "seek/destroy" assault. The multiday, two-part mission would begin with a U.S. initiated "cyber-attack" on communication devices which would encompass a several block area around the enemy complex. The electronic disruption would occur minutes before a "fast-rope" insertion onto a prominent rooftop of the jointly occupied Taliban/al-Qaeda base, which they were to infiltrate in order to locate a central communication center.

After obliterating the enemy's intelligence hub, the covert operatives were to trek several miles further "in-country" and holdup through the daylight hours inside the pastoral huts of "friendly" Afghani families who were compensated in advance for their cooperation. After darkness set in on the following moonless night, the commandos would hike several more miles to a thoroughly guarded, munitions storage facility. Once they had detonated the weapons and ammunition, Poteet and his group were to hastily make their way by foot two miles up a broad, dry wadi (riverbed) which lay adjacent to the munitions facility. Upon reaching a predetermined extraction site, the Special Task Force would radio for the Black Hawks.

The commander was concise about the mission's objective. He summed up the operation in five, laconic statements: "Commandeer each target. Kill all combatants. Secure or destroy all vital information. Destroy all munitions. Take no prisoners. Gentlemen I want you in and out of that hostile 'theater' in less than forty-eight hours, and I want nothing left behind but destruction."

The following day, the newly combined task force flew from Panzer in the C-17 to Bagram Airfield in northeastern Afghanistan. The last leg of their "hop" was on a spacious Ch-47 Chinook helicopter that transported the mix of commandos and all of their gear from Bagram to an F.O.B. (Forward Operating Base) situated on the very edge of Taliban controlled territory.

At this forward-most base, Travis met for the first time a unique squad of warriors that he had often heard about but never had seen. Three Airmen of a Special Operations Weather Team (SOWT) had briefly returned to the F.O.B. from an "in-country" assignment to assist Operations Command in the planning of Travis' two-part mission. The three meteorologists had unique training that prepared them to operate behind enemy lines and act as an environmental reconnaissance unit in order to gather, as well as interpret weather/environmental intelligence. These men were often the first commandos to penetrate a hostile or occupied territory for the critical purpose of assessing the environmental conditions of a "strike" zone. The optimal "when" and "where"of a covert attack could not be determined without the pivotal information supplied by these critical-skills combatants. Travis remembers easily relating to those weather specialists because they tended to be "lone operatives" much like he considered himself to be. He often touted: "Loners get excited when there's no support, and the odds of getting in and out alive are stacked against us."

After some casual chat, the senior SOWT member gave Poteet a little inside information about their upcoming assault. He told Travis to be sure and hold onto his dog during the flight to the target, because they were predicting the low-elevation winds to be strong and mixed on the dark night of their designated launch.

On the first night of the new moon, Travis Poteet and Razor, along with the rest of their Six-Man-Element, joined eight operators from the multi-branch assault team for a final briefing before boarding two modified, Black Hawk helicopters. Operations Command had directed the pilots of the attack helicopters to approach the mission's insertion point by using a "nap-of-the-earth" (NOE) flight pattern. A low-altitude, NOE course would give the commandos the best chance of avoiding detection by enemy radar as they advanced toward the al-Qaeda controlled complex. Taking advantage of the moonless night, the flight crew would "hug the ground" using their panoramic night vision technology to exploit geographic features of the landscape as cover. Their strategy was to fly the Black Hawks into valleys, below treetops, and between knolls all the way to the insertion point atop the tallest structure within the terrorist stronghold.

Just as the tactical weathermen promised, the wind gusts were potent and whipping up dust clouds all through base camp as the commandos walked to the waiting aircraft. Climbing into the helicopter, the men prepared as best they could for what was sure to be a rough, nauseating ride with the NOE flight and strong wind. Like his comrades, Travis tightened down all of his gear bindings and safety belts. He also took an extra precaution to strap Razor's harness unusually close to his own. The new handler was not only concerned about the trip to the target, but for the "fast roping" insertion once they got there. "Fast roping" with a dog in his hand was challenging enough without the dark and gusty conditions to complicate matters.

Straight off the launching pad the commandos felt the ominous grip of the wind take hold of their helicopters. The highly skilled pilots wrestled with the intangible force for control of their crafts, no differently than a captain strains at the helm of a small vessel amidst a wild sea. The trip to the terrorist complex amounted to an unbroken series of neck-straining pitches and gut-wrenching undulations for both man and beast. Although connected by harnesses and trapped between Travis' legs the entire flight, Razor had his four feet spread far apart, desperately trying to dig his nails into the steel deck and gain some purchase. By the time the men reached their destination, it was a consensus among the warriors aboard the helicopters that "fast roping" into an al-Qaeda camp during high winds would be less troubling than the unsettling ride to get there.

Reaching the target site, the Black Hawks hovered over opposite ends of a large flat-roofed building at the edge of the terrorists' compound. The night's stiff winds really taxed the flight crews as they strained to hold their aircraft steady during the "fast-roping" deployment. Although a relatively large surface, the roof serving as a landing pad for the commandos was only spacious enough to accommodate the two helicopters as long as they held closely to their respective ends of the structure. For the "operators," the timing of each descent had to be coordinated with the aircraft's momentary alignment over the roof, and not the ground that was three stories further below. As each commando took hold of the rope for his turn to disembark, a flight crewman watched for the rooftop which floated in and out of view. When the Black Hawk was sufficiently over the landing mark, the crewman would slap the "operator" on the shoulder and shout "Go!" The pilot could only hold the helicopter over the "sweet spot" for a brief moment, which afforded the descending "operators" no room for hesitation. Ready or not, when the man said "go," each commando stepped off into the darkness clutching the lifeline with two gloved hands to hopefully slide down to the waiting platform.

Since Travis and Razor were "fast roping" as a team, they would be connected to the mechanical descender which first had to be attached to the line. Given that requirement and the furtive need to unload as expeditiously as possible, Poteet was designated the lead man out of his helicopter. The first Black Hawk over the drop-zone had already begun to unload as Poteet's aircraft struggled to get into position. On the crewman's cue, Poteet and Razor began their slide across the steel deck towards the open bay. The helicopter's pitching and bouncing made connecting to the descender a three-man job, just to keep from losing someone out the gaping doorway. Hooked into the device and teetering on the threshold of the open bay, Travis used his right arm to hold Razor tightly against his body while he clutched the rope with his gloved left hand. In those tense moments waiting for the "jump" signal, Poteet wasn't as worried about the mechanized descent as he was getting on the ground before the inevitable gunfire broke out.

Unfortunately, the crewman was consumed with the timing of proper roof alignment and the "go" signal, and he failed to mention to Poteet that the rope was blowing at a severe horizontal angle due to the heavy, rotor "wash" and high winds. If Travis had been "fast roping" solo with both hands and feet gripping the line, the extreme angle of the rope wouldn't have posed an insurmountable problem. However, that's not the case with a K-9 team who counts on the braking effect of the descender to assist his single-hand grip in slowing a descent. With the line blowing at a severe angle, there is a danger of the descender not engaging from lack of friction. Only seconds had ticked by once Travis had clipped into the descender before he felt a slap on the shoulder and heard "Go, Poteet!" The time for thinking was over. Travis launched Razor out the door with his right hand, clung to the rope with his left, and stepped out of the Black Hawk to apply friction-grabbing weight on the descender. Instantly, Travis could feel the overwhelming strain on his left arm and realized in a flash that his device did not fully engage because of lack of friction due to the rope's horizontal angle. Force from the heavy rotor wash and strong wind had blown the rope severely outward causing the K-9 team to slide down the line at catastrophic speed. Rocketing into the night air, Travis and Razor were nearly parallel to the roof as he desperately tried to assist his left arm by trapping the line between his boots in an attempt to slow their velocity. Looking down at his companion, Travis pulled Razor close to his chest in order to protect him from the impact when an explosion of pain silenced his consciousness.

A K-9 team commencing to "Fast Rope."

The very moment the K-9 team stepped out of the launching bay, the assisting crewman recognized that they were in a virtual free-fall and hollered "Dog Down" over the "coms" to the commandos on the ground. Gunfire was already being exchanged on top of the structure as Travis' comrades raced toward his end of the roof. Poteet's still body was lying supine and helmetless on the hard deck while still connected to the rope. Waiting for help to reach the K-9 team, the pilot worked feverishly to keep his aircraft hovering above the roof so as not to drag the two over the edge. The first commando to reach Poteet found Razor stunned from the impact, but perched intact on top of his handler. He quickly disconnected the handler and dog from the rope, and assessed their condition while another "operator" radioed for an emergency evacuation.

The flight crews finished offloading the remaining commandos as they communicated back and forth over the particulars of an extraction. Before an emergency plan could be implemented, Razor had shaken his temporary daze from the crash landing and had committed to taking control of the situation. Stepping between his unconscious handler and one of the attending commandos, Razor began to obsessively lick Travis' face. When the "operator" recklessly pushed Razor out of the way, the four-legged warrior jumped to a protective stance over Travis and dared interference with a brazen display of teeth.

Poteet's two comrades were faced with a time-sensitive problem; a gun-battle was escalating on the rooftop, a Black Hawk was preparing for an emergency hoist, and their canine teammate (whom they were unfamiliar with) had taken control of one of their wounded. A quick decision had to be made between two unpleasant alternatives. One option would be to subdue Razor by taking hold of his collar knowing that a mauling would likely ensue, or shoot their canine counterpart in order to rescue Travis. Either way, they had to act.

Stepping back from the K-9 team to execute their regretful but unanimous decision, one of the "operators" reluctantly lowered his M4's "red dot," laser-sight on Razor's torso. Flipping off the safety he complained out loud; "I can't believe we have to do this." Before his finger contacted the trigger, the men witnessed Travis slowly reaching up from his recumbent position to pet Razor, who was once again licking his handler's face. Both commandos called to Poteet as they moved towards their friend only to encounter more hostility from the war-dog. This time, however, Travis was coherent and able to intercede, so he commanded Razor to disengage and lie down.

Struggling to sit up, Travis listened to his friends' recount of the failed descent and the apparent flat-backed landing in the drop-zone which spared the K-9 team from broken bones. After requesting help to stand up and put his helmet back on, Travis directed his comrades to cancel the emergency evacuation order. The sinewy Poteet said, "We're not ready to go home yet. There's nothing broken on me or Razor, and we've come a long way to 'smoke' some terrorists. Don't mention anything about being unconscious either. We're here to fight and don't have time for concussion observation." The attending commandos were relieved to hear Poteet's wishes and gladly offered no protest. They had been counting on the tattooed, "shooter's" killing instinct for that mission, not to mention his dog's ability to expose ambushes and ferret out munitions.

Outside of an aching, and rapidly stiffening back, Travis didn't feel too bad after his crash landing. Preparing Razor to enter the embattled structure with a quick "once-over" and a vest-tightening, Travis saw no lingering signs of stress or anxiety from the free-fall. In fact, his canine partner was dancing and whining in anticipation of combat. Razor was ready to go to work, and he was clearly demonstrating that the bad descent that occurred only moments earlier left no damaging mark on his psyche. For years after reading the AA Report of that incident, Jeff used Razor's instant recovery from the failed "fast-roping" and immersion into combat as a testimony to superior genetics. Not that he needed vindication for the high-cost product that he supplied to the United States Military, but Jeff believed that this single experience justified his effort and expense to acquire such canine specimens for Colonel Edward's program or any other elite military group for that matter.

Poteet and Razor joined their element as they were making entry into the al-Qaeda communication center down a secondary and tiny stairway. The eight members of the other tactical team were simultaneously penetrating the stronghold through a primary passageway. The Strike Force encountered resistance from the moment they landed on the roof. Both teams were prepared for what they had been briefed to expect, a real gun battle. None of the commandos were running "slick" (removing protective plates from their vests to facilitate speed and comfort) on this mission. Even Razor was wearing his heavy "bullet protection." The "operators" were also caring an ample supply of M67 hand-grenades to make penetration into well defended compartments possible.

To open their way into the structure, Travis' element leader tossed an M67 into the tight stairway where much of the gunfire had come from. The small hand-propelled bomb would kill any living thing by fragmentation or rapid expansion of air pressure within five meters of its detonation point. The commandos were always careful not to harm the women and children living among the guerillas (minimizing the casualties of war was the main reason for not annihilating the Taliban/ al-Qaeda base with an air-strike, in addition to acquiring operational intelligence stored inside the building). However, innocent death or injury was inevitable within the context of close-quarter, urban conflicts as was evidenced by the mortally wounded woman that was dressed in sleeping clothes and lying at the entrance of the staircase.

As the element slowly made their way down the stairs, they had to walk on and around the bloody, dead bodies that were cluttering the narrow passage. Two reassurance rounds were fired into the torso of each collapsed guerilla as the element encountered them. Understandably, Razor was in a high state of stimulation and couldn't keep from taking a quick bite of the deceased targets as he "heeled" with Travis over their bodies. At the bottom of the stairs where the top floor of the structure opened up, the leader called "Dog" forward and asked if he were comfortable sending Razor across an expansive area to search a room that faced their position. Travis was confident that Razor would "zero in" on the partially opened door of the compartment, but he wanted to know that as an element they wouldn't delay in supporting his canine partner once he made entry. The leader put his hand on Travis' shoulder and said, "Poteet, we'll be right on his hairy ass. I don't want to lose that guy either."

With the leader's promise, Travis initiated the ritual that he'd gone through so many times with Franklin as his trainer. He held Razor's harness, disconnected the leash and gave him a few stimulating pats, then he pointed across the large space to the door standing ajar. Razor was vibrating with anticipation, waiting for the last step in the very familiar ritual.

Feeling his canine warrior humming and remembering Jeff's final words of instruction, Travis confirmed the direction of his dog's pricked-ears stare. He then quietly released the harness and whispered into Razor's ear, "Take 'em!" The canine commando crossed the unobstructed area so swiftly that he appeared as nothing more than a blur through Travis' NVGs. Razor's momentum didn't abate as his body impacted the targeted door nearly knocking it loose from its hinges.

Gunfire and screams bellowed from the room the instant Razor darted inside. The Element, who had split into two groups of three, quickly slid along opposite walls to make their way to the "hot" compartment just moments behind Razor. Entering the room simultaneously, Travis turned left to see Razor in a far corner violently thrashing a woman by her shoulder, at the same time the team leader veered right to return fire on a muzzle flash from an adjoining cell. Travis had no time or energy to spare over concern for the woman that he considered to be in the wrong place at the wrong time. Sharply commanding Razor to "release," Travis pulled a curtain back from the entrance to a deep recess and directed his animal counterpart to "search." Letting go of the mangled woman, Razor was on a "bee line" toward the recessed space when 7.62 rounds ripped through the curtain still partially covering the opening. Instinctively, Travis commanded Razor to "down" dropping him below and short of the bullets streaming from the recess. Taking advantage of an apparent reloading-pause in the gunfire, Travis turned his M4 barrel into the dark space and sprayed it with 5.56s in preparation for Razor who was eagerly waiting on his "down." When the last bullet left his weapon, Poteet sent his companion in to "search." Travis followed after Razor who had already engaged a guerilla hiding far in the back under a makeshift bed. As Razor was forcefully trying to extract the armed man from his concealment, another combatant was violently kicking the dog-commando to drive him away. Although having his AK-47 pointing toward the curtained doorway, the kicking-guerilla was preoccupied with Razor which allowed Travis the second and a half he needed to discharge three unanswered rounds into the enemy's torso and head. Thoroughly enraged from the two-on-one altercation, Razor required three stern commands before he finally released the quarry and stepped back. With only inches between Razor and the combatant, Travis unloaded a couple of shots under the bed to end the battle.

Before joining his comrades, Travis took the time to look over Razor for injuries. The post- struggle exam was one of Franklin's policies that all of his handlers took seriously. Owing to a war-dog's high-energy state (a condition very capable of masking serious damage) during a foray, and the obvious fact that the four-legged commando can't describe physical sensations as his human counterpart can, an immediate and thorough "once over" is a critical measure for canine health and safety. Routinely, Travis also checked Razor's skin elasticity as part of the exam. Jeff showed Poteet how to squeeze and pull Razor's skin away from the withers and judge by its thickness and rubbery snap-back (or lack thereof) what state of hydration the war-dog was in. If Razor's skin felt thin rather than plump and was slow to snap back to its normal condition against the shoulders, that meant Razor was lacking in fluid and was in danger of impaired performance, no differently than a human being in that same state. Whenever Poteet seized an opportunity to test Razor's hydration, he also offered him a drink and took one himself. This routine helped the K-9 team keep on top of the constant threat of dehydration that was an inextricable part of Middle Eastern operations. Efforts to keep hydrated also led Travis into the habit of perpetually spying for caches of sealed water bottles while "in country."

Once the combined Strike Force cleared the al-Qaeda compound they began the hurried and tedious task of collecting intelligence and destroying machinery. Capitalizing on broken enemy communications from the U.S. led cyber-attack, the commandos were able to thoroughly destroy the terrorist information center without the immediate risk of enemy reinforcements. Although not as pressed for time as they usually were, the combined force had completed their objective and were marching out into the countryside toward the "friendly" homesteads in less than thirty minutes.

Poteet had sheltered with designated "friendlies" on previous missions, and he hated it. He didn't consider any neighbors or acquaintances of the enemy his friends. He didn't trust them, he considered them dirty and he never slept in their presence. Travis' distrust toward "friendlies" was solidified by an unforgettable event that occurred the previous year. A fellow commando was in Afghanistan traveling in a convoy led by an Air Force Combat Controller and an Afghani "friendly" in the front vehicle. When the convoy halted at a rebel checkpoint, the Afghani guide exited the front vehicle to secure permission to pass the armed guards. After a brief discussion with one of the soldiers, the guide was handed an AK-47 which he turned toward the convoy firing into the front vehicles, killing the Combat Controller. To Travis, "shacking up" with the locals was one of the uglier parts of this mission. However, he had Razor as company this time, and he planned on getting a little rest while his ferocious body guard maintained watch.

Sixteen

INTO THE KAREZ

The sun wasn't far from coming up by the time the Strike Force had reached the scattering of pastoral huts that were spread far and wide. Poteet's group traditionally used the "rock- paper-scissors" method for selecting the sleeping arrangements. Travis really didn't care which family he got stuck him with; he hated them all. Standing outside of his assigned hut's miniature doorway, Poteet called for all the occupants to come outside and be counted. Being very stern in both Pashto and Dari, Travis announced that he was an armed U.S. warrior and he was taking temporary control of their home. A mature couple, along with their adult daughter, slowly made their way out to greet the American. No words were exchanged as the Afghanis stared at Travis, who was fully outfitted in battle gear, like he was a cyborg from an alien planet. If he had cared at all about the rural family's perception of the situation, Travis could have described the non-verbal meeting as awkward. Since he had absolutely no concern over their feelings, Travis remembers the experience as simply business-like.

In preparation for a potentially bad outcome, Poteet had placed Razor on a "down/stay" around the side of the dwelling, out of sight and harm's way. Satisfied that all of the occupants evacuated the dwelling, Travis ordered them to file back inside in front of him. Leading with his M4, literally over the shoulder of the daughter, Travis held on to her gown as the two entered the shelter as a unit. After easily clearing the small residence that was devoid of interior rooms or offsets, Poteet claimed one corner of the dirt-floor residence as his space. Using a small collapsible shovel that he brought along for that specific purpose, Travis drew a semicircle from one wall to the next, outlining an area just large enough to sleep in. Then he proceeded to dig out a shallow fox-hole, piling up the dirt along the semicircle perimeter. He confessed to his Afghani roommates that this measure was an attempt to keep their bugs and filth away from him. It also was a means to peaceful living. Pointing over the freshly dug ridge of dirt, Poteet said, "That's my space. Stay out of it and we'll get along fine. Approach my space and I'll kill you, and I mean I'll kill all three of you. Understand? I'm not your friend. Oh yeah, I also have a surprise you're not going to like."

With that, Travis called for Razor who charged into the hut displaying a high tail and an expression full of anticipation. Both women shrieked in horror at Razor's appearance, and all three Afghanis backed against a far wall.

By that time in the Afghani campaign, the U. S. war-dogs, especially Jeff's elite, canine commandos had amassed a ferocious reputation and were generally feared throughout the countryside. Laughing at their terrified reaction, Travis commented, "His name is Razor, and he's not your friend either. He doesn't sleep, so he'll be watching every move you make. Keep in mind that this dog likes to hurt people, so be very careful around him."

Settling into the foxhole with Razor was an entirely different experience for Travis than what he was used to. When he thinks back on that mission, Travis recalls for the first time feeling at ease in the company of "friendlies." Sitting in the dugout space with his back against the wall, Poteet dozed in and out as he clutched his Sig Sauer 9mm with one hand and calmly stroked Razor with the other. For hours the canine commando closely studied their Middle Eastern roommates. Having his sentry on guard afforded Travis the freedom to reminisce about the previous night's mission and dream about getting back to basecamp so he could send Franklin the stellar report on Razor's first operation.

When darkness set in that following night, chatter over the communications headset woke Travis from a light slumber. The Strike Force leader was rousting both groups of commandos for their evening trek to the al-Qaeda hideout. It was time for the K-9 team to take a bathroom break, ingest some calories and water (donated by the Afghani family), say good-bye to their frightened hosts and hookup with his element for the lengthy hike to the terrorists' storage facility.

The evening was passing by quickly as the Strike Force laboriously made its way across the broken terrain toward their target. The familiar anxiety of running out of night before completing a mission seemed to be an inextricable part of covert operations, especially when the difficulty of getting to the strike zone is underestimated. By the time they reached their destination, the commandos would need every minute of

Precious shade for the canine warrior while on a water break.

darkness that remained to take over the guarded storage facility and escape via the wadi.

Before their cross-country hike began, the Strike Force leader approached Poteet about employing Razor to sweep the compound area, excluding the main structure, for stockpiled munitions the very moment the exterior guards were eliminated. The leader had received last minute intelligence indicating that most of the terrorists' arms and ammunition could be scattered about the communal outbuildings, or they may be buried in caches connected to the irrigation tunnels that lie just outside the complex. The leader was left to believe that the storage facility itself might be used primarily for housing guerillas.

The assault was non-mechanized, which allowed the Strike Force to catch the inhabitants of the storage complex completely off guard. As the commandos approached the periphery of the compound, all was quiet in the large building and the few, outlying dwellings. Thick vegetation atop elevated topography sandwiched the area on two sides which provided ideal, covered positions for guerilla lookouts or snipers. The first order of business for the Strike Force was to bring forward their two long- distance shooters and eliminate any lookout/snipers from the elevated cover with suppressed rifle-fire. After half an hour of careful searching through their "night scopes," the "shooters" found and eliminated two armed guerillas that were well ensconced in the high-brush surrounding the complex.

Receiving the "all clear" from his shooters, the Strike Force leader ordered his men to divide into two groups and begin a quiet search among the outlying structures and communal grounds. The large, central building was purposely left for last. Poteet and one other "operator" were held back so that they could immediately begin the munitions sweep as each section of the complex was cleared of armed resistance.

The smallest and most distant of the outbuildings was found unoccupied and unguarded, so Poteet was called up with Razor right away to look for weapons and ammunition. As the K-9 Team stealthily snaked their way toward the small structure, Razor was on hyper-alert and insisted on forging ahead of Travis' left leg. His mind was definitely bent toward a struggle of the kind he was so engrossed with the night before.

Knowing that Poteet and Razor could reach the pinnacle of team performance, Franklin had pushed the two through countless additional sessions of "heeling" practice until they attained near perfection in synchronized movement. Jeff wanted to feel confident that his neophyte K-9 Unit would be ready for the challenges of their unusually dangerous first mission.

Although in the midst of authentic tactical maneuvers, Poteet was a true disciple of Jeff Franklin's, and he had no intention of giving Razor a "free pass" on poor heeling just because they were in combat. Moving with Razor to the empty dwelling's blindside, Travis continued the "heeling" pattern with his companion just long enough to apply a series of sharp, collar corrections in order to regain precise "heeling." Once he was satisfied with his dog's focus, Travis pulled out Razor's ball for a brief bit of play and mental alignment with munition searching rather than guerilla fighting.

Sweeping the small, multi-room construction from the front door to the rear cubbies, Razor was attentive and meticulous, but no explosives or munitions were found. Travis did comment to his fellow operator about his dog's high interest (minus a definite indication) in the dirt floor of each room. Upon further inspection, the two men could see that the floors had all been recently excavated.

Excluding Razor's discovery of some partially, buried fuses, spent casings and empty ammunition boxes, the second structure was also devoid of any munitions cache. Frustrated, from the lack of finds in either structure, save for the freshly disturbed, dirt floors, the K-9 Team turned their attention toward the grounds surrounding the two outbuildings. This area of the complex was flat, open, and extended outward in the direction of the distant mountains.

Hungry to locate something of worth, Travis connected Razor to his ten-meter long-line and directed him to "find." The canine commando searched with his nose to the ground in a zigzag pattern, moving slowly and methodically according to his handler's signals. Razor's enthusiasm intensified and his pace accelerated as he gradually worked his way across the compound's communal yard and out into the periphery. Rapidly moving farther into the countryside and away from the Strike Force, Travis had to call Razor from his ebullient hunt before they found themselves compromised in open territory and too far from support.

Clearly hot on the enemy trail of armaments, the excited searching dog was hard to reel-in that morning. Razor was whining and rearing up on his hind legs as Travis switched him back to his short "heeling" leash. Apologizing to his partner for the premature "call off," Travis knelt beside Razor and soothed him with some calm promises about returning to the search before all was said and done. As he settled his dog with a few heavy strokes, Poteet aligned his vision with that of Razor's rigid stare. Looking out into the darkness through his NVGs, Travis could make out the phantasmal, green image of his dog's focus. It appeared to be a small entrance to a mine or cave. Travis could also see an evenly spaced row of large, dirt mounds that were arranged in a straight line and faded in the distance as they drew closer to the mountains. Poteet didn't wonder long about the landscape features and their worth to his dog before "butterflies" hit him like a queasy hammer. He whispered to Razor, "That's the frickin' karez! So that's why their floors were dug up.

They knew we were coming and stashed their munitions in the tunnels. Let's get back to the compound and round up a posse."

On a previous Middle Eastern tour, Poteet was part of a mechanized Special Task Force that encountered a lethal Taliban ambush. Like ghouls from hell, more than two dozen guerillas spilled out from subterranean tunnels to launch their attack. Fully armed with PKMs and Rocket Propelled Grenades, the assassins delivered a swift and staggering blow to the Task Force, and then retreated back into the earth from where they came, all in a matter of minutes. Travis remembered how he and his group were caught so off guard. He said, "We were bewildered in the moments following the ambush in how to conduct a 'strike-back'. It felt as though they were supernatural demons who appeared in a flash to pummel us and then disappeared without a trace before we had a chance to retaliate." That's when somebody in Poteet's group mentioned the karez and the particularly treacherous nature of subterranean warfare, which was so dreaded by U.S. troops during the Vietnam War when the enemy had to be routinely cleared from their underground tunnels.

The karez is an ancient network of hand-dug, irrigation tunnels that spread from the mountainous regions in Afghanistan throughout countless miles of dry plains. These tunnels or underground channels allow water to flow from the orographic water tables to the homesteads at lower elevations. A straight line of vertical wells or access shafts (about thirty meters apart and identified by the spoils around the opening) leading from the mountains to the plains is a dead giveaway for a channel hidden below.

At the water's source in the higher elevations, where the horizontal tunnel construction actually begins, a well can reach depths in excess of one hundred and fifty meters. As the irrigation channel is dug, more vertical shafts are needed for excavation purposes to gradually extend the gently sloping tunnel toward the lower flat-ground (in some cases many kilometers). Numerous subterranean channels eventually surface to expose the life-giving water as it flows into narrow, open canals. Residential areas naturally spring up around these wells and canals which amount to a true oasis within the arid environment of Afghanistan.

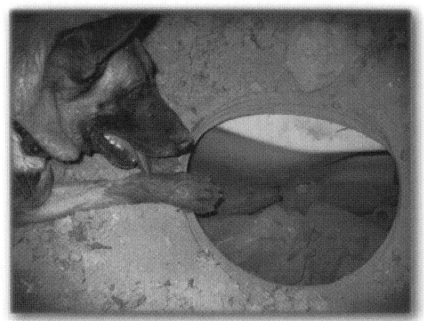

The enemies' buried explosives could not elude the trained canine nose.

Because the tunnels are completely excavated by local men with handheld tools, the karez could be considered a network of manmade caves. They are spacious enough and have been modified (by additional burrowing) in many cases to accommodate human beings in a number of ways. Throughout history, the Afghanis have used the irrigation system for storage (munitions and supplies), habitation (over extended periods), and mobilization (guerilla troops).

The eerie ambush from underground stayed with Poteet for a long while. In fact, one of his first tasks when he returned to civilization from that mission was to research the elaborate, irrigation systems of Afghanistan and their multifarious uses throughout history. During his investigation Travis discovered that the Afghanis from as far back as the invasion of Genghis Kahn have used the karez as a means of defense. In more recent times the Mujahedeen guerillas successfully used the catacomb-like tunnels from which to launch attacks and to evade hostile Soviet troops during their ten-year occupation from 1979 to 1989.

The K-9 team double-timed it back to the main, multi-storied structure to join the Strike Force as they solidified plans for entry. Rejoining his group, Travis immediately called out to the Force leader by his nickname and passed along his theory; "Boss, I don't think there's anything left to find in this entire complex, I believe it's all been moved into the karez." Justifiably tense, the Force leader lashed back at Poteet, "What in the hell are you talking about, and what's a karez?" Boss gave Poteet one minute to describe the irrigation network and divulge his theory on how al-Qaeda may be using it. Afterwards, he sent the K-9 team and another shooter to guard the back entrance of the building and take down the "squirters" (fleeing antagonists) as they poured out.

Crouching with his dog at a rear corner of the structure (opposite his comrade), Travis flipped his M4's safety off and unleashed Razor. He was ready to shoot and send his dog at the same time in the event the enemy escaped in large numbers. Dragging down "squirters" was Razor's favorite exercise among all of Franklin's training scenarios. The canine commando could tell by the set-up of men storming the front, while he and his handler lay hidden in the back, that fleeing prey would soon appear. Razor was so eager to break into the real-life action that he emitted a slight, vibrating whine with every exhale as he and Travis stared at the back door and windows.

Quietly forcing entry through the side windows and the front door simultaneously, the commandos stepped into the lower level of the building to find no living beings, but only some scattered piles of bottled water and rations. Watching from the outside, Travis saw his fellow operators slip into the structure. He braced himself for the "fire fight" and shook Razor's harness as if to say, "It's going down. Get ready!" However, silence is all that came from the guerilla hideout. Waiting in their designated spot, Poteet and Razor listened as the commandos crept up two separate stairwells to the second floor. An explosion of hysterical screams poured out from the second story windows as Poteet exchanged "all ready" signals with the other shooter, but no gunfire followed. More shrieks and wails from the top-floor windows, and still no rounds were exchanged. So far, the operators had only encountered clusters of sleeping women and children. By the time the Strike Force breached the roof, Travis had already stood up, returned his weapon to safe, and re-leashed Razor. He felt sure there were no al-Qaeda soldiers hiding inside the compound. Razor and his viscera had all but confirmed the location of their new lair.

Frustrated from the complete lack of success, the Force leader huddled his men outside of the makeshift dormitory and asked Poteet to divulge his thoughts to the group. Travis' karez theory seemed plausible to the band of warriors, but the difficult question of how to handle the tunnel-search remained. One of the operators suggested that they copy the Vietnam War strategy and soften the subterranean hide-out with grenades dropped in from the shafts, then send in a few men to clear the tunnel. Travis volunteered immediately to spearhead the underground search with Razor, saying that this task was tailor-made for a K-9 team. Travis boasted that none in their group could flush the enemy from side chambers and search for munitions more efficiently than Razor.

Looking directly at Poteet and Razor, Boss said that he didn't like the idea of sending members of his team into a death trap. Despite being keenly aware of the imminent dangers linked to such a project, Travis' response to the leader's concern was calm, "If Franklin were here, he'd take Razor into the karez. This is the best dog to have come through the commando program, and Franklin has the two of us ready to meet any challenge. Besides, I have a score to settle with those 'subterranean devils'."

"Well night is fading fast, so the talkin's over anyway. Let's do it!" With those final words from Boss, the commandos filed in behind the K-9 team and marched out of the al-Qaeda compound en route to the karez.

Approaching the mouth of the tunnel, the Strike Force minimized their exposure by splitting into two ranks and flanking the entrance. Boss assigned six men to position themselves (one man per well) over the first half dozen wells arranged in a line that spanned a distance of about a hundred and fifty meters. Following signals from the Strike Leader, the six commandos armed their M67 Fragmentation Grenades and simultaneously dropped them into their designated shafts. The rumble and roar from the underground explosion felt nothing short of cataclysmic. After the synchronized detonation, the "operators" were convinced that nothing living could remain in the first two hundred meters of the subterranean hideout.

Waiting for the air to clear inside the tunnel, Travis stood outside of its entrance along the edge of the open canal and meticulously executed his gear-check ritual. Connecting the long-line to Razor's harness, as the two peered into the wet, dark hole, Travis talked to his dog as if he were human about the tight quarters and slippery terrain they were about to face. Debating over whether or not Razor should wear boots, the handler deferred to his dog's preference to operate barefoot which allowed him to spread his toes for maximum purchase. Possessing the characteristics of a loner, Poteet, usually found it challenging to be communicative with his teammates; however, he had no such hang-up with Razor. Travis even thought it was odd how he readily chatted with his four-legged companion, who so quickly evolved into his best friend. Poteet felt that people in general were deficient and disappointing. However, Travis believed that his dog was a perfect specimen and fully worthy of his respect and admiration. So, it became part of Poteet's combat ritual to talk over plans with Razor, and that seemed to comfort them both.

After a short time passed, the dank air wafting out of the underground world was still laced with the smell of hot metal from the detonated grenades, but it didn't seem toxic. Also, a light stream of water once again flowed from the tunnel after being disrupted by the explosions. The time had come, and the entry plan was set. Eight men were positioned along the line of wells at the surface ready to deal with flushed-out guerillas and defend against intruders. Two of Travis' comrades would follow a substantial distance behind him and Razor as they pushed through the karez, and two commandos would hold at the entrance with the leader as back-up.

Razor was the first to enter into the wet hole-in-the-ground with a directive to "search." Travis had the handle of the ten-meter line secured to his vest which allowed both of his hands to be free to operate his M4 and catch himself as he slid along the wet floor of the tunnel. Razor, who was attached to the other end of the line, would be expected to operate by voice commands to "search" (concentrate on combatants), "wait," "find" (focus on munitions), "down," or "heel." Given the terrible fighting conditions (countless hidden side chambers, no cover from gunfire in the relatively narrow passage, and a slick to sloppy surface for footing) and the inability to effectively back-up his dog, Travis elected to keep Razor fixed within ten meters of his M4. Consequently, the canine commando would be restricted to functioning as an early warning system rather than a seek-and-destroy weapon. Poteet felt very uncomfortable having Razor so exposed and limited in fighting options, but he couldn't think of a better way to manage the task given the circumstances.

Travis braced himself for Razor's impact at the end of the line before he entered the tunnel behind him. Cautiously stepping into the running water, Travis turned to the Force leader and asked, "Boss, if it goes bad for us, don't leave my Razor down here to rot." The leader pointed at Poteet and said, "No man left behind, Poteet! And that includes Razor. If I hear of any trouble, we're comin' to get you, hell or high water. No body dies today!" Travis flashed the leader a "thumbs up" and followed his dog into the darkness.

Razor was more than eager to meet up with some trolls, which he proved with every step by straining against the long-line. Travis had to repeatedly communicate to his companion, "Easy, Raz! Easy. We'll get to 'em." Razor effortlessly plowed through the first crater (left by one of the grenades) filled with water while Travis struggled to stay on his feet. Travis appreciated his NVG's more inside the karez than he ever had on any other mission. He couldn't imagine how frightening it must have been for the poor soldiers clearing tunnels in Vietnam with only a handheld flashlight and a 45 pistol.

Travis took a spill in the third crater and hollered for Razor to "wait." Just past the fourth well the K-9 team encountered the first adjunct chambers, one on either side of the tunnel. Both excavated sites bore evidence of habitation, but no munitions. Struggling to get through the fifth water-filled hole, Travis felt the long-line go slack. Looking ahead Travis saw Razor sitting to the right with his nose pointing straight up.

Cautiously approaching his alert companion, Poteet looked up and called into his radio, "Bingo! Razor just found a bundle of AK-47s hanging in a depression over a crate of ammunition." A short distance later, the K-9 team came across a larger depression packed with RPGs and several 7.62 machine guns. Passing the seventh shaft, the subterranean Assault Team moved deeper underground as the commandos on the surface tracked them.

Following the gently sloping karez as it headed toward the mountains, the long-line dropped to slack once more, and Travis noticed Razor locked on alert, standing in the middle of the tunnel and staring straight ahead. Travis whispered into his headset, "Dog on alert. We have live targets upfront." As the Task Force leader called for Poteet to halt, shots rang out from a dark recess up ahead of the K-9 team. Travis crashed to the ground hollering for Razor to "down." Scrambling to his knees, Travis lit up both sides of tunnel with his M4. More gunfire from the recess forced Poteet into desperate action. He cut Razor free from his vest and commanded, "Take 'em!" Like a bolt, the canine commando charged down the wet tunnel and leapt into a depression.

So effective and so feared, Franklin had them ready for battle.

Travis was sliding along the tunnel wall toward his partner and the horrendous sounds of a life-or-death struggle when another guerilla appeared from a cavity on the opposite side of the corridor. Instinctively, Poteet aligned his sights and squeezed his trigger twice, dropping the combatant before he had a chance to act on the American predator that was advancing in the almost total darkness. Looking back toward Razor, Travis saw that the feisty Dutchy had pulled his adversary out into the tunnel, so Travis shouted for him to "release" and "heel," then sent two 5.56 rounds into the guerilla the very moment his dog afforded him a clear shot.

Although blood-spattered and breathing heavily, Razor appeared to be in good shape when he returned to his handler's side. Poteet could hear Boss calling out "Dog," over the radio while he and the other commandos raced to their aid. Travis answered back, "We're good!" Razor and I 'smoked' two targets and we're moving on."

The underground battle compelled a number of combatants at distant wells to flee the tunnel by climbing up rope ladders. They climbed up to the waiting commandos and a gunfight when they reached the surface, however. The karez was proving to be the hotspot that Travis had suspected.

Re-attaching the long-line to Razor's vest, Poteet directed him to search once again. Full of zeal from his recent, lethal encounter, the four-legged "operator" vigorously pulled ahead causing Travis to slip and slide in tow. Under wells nine and ten, the K-9 team warily came upon two dead guerillas that had dropped from the surface battle. Travis wasted no time firing two shots into both inanimate combatants just to make sure that there was no life left in their physical forms.

Once stepping over the bodies, Razor didn't go far before he doubled back and put his front feet up on the tunnel wall. Travis carefully closed in on Razor who gradually settled into a sit with his eyes fixed on the wall. Poteet was on high alert, continuously scanning from side to side as he crept up on his dog. Razor's focus on the wall was steady and unbroken. He didn't even twitch when Travis came up to pet him. Looking over the top of his dog, Travis could see a large man-made cavern just above his head. Unleashing Razor, Poteet slung his M4 around so that he could shove his dog up into the hollow for a closer investigation. After a quarter minute of silence, Travis called Razor back to the edge of the cavity to check in. He came readily, but was immediately drawn back in by some powerful interest. Feeling compelled to follow, Poteet radioed back to Boss that Razor was on a possible munitions alert in a high cavity close to well ten and he was climbing up to explore. The Force leader insisted that Poteet wait for them. Unfortunately, his directive fell on the deaf ears of a "loner," who was already scrambling into the elevated hole.

Before Travis could climb to his feet, he saw that Razor was sitting in front of a stockpile of ammunition and crated firearms. Crawling over to his tail-wagging companion, Travis praised Razor and promised him some well-earned ball-play as soon as they resurfaced. When Poteet stood up to marvel over the size of Razor's find, a light from a high, deep recess across the tunnel illuminated their cavern. With no thought sequence, Poteet's fast-twitch muscles grabbed the M4 hanging at his waist and squeezed off shots at the light while calling for Razor to "jump." Sniper-fire chewed up the cavity walls as Poteet leapt from the hollow hoping that his companion was right behind. Landing hard and slamming into the tunnel wall before coming to a halt, Travis' left arm was throbbing with pain as he adjusted his goggles and struggled to sit up. Seeing no apparent wound or blood, Travis surmised that he must have shattered a bone during the fall, so he instantly turned his thoughts toward Razor. Poteet didn't see his friend standing in the cavity or on the ground. He was flooded with bad feelings over Razor's whereabouts, but there was no time to investigate given his critical situation.

Gloomy thoughts filled Travis' mind as the light from the recess skimmed towards him. It took less than two seconds for Poteet's feelings of desperation to turn into burning rage over the prospect of losing Razor. Wrestling his M4 around with his one operable arm, Travis shouldered his weapon as he rocked forward on his knees. His eyes were glued to the high cavity as the sniper tentatively peered around the edge of the opening, exposing a bit of his torso. At that critical moment Travis should have taken a "kill shot." However, he was so consumed with hate over the loss of his companion by that time, he purposely allowed a dangerous second to pass just to be certain that his enemy could see death looking back at him over the barrel of the M4. Poteet dumped multiple rounds into the sniper's body causing him to fall from the recess onto the tunnel floor. There, Travis shot him again, for his friend.

Poteet's cognitive universe became empty and dismal in the ten seconds that passed from the time he'd leapt from the cavity. Slumping against the tunnel wall on his right shoulder, Travis imagined he heard Razor's familiar whimper deep in the recesses of his mind. It was very faint, but seemingly so real. The thought of that friendly sound made the depressing act of searching for his companion's body almost unbearable for the hardened warrior.

Still on his knees, Travis shuffled around to get his back against the wall for support when the dreamy whimper of his dog called from memory once again. It seemed so close that time he could imagine touching Razor. Settling against the wall, Poteet would have sworn he could smell dog breath. Knowing that wasn't possible, he blamed the surreal experience on his weakness of emotional attachment that he had vowed never to have for anyone or anything. Wrestling with his grief, Poteet shoved the NVGs up to his helmet, when he felt an unmistakably authentic lick on the side of his face. Jolted into hyper awareness, Travis quickly reached out to feel his living, breathing Razor, standing only inches away. His devoted companion had been happily standing behind Travis the entire time, waiting for orders. Razor had shadowed his team leader from the moment he heard "Jump." Putting his face against Razor's, Travis confessed, "My friend, you've become way too important to me."

For Poteet, all the world was good again. The fact that he was exhausted and deep in the karez with a broken arm felt insignificant after Razor's return from the "imagined dead." To think that they were walking out of the tunnel together caused Travis to chuckle, and that was the scene that Boss and the "back up" commandos walked up to: dead guerillas lying next to their fellow warrior who was sitting in the mud with a broken arm and laughing while Razor climbed all over him.

After effectively detonating the caches of munitions found in the karez, the Strike Force was swiftly and adeptly extracted from the nearby wadi in broad daylight. The mission was recorded as a consummate success, and particular appreciation was given to the K-9 team and the overall contribution that Jeff Franklin's canines brought to the Special Task Force Operations.

On return to Base Camp, Travis Poteet was shipped back to the States (against his will) to have his strained back and debilitated arm treated. He was forced to leave Razor behind for a new handler who was assigned to finish that tour of duty. For the months that Razor remained in the Middle East, Travis obsessively worked his way back to health and a dog-handler's position. He made a promise to himself and to Jeff that he would one day be fit for a K-9 team.

Travis made good on his promise, and by the time that Razor made it back home for rest/recovery, he was once again in peak physical condition and at the top of handlers' class. Jeff gave Travis special consideration on his return to the program and let him choose the dog of his choice for his next tour of duty. Everyone involved with the Canine Commando program knew that Jeff's offering to Travis was only ceremonial because the recovered handler had talked of nothing but "his dog" Razor since returning home. Poteet and Razor went on to serve as Franklin's quintessential K-9 team for two more active tours, and both survived their service in the Special Tactics Group to reach retirement together.

I met Travis Poteet and Razor for an interview when they were no longer assigned to active duty, but they were still a team. I asked Travis to reflect back on his years with Jeff Franklin, and we talked about many aspects of the Canine Commando program. Then I asked him one final question, "As the experienced and respected warrior that you are, what would you like to have seen Jeff do differently in regard to the program or your and Razor's training?" Sitting across from me,

Travis studied his courageous and faithful companion, who was relaxed on a "down" beside his chair. Calmly petting Razor's head while he thought over my question, Poteet looked up and answered, "There was nothing for him to do differently. Franklin had us prepared for battle."

Afterword

Semper fidelis.

In the last quarter of 2011, four of Jeff's K-9 Commando teams took part in a U.S. Military, large-scale Full Mission Profile (F.M.P.) in North Carolina. The F.M.P. was a joint training exercise involving multiple service branches of the Armed Forces as well as Colonel Edward's Tactical Operations Command that was based in Virginia and a competing task force command from California. A large-scale F.M.P. affords the human and mechanized components of various military service branches the opportunity to coordinate as well as integrate together in a real-life conflict scenario.

Live-fire, demolitions, air and watercraft deployment, as well as role-players are often utilized in this type of training exercise to simulate authentic battle conditions. High ranking commanders make use of F.M.Ps. to assess strategic functionality and effectiveness of the integral parts comprising a Joint Warfare offensive.

It's no secret among the military elite and their superiors that being the best at execution in any form of combat operation (real or practice) means nearly as much as a successful mission. Whenever the top tier operators have a chance to perform alongside one another during a joint training exercise, especially of the F.M.P. magnitude, the rivalry is fierce.

At one point in 2009, the colonel overseeing the task force in California commissioned one of his more enthusiastic captains to construct a working dog program of their own. The plan was to emulate the Canine Commando paradigm that Jeff built for Colonel Edward. After evaluating the submitted bids for the new contract, the Captain selected an ex-military dog handler with solid experience in police K-9 instruction.

Candidate selection and training began right away. Within eighteen months the California task force possessed multiple K-9 teams with limited deployment experience and a reasonable level of confidence in their own commando dogs' performance. Having been invited to also take part in the 2011 F.M.P., the Gunnery Sergeant directly in charge of the California canine program was eager to pit his teams' strike tactics and execution against that of Colonel Edward's men with Jeff's dogs.

On the opening morning of the large-scale, combat exercise, curiosity inspired Jeff and Gunnery Sgt. Hawk (Gunny) to drop in on the visiting California group to say hello. Walking into the opposing camp reminded Jeff of his college baseball days when he had the occasional opportunity to check out the competition. Energy was high as Jeff and Gunny wandered through the camp looking for the K-9 units and their commanding sergeant. Halfway through the jumble of military personnel and machinery, the two men heard ecstatic barking coming from the far side of the latrine area. As Jeff and Sgt. Hawk approached the commotion they saw that the handlers were already geared up and running their dogs through some basic drills while their trainer observed. Even though the two had never met, the California trainer recognized Jeff from a recent accommodations ceremony and waived him over.

The two trainers talked shop for a bit while Gunny watched the K-9 teams take their turn locating a hidden decoy who was conspicuously perched on a low branch of a scrubby pine tree. Each dog in their searching effort seemed eager but much too distracted by the clamor of camp and wildlife activity to focus on their straightforward task. After the many hours of watching the K-9 teams under Jeff's instruction, Gunny had developed an appreciation for human/canine coordination that he saw none of with the California group. Working individually in a sequence, the four dogs took their turn resembling a loose cannon crashing around and running helter-skelter through the target area.

One at a time, the California dogs would race through but never alert on the decoy's obvious scent plume that must have engulfed the area around the small pine tree where he had been waiting for some time. Gunny was perplexed as to why the handlers appeared powerless and unconcerned about retrieving their wild canines and redirecting their searching pattern.

Eventually the decoy used audible cues to lure each frustrated dog into a "hold-and-bark" pattern at the base of the tree. Once cued in to the decoy's location all four canines demonstrated a gamey response in trying to climb the tree to engage their quarry. Allowing for a sufficient period of intense "holding-and-barking," the decoy dropped out of the tree and physically sparred with each dog. Although proving to be battle worthy in regards to aggression during the physical conflict, the canines from California lacked across the board in their bite depth and duration. And no surprise to Gunny, after observing the lack of discipline during the searching exercise, there was no hint of a "cease fighting" response for any of the dogs. All four unruly animals had to be physically removed from the decoy and drug from the sparring scene in order to regain any kind of composure.

Sgt. Hawk was the first to admit that he's no professional dog trainer, however, he knew enough about the process from working closely with Jeff over the years to recognize the lack of self-control and tactical protocol in the K-9 teams. The dogs themselves were athletic according to Gunny, and although not the robust specimens that he's used to seeing with Jeff's handlers, they did appear to be of quality breeding. Unfortunately, their overall lack of concentration and handler responsiveness, made it difficult to determine whether or not they were commando material. Combat-savvy Sgt. Hawk saw in only a few minutes that the instruction needed to prepare the men and dogs from California for the demands of tactical operations was missing.

Once the last dog had been pried free from the decoy, Gunny conveyed to Jeff the need to return to camp for strategic meetings regarding the next day's start of the Joint Training Exercise. On the walk back to their post, Jeff and Gunny compared observation notes about the opposing team's performance and training philosophy. Both men were in full agreement that the cavalier training style which the California instructor described to Jeff in great detail, produced the inadequate results that Gunny witnessed in the four K-9 teams during their search and apprehension exercises.

Following the visit with his arrogant competition, Jeff surmised that the relaxed standards set for the California dogs must have filtered down from the highest-ranking officers within their task force. If not, none of the K-9 teams would have been deemed ready for such a large F.M.P., let alone actual deployments. Gunny closed the discussion on the competing canine commando program with his final portentous comments;

"Colonel or no Colonel, I wouldn't allow those California dog teams to accompany us on any kind of mission. I guess I'm accustomed to the tight 'Franklin' structure of our program and anything short of that makes me think of disruption and disaster. They're not in our league, Jeff, so no worries about any 'higher-ups' bustin' your chops. You set the standard. Don't forget that."

Back at camp Jeff prepped his men and dogs for the F.M.P. just like he did for an actual deployment. There was only one difference as far as execution was concerned, that was the use of simulated ammunition instead of live rounds. Once in his commando-dog instruction mode, the thought of the other task force and their dogs never crossed Jeff's mind. He viewed the Joint Training Exercise not as a competition or pretend battle, but as one more opportunity to hone the skills of his K-9 units and increase their odds of returning from war zones safely.

Colonel Edward's Tactical Operations Command and the California task force were positioned on opposite ends of the designated combat zone which was quite extensive. As a consequence, Jeff and Gunny were never privy to the California group's activity. The colonels along with their captains, on the other hand, routinely observed from every vantage point and advised as an overseeing "think-tank" during the simulated, multi-day mission.

The dog teams from both of the specialized commands were called into action almost immediately on the first day of engagement. At the close of the second day of the simulated campaign, Gunny was informed by his captain that all four of the California K-9 teams had been sent home with their sergeant, and the trainer had been dismissed on the spot by their captain who was the officer in charge. It was relayed to Gunny that the colonel from the California Command was embarrassed by the performance of his commando dog-teams as compared to that of Colonel Edward's, and he couldn't tolerate another day of it.

Over the following week of maneuvers, the captain of the California task force, at Colonel Edward's invitation, was given open access to observe the training/execution practices of the K-9 teams under Jeff's direction. Near the close of the large-scale combat exercise, the captain from California approached his colonel and pointed directly at Franklin, who was standing next to his four K-9 teams, and said; "I want that man." Not long after returning to their home station, the colonel overseeing the California group contacted Colonel Edward with an unprecedented request. Even though usually competing against one another for status, first access to innovative equipment, and high-profile missions, the colonel from California asked Colonel Edward if Franklin could be afforded the freedom to also head-up their tactical canine training. Colonel Edward reluctantly agreed, saying that the need for bilateral effectiveness in the fight against their common enemy, terrorism, was far more important than top ranking among the elite task forces.

South American Anti-Terrorism Special Forces Group.

In less than three months, Jeff was setting up shop in California and laying the foundation for the second Canine Commando program. At the time of this writing, Franklin and his dogs are still one of the only non-competitive forms of cooperation between the U.S. Military's two most specialized commands. In addition to overseeing the U. S. Canine Commando teams, Jeff has also outfitted numerous foreign national police forces with tactical warfare dogs. In between his trips to Europe and South America, Jeff routinely places police dogs into departments around the United States. After twenty-six years as a professional dog-man, Franklin is still passionate about his trade. He continues to sleep little and labor much, relentlessly pursuing the perfect working dog and refining his training techniques.

About the Author

Matthew Duffy continues to write and train dogs in the hilly country of Southern Indiana.

Other Books by the Author

*Dog Training and Eight Faces of Aggressive
Behavior
(A Master's Solution to Barkers, Growlers, and Biters)*

Also

*Ten Natural Steps to Training the Family Dog
(Building a Positive Relationship)*

Manufactured by Amazon.ca
Bolton, ON

24623606R00190